FAMILIES DIVIDED

The impact of migrant labour in Lesotho

AFRICAN STUDIES SERIES 29

BOOKS IN THIS SERIES

FAMILIES DIVIDED

The impact of migrant
labour in Lesotho

COLIN MURRAY
Research Fellow in Sociology
University of Liverpool

RAVAN   JOHANNESBURG

Published in South Africa by Ravan Press (Pty) Ltd.,
409–416 Dunwell, 35 Jorissen Street,
Braamfontein, Johannesburg 2001, South Africa.

© Cambridge University Press 1981

First published 1981

Printed in Malta by Interprint Limited

ISBN 0 86975 203 0

To the dead
especially Semahla, Motloang and 'MaLineo
and to the living
especially Moetsuoa, Mahashe, 'MaTšehla, Nkiling and 'MaBatho

Contents

Contents

Tables

Figures

Preface

In 1863 Lesotho was described as 'the granary of the Free State and parts of the [Cape] Colony' (CB: 459). Today it is an impoverished labour reserve. A study of this transformation poses urgent and fundamental questions. What are the effects of an increasingly refined application of the machinery of apartheid, not only inside but also outside the political boundaries of South Africa? How is it possible to condone high unemployment, extreme poverty and social deprivation in the labour reserves of the rural periphery, while the coffers of the South African state are swelled by the gold boom of the 1970s? How can the systematic destruction of family life through mass labour migration be reconciled with the principle of self-determination which is supposedly enshrined in the granting of political independence, both to the erstwhile British territories of Botswana, Lesotho and Swaziland and to the Bantustans within South Africa?

In this book I present empirical evidence relating to some aspects of the transformation of Lesotho from granary to labour reserve. I also analyse the impact of this transformation on the lives of migrants and their families. The material is mainly drawn from a period of two years' anthropological fieldwork in five villages in 1972–4 and from a further brief visit in 1978. The book is not therefore a history of labour migration from Lesotho. Nor is it a full account of the social, economic and political changes that have taken place. But the way I have written it reflects two convictions in particular. One is that no aspect of contemporary village life can be understood without central reference to the dependence of villagers for their livelihood on earnings derived from the export of labour. The other is that this dependence must be understood in its proper historical context.

In Chapter 1, accordingly, I outline the historical background to Lesotho's predicament and offer an analysis of contemporary trends in the political economy of migrant labour. In Chapter 2 I illustrate the experience of particular migrants and discuss the problems of analysing household composition in circumstances where household members move repetitively between home in Lesotho and work-place in South Africa. Chapter 3 offers an account firstly of the political context in which rights to arable land are administered, and secondly of the most important agricultural operations. I then draw on the evidence in Chapters 2 and 3, together with the results of other empirical studies undertaken in Lesotho, to undermine conventional wisdom on the relationship between migrant earnings and domestic agriculture, and to propose a more realistic assessment of differentiation in rural communities.

In Chapter 5 I question the usefulness of well-known descriptive stereotypes of the family such as the extended family and the nuclear family; seek to clarify the empirical evidence relating to processes of family constitution in Lesotho and elsewhere in the southern African periphery; and attempt to resolve some ambiguities in the ethnographic literature concerning Sesotho kinship structure. I conclude, in particular, that the apparent continuity of custom must be analysed as an integral and vital aspect of underlying structural transformation. Chapter 6 is an attempt to exemplify this argument with specific reference to marital transactions in Lesotho. High bridewealth in the mid-nineteenth century was a structural correlate of the process of political and economic differentiation between chiefs and commoners. High bridewealth in the late twentieth century is a mechanism by which migrants invest in the long term security of the rural social system and by which rural kin constitute claims over absent earners. Detailed case studies are used to substantiate the latter proposition. Chapter 7 concentrates specifically on the experience of women, as migrants themselves, as rural household managers left behind by migrant husbands, and as widows. They are at an acute structural disadvantage in the South African labour market; their conjugal careers are characterized by the separation of husband and wife; and they are economically vulnerable to the exigencies of migrant support.

In a short concluding Chapter I attempt to place the present work in comparative perspective, with reference to previous regional studies of migrant labour, to recent historiographical developments in southern African studies, and to some wider theoretical and political issues. The most important of these issues is the threat of mass unemployment which faces the people of Lesotho in the 1980s, as a result of changes in South African policies of labour recruitment.

I should like to acknowledge financial support from the following sources: the Chairman's Fund of the Anglo American Corporation of South Africa, which provided a generous grant for fieldwork in 1972–4, and to whose officers I am indebted for their unfailing courtesy and practical assistance; and the Research Fund of the London School of Economics, which made possible a brief visit to Lesotho in 1978.

My intellectual and personal debts are many and various. I should like particularly to thank Monica Wilson, who supervised the original field-work on which this book is based; Esther Goody, who supervised the Ph.D. thesis of which this book is a substantial revision; and Shula Marks, who gave me encouragement and stimulus and several opportunities to express ideas at her London seminars. She also commented very helpfully on the manuscript for this book. I should like to thank the following persons, severally, for their critical comment, support and hospitality: David Ambrose, William Beinart, Sandy Cairncross, Julian Clarke, David Cooper, John Gay, Judy Gay, Jeff Guy, Thabiso Mafisa, Pepe Roberts, John Sharp, Andrew Spiegel and Francis Wilson. I remain responsible for the views and the evidence presented below.

Above all, I thank my friends and erstwhile neighbours in northern Lesotho for an experience which I shall never forget. This book is dedicated to some of them, invidiously perhaps; and to Linda Pepper, who became known as 'MaBatho, and who bore the brunt of the writing.

Colin Murray
9 June 1980

Note on conventions

Orthography

In reference to the Southern Sotho with whom this book is concerned, I have retained the prefixes they use themselves. Collectively, they are Basotho. Their homes are in Lesotho. Individually, each is a Mosotho. They speak Sesotho, and Sesotho also pertains to any aspect of their culture. The old forms Basuto, Mosuto and Sesuto are used only in direct quotation. I have not followed the convention of dropping prefixes which is often adopted by ethnographers of Bantu-speaking peoples. In this case, the root Sotho is likely to cause confusion, for it is commonly used in a sense that embraces both the Tswana of Botswana and the western Transvaal, and the Pedi of the northern Transvaal.

There are two orthographies of Sesotho, one used in Lesotho itself, the other adopted for use in South Africa at a convention in 1959. In deference to the Basotho, who feel strongly about their linguistic and cultural identity, I use the Lesotho orthography in this book. It has several peculiarities. (1) A double consonant is invariably a prolongation of the single consonant: thus, *ho lla* (to cry) is quite distinct from *ho laola* (to divine). (2) An *l* before an *i* or a *u* is pronounced as a *d*: thus, the greeting *lumela* is pronounced *dumela*, and *bohali* (bridewealth) is pronounced *bohadi*. (3) An *š* is an aspirated *s*: thus, *matšeliso* (consolation, indemnity) in the Lesotho orthography is written *matshediso* in the South African orthography. (4) A *th* is an aspirated *t* and is not pronounced as *th* in English. Otherwise, there are no particular difficulties of pronunciation, except that differences of tone which are extremely important in Sesotho are not easily conveyed in the orthography: an example is *o* (third person singular pronoun) and *u* (second person pronoun) – the sound is the same but the tone is high in the first case and low in the second.

Currency

The currency in use in Lesotho throughout the 1970s was the South African rand. Its rate of exchange with the pound sterling was R2=£1 prior to devaluation of the pound in 1967, and the present rate of exchange is a fluctuating one. However, Basotho retain the use of £.s.d. (the pre-1961 currency) in speech and calculation for ordinary market purposes as well as, almost invariably, in the accountancy of bridewealth. This implies no computational problems as no account is taken of the devaluation of either currency. Basotho continue to translate between pounds and rands at the old prevailing rate of £1=R2, and this translation remains valid irrespective of floating official exchange rates. Lesotho's own currency, the Loti, was introduced in December 1979, initially at par with the rand.

Symbols used in text

The following symbols are used in the text:

△ ○   Living male, female

▲ ◉   Deceased male, female

△ ○   Full siblings

△ ○   Half siblings

△ ○   Marital relationship

△ ○   Sexual or extra-marital relationship

△ ○   Conjugal dissociation or divorce

Abbreviations

ACROL	Anglo Collieries Recruitment Organization of Lesotho
AHCM	Association of Home Countries of Migrants
ASB	Annual Statistical Bulletin
BCP	Basutoland Congress Party
BNP	Basutoland National Party
CAR	Colonial Annual Report
CB	*Chronicles of Basutoland* (Germond 1967)
FAO	Food and Agriculture Organization
FFYDP	First Five Year Development Plan
IBRD	International Bank for Reconstruction and Development
ILO	International Labour Office
LASA	Lesotho Agricultural Sector Analysis
NCOLA	Natal Coal Owners' Labour Association
NRC	Native Recruiting Corporation
PDL	Poverty Datum Line
PEMS	Paris Evangelical Mission Society
SAIRR	South African Institute of Race Relations
SALB	South African Labour Bulletin
SFYDP	Second Five Year Development Plan
SIDA	Swedish International Development Agency
TEBA	The Employment Bureau of Africa
USAID	United States Agency for International Development

1

From granary to labour reserve

The country and the people

The Kingdom of Lesotho is a small, barren and mountainous country entirely surrounded by the Republic of South Africa. It lies astride the watershed of southern Africa, amid the rugged peaks of the Drakensberg from which rise the tributaries of three great rivers – the Vaal, the Tugela and the Orange. The country is divided into four ecological zones (see Fig. 1.1). The Lowlands are a narrow strip of land lying west of the mountain ranges and less than 1,830 metres above sea level.[1] Dotted with flat-topped hills and scarred with erosion gullies known as dongas, they constitute less than 20 per cent of the total land area of 30,344 square kilometres. A conspicuous sandstone escarpment at a height of about 1,830m crosses the country along an axis from north-east to south-west. It divides the Lowlands from the Foothills, an irregular series of plateaux intersected by river valleys and the lower mountain spurs. Beyond the Foothills lie the Mountains, rising to a rolling upland plateau in the north-east at about 2,740m. The highest peak is Thabana Ntlenyana (3,841m) on the eastern escarpment. The mountain ranges are divided by a series of deep gorges running southwards and westwards, in which flow the Senqu or Orange river and its major tributaries such as the Malibamatšo and the Senqunyane. The Orange River Valley is conventionally distinguished as the fourth ecological zone.

Because of the high altitude, the climate of Lesotho is healthy and temperate. The average annual rainfall of about 700mm is concentrated in the summer months from October to April, and very little falls in the winter months from May to September. Rainfall varies considerably between years and Lesotho is subject to an extended drought in about one year in five. The country is also subject to extremes of temperature. The hottest months are December and January, with mean daily temperatures ranging up to 28°C in the Lowlands, while 40°C has been recorded. The coldest months are June and July, particularly in the

1

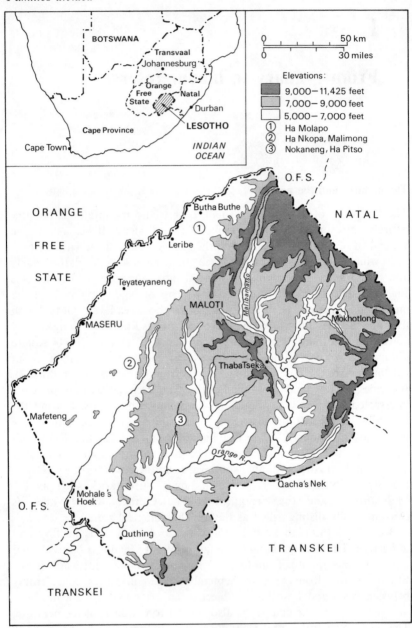

1.1 A map of Lesotho, showing relief, district administrative headquarters and approximate areas of fieldwork

Mountains where the temperature often falls below freezing, and may be as low as $-10°C$ (Bawden and Carroll 1968: 15). Night frosts are recorded regularly throughout the winter months. The higher peaks are capped with snow during June, July and August. Large areas of the Mountain zone are sometimes cut off by snow, and their inhabitants threatened by famine.

Lesotho is divided into ten administrative districts (Fig. 1.1). Six of these have their headquarters in the small towns or 'camps' connected by the main arterial road running north to south in the western Lowland belt. These are Butha Buthe, Leribe, Teyateyaneng, Maseru, Mafeteng and Mohale's Hoek. A seventh, Quthing, lies in the Orange River Valley in the south. The remaining three districts have Mountain headquarters: Mokhotlong, Thaba Taeka and Qacha's Nek. The capital Maseru was a small and dusty stone-built town of about 9,000 people in the early 1960s. Since independence in 1966 it has grown rapidly in size and population, having about 30,000 people in the early 1970s. The other towns remain much smaller.

More than 92 per cent of Lesotho's population live in the rural areas. They live in villages whose mean size varies between 94 persons per village in the district of Mohale's Hoek and 232 persons in Leribe district.[2] The actual range of variation in village size is much greater, from a minimum of about 40 to a maximum of about 1,000. Village homesteads in Lesotho are clustered around a central area, the chief's place (*moreneng*), and not dispersed across the landscape as in the Transkei and Zululand. This relatively concentrated settlement pattern is consistent both with highveld ecology (Sansom 1974) and with the Sotho political tradition (Kuper 1975). Villages huddle in folds of the undulating Lowland plain; they nestle beneath the flat-topped outcrops of the sandstone escarpment; they are perched on the lower mountain spurs; and they straddle the dolerite ridges which ascend into the steep ranges of the Maloti.

About 70 per cent of the population live in the Lowlands and Foothills, whereas the Mountains, the largest of the zones in area, are relatively sparsely populated. Resident population densities in 1976 were projected as 35 persons per km^2 in Lesotho as a whole, and 275 persons per km^2 of *available arable land*. The corresponding figures for the Lowlands only were 80 and 219 persons per km^2 (Monyake 1973: 90, 92). These figures illustrate the intensity of the pressure on the country's very limited land resources. The population has increased rapidly in the twentieth century, from 428,000 in 1911 to nearly 1,250,000 in 1976 (Table 1.1). In view of the large number of people who are away at work in South Africa at any one time, census practice since 1911 has been to

3

Families divided

Table 1.1. *African population of Lesotho, 1911–76.*

Year	Males A	B	Females A	B	Total A	B	C
1911	204,797	21,658	222,752	2,972	427,549	24,630	5.8
1921	260,675	37,827	283,472	9,314	544,147	47,141	8.7
1936	317,918	78,604	343,892	22,669	661,809	101,273	15.3
1946	342,340	95,697	347,579	32,331	689,919	128,028	18.6
1956	383,546	112,790	410,737	41,992	794,253	154,782	19.5
1966	463,437	96,350	502,476	19,550	965,913	115,900	12.0
1976	587,331	129,103	629,484	23,551	1,216,815	152,654	12.5

Key: A. *De jure* population (residents plus absentees). B. Absentees. C. Absentees as percentage of *de jure* population (B/A × 100).
Sources: Monyake (1974), and 1976 census preliminary results, Bureau of Statistics, Maseru.
Note: The number of absentees was not recorded in the 1946 census; the figure given is an interpolation based on the figures for 1936 and 1956. The 1976 figures are preliminary, and include approximately 5,000 non-Africans.

distinguish the *de facto* population – those present at the time of enumeration – from the *de jure* population – those present plus those recorded as absent members of households. The importance of this distinction is elaborated in Chapter 2. Table 1.1 shows the number of recorded absentees expressed as a percentage of the total population for each census year.

Almost all of the country's inhabitants refer to themselves as Basotho. Their language, Sesotho, is classified by comparative linguists as Southern Sotho, one of three language clusters which belong to the Sotho language group of the South-eastern zone of Bantu languages (Doke 1967). The other two clusters in the group are Northern Sotho, spoken in the northern and eastern Transvaal, and Tswana or Setswana, spoken in the northern Cape, the western Transvaal and Botswana. The relative uniformity of Southern Sotho is attributable to the incorporation of various Sotho clans under one political authority, the chief Moshoeshoe I, in the second quarter of the nineteenth century, following the devastating upheaval known to the Basotho as the *lifaqane*.[3] These clans formed the Basotho nation, whose territorial base was the western foothills of the Maloti range of the Drakensberg and the lowlands of the Caledon valley. They lost their independence in 1868 during a debilitating war with the Afrikaners of the Orange Free State, when Moshoeshoe sought British protection in order to prevent further loss of land. For nearly a hundred years Basutoland was subject to British over-rule, until in 1966 it emerged as the independent Kingdom of

4

Lesotho. Today the Basotho of Moshoeshoe, as they describe themselves, are distributed between Lesotho itself, the tiny barren Southern Sotho Bantustan of Qwaqwa, on the northern edge of Lesotho; two other Bantustans – the Transkei and Bophuthatswana (see Fig. 1.4); and the 'white' farming areas and industrial centres of the Orange Free State and the southern Transvaal.

The following brief review of events at the national level since independence is intended only to facilitate understanding of the intense factional rivalries which dominate politics at the village level. The developments that led to Lesotho's independence and the internal tensions that have prevailed since then have been fully described elsewhere.[4] These tensions have involved a variety of political forces of which the most important are the monarchy, represented by King Moshoeshoe II; the ruling Basutoland National Party (BNP) led by Chief Leabua Jonathan; and the opposition Basutoland Congress Party (BCP) led by Ntsu Mokhehle. By and large, the BNP has the support of the Catholic church, large traders and many of the chiefs; whereas the BCP, Pan-African and socialist in orientation, derives its popular support from commoners, migrant workers, teachers and some small traders (Breytenbach 1975; Ström 1978). Although Chief Jonathan's government has a very limited capacity to change the conditions under which the majority of the citizens of Lesotho spend their working lives, it is of course a more politically accessible target for the expression of their frustrations than the South African government.

The first post-independence elections were held in January 1970. The result would have been a victory for the BCP, but Jonathan declared a state of emergency, suspended the constitution, arrested opposition leaders and put the king under house arrest. He took these steps under pressure from hard-line cabinet ministers, in order to pre-empt the electoral defeat of the BNP. Violence flared up as a result and several hundred people were killed in various parts of the country. Chief Jonathan subsequently attempted to 'abolish politics' in the interests of national reconciliation and concerted action for development. He established an Interim National Assembly in 1973 but this was boycotted by Mokhehle and several of his followers because members of the Assembly were to be effectively nominated by Jonathan and not elected.[5] An abortive outbreak of violence in January 1974 was harshly repressed by the police and the para-military Police Mobile Unit. Following this the BCP split into an 'official' section under Gerard Ramoreboli, who was incorporated into the cabinet late in 1975 as Minister of Justice, and an 'unofficial' but much larger section which remained loyal to the exiled Mokhehle.

5

Families divided

Meanwhile Chief Jonathan was developing a foreign policy more explicitly hostile towards apartheid. As a staunchly conservative 'anti-communist' he had had the South African government's support against his political opponents in the early years of independence. But from about 1971 onwards this amicable relationship steadily soured. Tensions arose over South African pressure against investment by certain multinational companies in subsidiaries in Lesotho (Ström 1978: 115; also Selwyn 1975); over specific incidents such as the shooting of five Basotho miners by South African police at Western Deep Level mine in September 1973; over Lesotho's claims before the United Nations to 'conquered territory' in the Orange Free State, an area whose precise dimensions have not been publicly declared, but it includes the tract of land between the Caledon and the Orange which the Basotho lost by the two Treaties of Aliwal North in 1858 and 1869;[6] and over the common border with the Transkei following the latter's 'independence' in 1976 which was unrecognized by Lesotho. More generally, the anticipated benefits to Lesotho of a friendly relationship with South Africa had not materialized; little technical or financial assistance was forthcoming; and it proved impossible to reach agreement for South Africa to purchase water from the Oxbow–Malibamatšo hydro-electric scheme which had been proposed in the First Five Year Plan. In response to such difficulties the Lesotho government pursued a more open and aggressive foreign policy. Various diplomatic initiatives were undertaken which allowed Lesotho to diversify and multiply its sources of international aid (Ström 1978; Hirschmann 1979) and to conclude a series of agreements with Mozambique and other socialist countries.

However, there were also internal considerations behind this shift of orientation in foreign policy. Jonathan's domestic political credibility and his attempts to undermine the popular challenge of the BCP depended in part on an approach more overtly critical of South African policies. It appears that the government's increasingly sophisticated capacity to articulate its grievances against South Africa has allowed the BNP to steal some of the BCP's thunder in this respect. Lesotho's diplomatic aggression sufficiently irritated Prime Ministers Vorster and Botha to give rise to persistent rumours of collaboration between the South African security police and armed BCP insurgents who, representing the self-styled Liberation Party (*Lekhotla la Topollo*), infiltrated the northern mountains of Lesotho towards the end of 1979. A series of violent incidents, involving these insurgents and members of the Police Mobile Unit, led to an exodus of several hundred refugees from Makhoakhoeng to the Free State town of Bethlehem, where they were placed in a fenced encampment by the South African authorities. These

6

events induced speculation over the ruling party's connections with the mainstream of the South African liberation movement.

The failure of economic dualism

There is a well-established tradition in South African economic historiography which attempts to explain poverty in the labour reserves by invoking African failure to respond to changing conditions and, specifically, features intrinsic to African social structure which inhibit the capacity to innovate. The report of the Native Economic Commission in 1932, for example, drew attention to the absence of a saving propensity, the force of indigenous sanctions which discourage individual initiative, and the unwisdom of commoners attaining wealth which upsets the accepted proprieties of rank (Houghton and Dagut 1973: 73). This tradition of economic dualism is most clearly elaborated in D. Hobart Houghton's standard text book on the South African economy (1973). In successive editions he discusses the differences between 'market-oriented' (white) farming, characterized by a 'scientific and experimental' approach, and 'subsistence' (black) farming, characterized by a 'traditional' approach, as 'so great that they cannot conveniently be treated together' (1973: 46; also Sadie 1960). In this way the theory of economic dualism posits the co-existence of discrete economic sectors, most commonly a 'static traditional sector' and a 'progressive industrial sector' (Houghton 1974: 406). Poverty and lack of development are here represented as aspects of an original state, for which the remedy is seen as progressive economic incorporation.

Writers on Lesotho, particularly those associated with the Africa Institute in Pretoria, are well represented in this tradition. For example, Leistner attributed the underdevelopment of Lesotho to 'the remarkable tenacity of traditional institutions, concepts and values' (1966: 35–6). In a thesis on 'Problems and prospects of the economic development of agriculture in Lesotho', Jack Williams identified a phenomenon which he called 'socio-cultural congruity', made up of three elements: the irrational and sustained belief in superstition and magic; the sharing propensity supposedly inherent in extended family institutions; and a collective impulse not to behave conspicuously. All these factors, he alleged, 'impinge on rational decision-making at the farm level' (1970: 251).

The objections to this sort of argument may be summarized as follows. Firstly, as Merle Lipton (1977) has shown, the differences in productivity between white farming and black farming are not in fact as great as official statistics and white mythology represent them to be. Secondly, even if official figures are taken seriously, the comparison shown in Table

7

Table 1.2. *Comparison of maize yields, 1950–70*

| | (100 kg per hectare) | | |
| | South Africa | | Lesotho[c] |
Year	White farmers[a]	African peasants	
1950	7.4	5.7[b]	11.9
1960	9.1	2.1[a]	7.4
1970	11.9	2.3[a]	5.1

Sources: (a) Houghton (1973: 267); (b) Converted from Houghton and Walton (1952: 162); (c) Table 1.3 below.

1.2 between maize productivity in Lesotho and that of African 'peasants' and white farmers in South Africa over the years 1950 to 1970 suggests that substantial differences in productivity are relatively recent. Thirdly, if productivity is assessed in terms of net value added, that is by relating the value of output to the cost of inputs, then it is possible, even probable, that small-scale black farming represents a more efficient alloc..tion of resources than large-scale white farming (Lipton 1977).

These criticisms illustrate the static and impoverished quality not of traditional agriculture but of dualist theory. There is little evidence to justify Houghton's attribution of the contemporary differences between the sectors to the 'scientific and experimental' approach of white farmers and the 'traditional' approach of black farmers. On the contrary, the differences are best explained in terms of generous political support and capital provision made available to white farmers by the South African state and in terms of specific political and economic discrimination by the state against black farmers (F. Wilson 1971; Morris 1976). There is now plenty of evidence to demonstrate that there was a widespread and vigorous response by Africans to new market opportunities in the late nineteenth century (M. Wilson 1971; Beinart 1973); but that those opportunities were increasingly circumscribed by instruments of discrimination such as the Land Act of 1913, by constriction of access to markets and capital, and by increasing dependence on the export of labour. Colin Bundy's book *The Rise and Fall of the South African Peasantry* (1979) clearly documents this process of underdevelopment in the Transkei, the Ciskei, Natal and the Transvaal. As will be seen, Lesotho provides a particularly virulent example of the process. The essays in Palmer and Parsons (1977) illustrate a similar story further north, in Zimbabwe, Botswana and Zambia. At different times in different places, an initial period of prosperity was followed by a long spiral of decline.

Thus the failure of economic dualism consists in the following points. On the one hand, a relationship between the two sectors of the economy is, of necessity, recognized; for example, oscillating migrants, as 'Men of Two Worlds' (Houghton 1973: 82–99), move repetitively between them. On the other hand, explanation of the difference between the two sectors proceeds by invoking features that are allegedly intrinsic and implicitly exclusive to each sector, respectively. This central contradiction remains unresolved because the particular relationship between the two sectors is not itself regarded as problematic. Rather, it is regarded as a natural consequence of the existing distribution of resources, skills and attitudes of mind. In this way proponents of dualist theory tend to construct analytical boundaries that coincide with the physical boundaries between the sectors. Neglect of economic history is an indispensable condition of this construction; and the habit of reductionism is its inevitable corollary.

Some of these problems are to be found in analyses of Lesotho's predicament which can otherwise be taken much more seriously than those of Leistner and Williams cited above. For example, Hugh Ashton, the principal modern ethnographer of the Basotho, ascribed low agricultural productivity in the 1930s partly to a lack of capital equipment, partly to a shortage of male labour – both very plausible reasons – and partly to a prevalent attitude of indifference. 'The Mosotho is not an agriculturalist by tradition, and tends to regard agriculture as women's work (which it used to be), and even if he does not positively despise it, he just is not interested or enthusiastic about it.' Owing to the ready availability of employment in South Africa, the Basotho lacked any 'driving incentive ... to develop their lands and improve their agriculture' (Ashton 1939: 155).

Much more recently, Sandra Wallman (1972) argued that a complex syndrome of factors constrains the individual Mosotho from making any effort to improve his lot and from co-operating with development initiatives. She concluded that

non-development in Lesotho is a function of a complex of poverty, migration and ideology, and can only be successfully treated when attention is paid to the whole syndrome. It is easy to prescribe negatively, economic development will not be assured by an injection of cash to cure the poverty, nor by a tourniquet to stop the flow of migrants, nor by an amphetamine to lift the pessimism, nor by any one specialist effort alone. More positively – and therefore more diffidently – I would venture that the present emphasis on agricultural development for Lesotho will continue to be nugatory in so far as it exacerbates the unfavourable contrast with urban South Africa (1972: 260).

Wallman is surely right to insist on the connections between the various elements in the syndrome and also on the 'unfavourable contrast' between poverty in Lesotho and wealth in the industrial heartland of

9

South Africa. But the emphasis in her article is on the way in which 'the economic facts of village life in Lesotho are perpetuated by their effect on the individual villager' (1972: 251). In so far as these arguments are based on the premise that lack of development is to be explained in terms of individuals' perception of their predicament, they are both reductionist and ahistorical. Ashton's diagnosis of complacency in the 1930s and Wallman's diagnosis of pessimism in the 1960s are both, no doubt, of incidental relevance. They are not in themselves adequate explanations of poverty or 'non-development'.

The following review of Lesotho's economic history, albeit brief and provisional, makes it clear that the appropriate question is not 'Why are the Basotho still poor?' but 'How have the Basotho become poor?'.[7] This review also exposes as bizarre and self-contradictory Wallman's assertion in a later article that the contemporary 'facts of life' – poverty and economic dependence – may be regarded as conditions 'intrinsic to Lesotho, having no necessary reference to the presence of South Africa' (1976: 105–6). In the first place, Wallman herself had already acknowledged the importance of the long conflict with the Boers over land. Its resolution in 1869 determined the present boundaries of Lesotho, to the considerable disadvantage of the Basotho, and this partly explains the present shortage of land and gross over-crowding of population. In the second place, similar conditions are 'intrinsic' to the Transkei, Ciskei, KwaZulu and most of the other reserve areas in South Africa which have been constituted as African 'homelands'. Yet these, Wallman would doubtless acknowledge, have everything to do with the presence of South Africa. 'Foreign' identity is relative, as the citizens of Transkei, Bophuthatswana and Venda have discovered.

The decline of agriculture and the exodus of labour

The year 1870 was a historical watershed for the Basotho. Moshoeshoe, the founder of the nation, died in March of that year. His people had just emerged from a crippling war (1865–8) with the Afrikaners of the Orange Free State and had been incorporated, at Moshoeshoe's request, into the British imperial fold. The present boundaries of Lesotho were fixed in the Treaty of Aliwal North of 1869, by which the Basotho were forced to cede much of the land they had previously occupied and farmed (Sanders 1975: 306–7).

Basutoland was administered by the Government of the Cape Colony for a brief and somewhat unhappy period, 1871–84. The first Governor's Agent, Charles Griffith, reported that as a result of the war with the Free State the Basotho had been reduced to famine and near-destitution through the loss of their livestock and inability to reap their crops. They recovered remarkably quickly, however, so that by 1873 they presented the appearance of a 'thriving and well-ordered people' (Burman 1976: 42–6). This recovery was largely due to the discovery of diamonds in 1867 in the arid wastes of the northern Cape Colony, which brought about the first of South Africa's major mineral booms. It rapidly and irreversibly incorporated the Basotho into a larger economic system. The missionaries of the Paris Evangelical Mission Society (PEMS) were well placed to record the vigorous response of the Basotho to boom conditions:

Hitherto our Basuto have all remained quietly at home, and the movement which is taking place beyond their frontiers has produced no other effect than to increase the export of wheat and other cereals to a most remarkable degree. While the district in which the diamonds are found is of desperate aridity, the valleys of Basutoland, composed as they are of a deep layer of vegetable mould, watered by numerous streams and favoured with regular rains in the good season, require little more than a modicum of work to cover themselves with the richest crops (CB: 319).

The Basotho bought ploughs, planted assiduously and sold the grain to meet the needs of the distant mining camps. They responded to the incentives of the market with such zeal and success that, on the one hand, the missionaries expressed anxiety lest their material prosperity endanger their spiritual progress (CB: 322) and, on the other hand, the *Friend of the Free State* was moved to remark, 'Nowhere else in South Africa is there a more naturally industrious nation, as honest and as peacable as the Basuto' (CB: 319). In 1873 they exported 100,000 bags of grain – maize, wheat and sorghum – and 2,000 bags of wool. In the same year goods of British or foreign manufacture worth about £150,000 were imported into the country. As Griffith remarked, 'the Colonial revenue must benefit very considerably by the Basuto trade' (Burman 1976: 46).

The boom generated an acute inflationary impetus and some Basotho started migrating to the diggings in response to the demand for labour. Migration was not new in itself: Basotho had been dispersed as a result of the ravages of the *lifaqane*; and before the war with the Free State many of Moshoeshoe's subjects had undertaken short contracts of seasonal labour on the farms of the Cape and elsewhere; many also had spent their wages on or traded grain for guns and livestock (Kimble 1976: 1–9). The discovery of diamonds, however, gave new impetus to the pattern of migration. A comment on the first population census of 1975 referred to 'the multitude who have temporarily absented themselves in search of employment in the Cape Colony, or the diamond mines, or elsewhere' (CB: 326). It was estimated that 'by 1875, out of a total

11

population of 127,325 ... 15,000 men were getting passes to work outside the territory for long or short periods, and by 1884 this number had doubled itself' (Ashton 1952: 162). During this period it seems that migration was 'discretionary' rather than 'necessary' (cf. Arrighi 1973), although it is difficult from the reports available to distinguish between richer and poorer sections of the peasantry. Certainly the senior chiefs were much better off than most – through their control and distribution of livestock, their right to tribute labour, and thence an ability to plough far more land. There were also other perquisites. For example Molapo, second son of Moshoeshoe and senior chief in the Leribe district, received £800 a year out of the hut-tax collected from his people, and also at least £1 from every labour migrant out of his earnings (Taylor 1972: 44). It appears that most migrants went in order to acquire guns, horses, livestock, ploughs and manufactured articles. Many Basotho continued, however, to make an excellent livelihood from the sale of grain. In 1880 the Acting Governor's Agent Emile Rolland gave the following estimates of the aggregate income of Basotho (Kimble 1976: 16):

sale of grain	£400,000
export of wool and other produce	75,000
earnings of labourers and transport-riders	100,000

Such figures must be treated with caution, but they indicate that the production and export of grain was the most important source of income in the 1870s.

The period of prosperity was short-lived. Cereals and livestock products were subject to the vicissitudes of drought, epizootics and economic depression; and from the 1880s onwards market conditions were decisively affected by political and economic factors outside the control of the Basotho. Meanwhile population expansion in the Lowlands and political pressures arising out of the Gun War in 1880–1, when the Basotho successfully resisted the Cape administration's attempt to disarm them, led to rapid settlement of the Mountains. There was a severe recession in 1882–6 (Houghton and Dagut 1972: 226), and a savage drought brought widespread famine in 1884 (CB: 466–7). Gold fever hit the Witwatersrand in 1886 and precipitated another boom but this time the export market for grain from Basutoland was adversely affected by a prohibition on imports imposed by the Transvaal and by competition from American and Australian grain, which could be cheaply transported by the newly constructed railway from the Cape to Kimberley. A missionary noted in 1887: 'The population is rapidly increasing, the fields are becoming exhausted, the pastures diminishing, stock farming yields more disappointments than profits. The establishment of the railway has profoundly modified the economic situation of Basutoland. It produces less and finds no outlet for its products' (CB: 469).

In 1893 the Orange Free State attempted to impose a tariff on grain from Basutoland in order to protect the market of the white farmers who had turned from stock rearing to growing crops. This rendered it difficult for the Basotho to sell their grain and so inhibited mercantile exchange in Basutoland; but, as the acting Resident Commissioner Godfrey Lagden pointed out, the boycott also threatened the interests of the large merchants of the Free State who supplied the Basutoland traders (CAR 1893–4). The disastrous outbreak of rinderpest in 1896 wiped out up to 90 per cent of the cattle (CB: 475; Pim 1935: 30) and also caused a 'remarkable falling off' in the number of Basotho who migrated in search of work, because of quarantine regulations in the Free State (CAR 1896–7). The Basotho resourcefully adapted to the loss of their livestock: they used their horses for ploughing and transport (CAR 1896–7) and they arranged marital mortgages by counting stones as surety for future instalments of bridewealth cattle (CB: 473). However, the following year there was a fierce drought, and the wheat crop failed entirely. 'Famine threatens the majority of these poor people' (CB: 476; CAR 1897–8).

The Anglo-Boer war of 1899–1902 closed the usual outlets for export of grain and it was followed by another depression and a drought. The comments of the Government Secretary in the first decade of the twentieth century best reveal the fluctuating conditions which began to undermine what had been a consistently favourable balance of trade. In 1905 the wheat crop failed and low market prices led to a general scarcity of money, while 'grain and produce of all kinds have naturally gone to pieces through drought and locusts' (CAR 1905–6). The year 1907 saw 'a great improvement on the previous years of drought' (CAR 1906–7); but in 1908–9 the wheat crop was destroyed by lice and the maize crop by drought, though exports of wool and mohair steadily increased (CAR 1908–9). The 1911 census recorded a population of 427,549 Basotho, including 24,630 absentees (Table 1.1). The PEMS journal *Leselinyana* discerned the writing on the wall:

Were the population to continue to increase, the situation would become truly critical within a few years, unless other means of livelihood were provided for the Basuto. They would be forced to migrate in large numbers to offer their services to the Europeans of the neighbouring countries which are less densely populated, but where their social conditions would deteriorate and where, above all, they would lose their independence (CB: 480).

As we have seen, Basotho had already been migrating in considerable numbers – 20,000 labour passes were reported in 1892, for example (CAR 1892–3) – in response to fluctuating economic conditions. In 1903 the

Resident Commissioner commended those who had gone out to work for their industrious character in this respect. Significantly, however, he also noted that the minimum wage necessary to attract Basotho was £2.10s a month with food; and that they seemed able to find nearer and more attractive employment than on the Johannesburg gold mines (CAR 1902–3), where wages were £1.10s a month at the time (F. Wilson 1972a: 4). In 1907 the Government Secretary suggested, on the evidence of labour passes issued to Basotho, that

as the population increases and the country fills up the native population is showing a tendency to divide itself into two distinct classes of labour, namely the agriculturalist and the mine labourer. It would appear that year in and year out the latter goes to his work at the mines while, on the other hand, it appears that the native farmer who, on bad years, went out to 'miscellaneous' farm and domestic labour, in a good year remains at home and tills his land (CAR 1906–7).

It is probable that most mine labourers were younger men who had not yet acquired land or livestock; that migration for them was necessary rather than discretionary; and that a substantial increase in the number of labour passes issued during the first decade of the century reflected a steadily declining *per capita* income from agriculture. However, the fact that poor harvests were consistently reflected in low imports of manufactured goods during this period suggests that the sale of grain and livestock products was still the most important means of generating a cash flow inside the country.

The First World War sustained high prices in wool and grain and the Basotho were able to take advantage of this – maize production was particularly vigorous. Wheat exports in 1919 were a record 256,000 bags (Pim 1935: 191), which prompted an optimistic official disclaimer of 'the theory which is sometimes propounded that the wheat lands of Basutoland are "worked out"' (CAR 1919–20). The volume of exports fluctuated through the 1920s but reached a peak in 1928, the last year that 100,000 bags of maize were exported from Basutoland. Wool and mohair were by far the most important exports at this time (Pim 1935: Appendix v). The market prices of most commodities also fluctuated but only fell markedly after the 1929 slump. The record of labour passes issued during the decade does not indicate any overall increase in the number of labour migrants (Pim 1935: Appendix viii). The number of passes is not of course synonymous with the number of absentees at any one time. But the totals represent more than 50 per cent of the adult males, which suggests that most rural households had long since come to depend on migration as a necessary element in their strategies of survival.

The early 1930s were disastrous. Wool prices collapsed as a result of the massive recession in world trade which followed the 1929 slump. The

14

coincidence of acute economic depression with an exceptional drought in 1932–3 led to devastating losses of livestock. Sir Alan Pim reported a loss of 30 per cent of sheep and 50 per cent of goats between the years 1931 and 1934; and 'that the losses in cattle have been serious is well known but whether these amount to 30 per cent, to 40 per cent, 50 per cent or even over, can only be guessed at' (Pim 1935: 147). Wheat production survived and recovered but maize did not: in 1933 more than 350,000 bags of maize had to be imported (see Fig. 1.2). At the same time a resurgence in the price of gold stimulated the expansion of mining production and enormously increased the demand for labour on the gold mines: total numbers in employment increased from 241,000 men in 1933 to 365,000 in 1939 (F. Wilson 1972a: 83). During the 1930s and 1940s, in response both to this demand and to unfavourable economic conditions at home, very large numbers of emigrants from Basutoland left the country and were absorbed into the towns of South Africa. The scale of this emigration, offsetting natural increase, explains why no increase in the resident population was recorded between the censuses of 1936 and 1946 (see Table 1.1).

Rural poverty in this period was widespread but by no means universal. Ashton's analysis of differentiation, based on fieldwork in the 1930s, is most revealing in this respect. I quote him at length:

The people's wealth has never been equally divided and, so far as historical times are concerned, there have always been rich and poor. In the old days the richest people were the chiefs and other important political authorities. Successful warriors and specialists came next, then the heads of small family groups, followed by the mass of the people. At the tail end came servants, who were mostly aliens. This uneven distribution of wealth continues to this day and has been intensified by the widening of the gap between rich and poor. Wealth is still a jealously guarded prerogative of political power. The end of inter-tribal fighting and of cattle raiding dried up the chiefs' special source of income through captured cattle, but they were compensated by the growing value of their prescriptive rights to all stray stock found in their districts, and by the steadily increasing revenue from court fines. They also continued to enjoy and, in some cases, unscrupulously exploited, their rights to land, grazing and free tribal labour; some also used their official position to further small private enterprises such as transport riding. Moreover, the more important chiefs received a cash allowance from the Government. The real value of these incomes was further increased by their growing disregard of the obligations that had traditionally been associated with wealth; instead of using the produce of their tribal lands and of their cattle to support the poor and to feed people attending the court, and those employed on the court work, many diverted it to their own personal use. In 1934, one chief, who kindly showed me his books, owned 200 cattle, 1,500 small stock and £20 cash, and an allowance of £100 (subsequently raised to £300) from the Administration. He was one of the wealthier chiefs, but not as wealthy as the late chief Jonathan, who died leaving an estate worth over £20,000 (Ashton 1952: 173).

Various sources corroborate this evidence that some chiefs were abusing their prerogatives. As it operated in the period up to 1938, the 'placing' system (described in Chapter 3) allowed the number of chiefs and the corresponding allocations of territorial authority to proliferate without control. This led to constant quarrels and litigation over obligations on the part of particular chiefs and of their subjects. It exposed the ordinary people to excessive and conflicting demands for tribute labour on the chiefs' fields (*lira*) and for other public tasks (see Sheddick 1954: 147–51). There were many complaints that chiefs were exercising their judicial powers arbitrarily, by imposing unjustified fines, appropriating stray stock and failing to meet their customary obligations of hospitality towards the people. These complaints were analysed in some detail by Lord Hailey (1953) in his monumental survey of *Native Administration in the British African Territories*; they are also clearly set out in the *Report on Constitutional Reform and Chieftainship Affairs* (Basutoland 1958). It may be suggested that commoners' bitterness over such abuses was particularly strong in the 1930s partly because, as one member of the National Council remarked, 'there are now as many chiefs in Basutoland as there are stars in the heavens' (Pim 1935: 48); but partly also because in this period many of the middle peasants as well as the poor were directly exposed to the effects of the slump in the commodity market in livestock products and grain.

At any rate, writing of the 1930s and 1940s, Ashton went on to observe that many people had no stock or land at all, and that 'they are poorly nourished and shabbily dressed, find difficulty in paying their tax, and can only afford one or two small cooking pots and implements such as hoes ... Their incomes are often inadequate for their simple requirements' (1952: 175). Accordingly, well over half the adult male population were away at any one time, working out of the country.

The social consequences of this maladjustment are unfortunate. The men live a life divided between their rural homes and the urban areas of the Union and, floating between the two, they miss the full benefits of both. As mine or industrial workers, their intermittent employment makes them difficult to organize and so reduces the opportunity of bargaining for better wages; their instability keeps their productivity and therefore their wages low, and their life in the towns is squalid and unhealthy both physically and socially. On the other hand, the knowledge that they can always get temporary, if ill-paid, work deprives them as peasants of any great incentive to farm properly or to make the most of their land and pastures, while their absence from home disrupts and impoverishes their social and economic life (Ashton 1952: 176–7).

Table 1.3. *Agricultural production in Lesotho, 1950–70.*

Year	Maize A	Maize B	Sorghum A	Sorghum B	Wheat A	Wheat B
1950	214	11.9	49	8.7	50	10.1
1960	121	7.4	54	7.8	58	8.5
1970	67	5.2	57	6.9	58	5.4

Key: A. Production in thousand metric tonnes. B. Yield in 100 kg per hectare (converted from 200 lb bags per acre).
Source: IBRD (1975: 38).

Economic decline has continued unabated in the post-war years. One index of this is a steady fall during the 1950s both in the absolute output of wool and mohair and in the relative value of wool (Morse 1960: 372–3). Another index is relative productivity in maize, sorghum and wheat recorded in the agricultural censuses of 1950, 1960 and 1970 (Table 1.3). Considerable variation between one season and the next means that it is dangerous to extrapolate a trend from figures ten years apart, but this evidence is at least suggestive of a continuing decline in agricultural productivity. Over this period of twenty years increasing population pressure led the people to plough up pasture and marginal land so that the total acreage brought under cultivation increased by 12 per cent. Wheat and sorghum acreages greatly increased, while production rose only marginally; maize acreage considerably decreased, and production was very much reduced. All three cereals, constituting more than 90 per cent of Lesotho's arable production in both volume and value (SFYDP: 74–5), showed a significant reduction in yield per unit area.

In a survey of a Lowland village in 1963 Sandra Wallman found that of thirty households whose economic profiles she plotted only four harvested enough grain to provide minimum subsistence for their members at the officially estimated requirement of 20 bags of grain per family of five persons; while the average harvest was less than half the consumption requirement (Wallman 1969: 68–9, 74).[8] Perhaps the best single index of the country's incapacity to feed its own people is the shift over the years from net export to net import of maize, the principal staple food. This shift is shown graphically in Fig. 1.2. By 1975 the five-year rolling average of annual maize imports had climbed to 330,000 bags.[9] It is likely, however, that this figure is a considerable

17

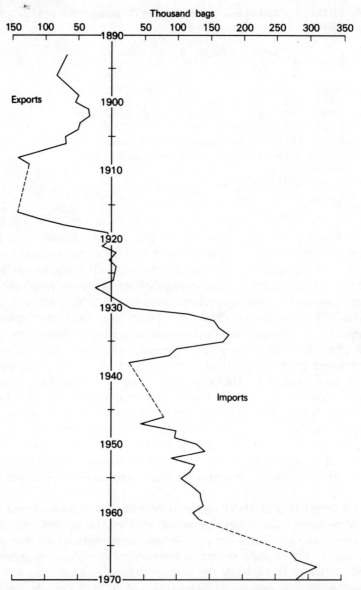

1.2 A graph showing net exports/imports of maize, Lesotho, 1890–1970, based on a 5-year rolling average
Sources: Pim (1935: 191–2); Morse (1960: 371–3); CARs; ASBs. Exports only, 1893–1918. No figures available for 1910–15, 1939–45 and 1963–5

18

underestimate of Lesotho's total imports of maize products, including donations from international agencies.

The decline of agriculture in Lesotho has been attributed to many factors: deterioration of the land through mono-cropping, over-grazing, exhaustion and severe erosion; insecurities in the system of land tenure which inhibit farmers from taking effective steps to conserve their agricultural holdings; population pressure which created an acute short-age of land relative to 'subsistence' requirements and which forced the exploitation of marginal land quite unsuitable for agriculture; and climatic vicissitudes such as drought, hail and frost which render agri-culture a risky enterprise in any circumstances and may inhibit farmers from making the necessary investment in intensive techniques.[10] The emphasis in both Five Year Plans in the 1970s has been on reversing this decline, both through regional development projects and through a proposal known as the Basic Agricultural Services Project. This was designed to create an infrastructure of roads, supply points and extension services and thereby to induce a 'gradual incremental improvement in farming practices and yields' (SFYDP: 86). The precedents are not encouraging. For reasons analysed by Wallman (1969) and Nobe and Seckler (1979), the history of development projects in Lesotho is one of almost unremitting failure to achieve their objectives.

Lesotho's present dependence on the export of labour to South Africa is starkly illustrated by the following facts. In 1976 there were only 27,500 Basotho employed inside the country (SFYDP: 42). Perhaps 200,000 migrants from Lesotho are regularly employed in South Africa, out of the country's total (1976) population of 1,217,000.[11] In 1977 nearly 130,000 men were employed in South African mines alone, supplying more than a quarter of the industry's complement of black labour (ASB 1978: 78). The earnings of these migrants far exceed Lesotho's Gross Domestic Product and, according to a recent survey (van der Wiel 1977), about 70 per cent of mean rural household income is derived from migrant earnings. Only about 6 per cent is derived from domestic crop production (see Chapter 4). The population of Lesotho today is aptly described as a rural proletariat which scratches about on the land.

In 1975 approximately four out of every five migrant labourers were employed in the South African mining industry, mainly in the gold mines and coal mines of the Transvaal, the Orange Free State and Natal (van der Wiel 1977: 30). All miners are recruited within the country by six licensed agencies which submit returns to the Department of Labour. The majority are contracted with The Employment Bureau of Africa (TEBA), known in Lesotho before 1977 as the Native Recruiting Corporation (NRC), which recruits on behalf of the South African

Table 1.4. *Lesotho citizens employed on South African mines, 1963–79.*

Year	Monthly average numbers employed	Year	Monthly average numbers employed
1963	58,678	1971	92,747
1964	62,653	1972	98,822
1965	66,527	1973	110,477
1966	80,951	1974	106,231
1967	77,414	1975	112,507
1968	80,310	1976	121,062
1969	83,053	1977	128,941
1970	87,384	1978	124,973
		1979	124,393

Source: Department of Labour, Maseru.

Chamber of Mines and represents most of the gold mines and some of the coal and platinum mines. Mining is the only sector of employment for which there are accurate figures relating to the number of migrants from Lesotho recruited each year and the average number of men in employment at any one time. These figures have been available only since 1963, when strict border controls were imposed by the South African authorities. Table 1.4 shows that the average number of men from Lesotho employed on South African mines more than doubled over the period 1963 to 1977.

It is extremely difficult to estimate the value of the earnings of migrant labourers that accrues to Lesotho. A large proportion of miners' earnings is officially recorded in the form of remittances and deferred pay. But migrants also send large amounts to their dependants in registered letters through the postal service, and there are no reliable figures for this unofficial flow of remittances. Further, on their return home migrants bring with them cash and goods bought with their earnings which may be considered part of the rural household's income in Lesotho. On the basis of a sample survey of 170 returning miners in 1973, McDowall (1973) estimated that approximately two-thirds of their total cash earnings in South Africa accrued to Lesotho in these ways; and from similar evidence van der Wiel estimated that the corresponding pro-portion in 1975 was 72 per cent (1977: 79). The value of net earnings unofficially estimated by these two investigators was R16 million in 1972–3 (McDowall 1973) and R100 million in 1976 (van der Wiel 1977: 79). These figures are broadly consistent with official estimates of R30 million in the financial year 1973–4, R46 million in 1974 and R55 million

Table 1.5. *Lesotho's trade figures,*
1973–76.

Year	(R million) Exports	Imports
1973	8.8	60.5
1974	9.8	81.7
1975	9.2	117.8
1976	14.6	179.6

Source: ASB (1977: 76, 84).

in 1974–5 (ASB 1977: 14; SFYDP: 260). This very substantial increase in the value of net earnings reflects the increase in average numbers of miners employed (Table 1.4) and, above all, the fact that mine wages quadrupled in nominal value over the period 1972 to 1976 (Table 1.7 below).

Since 1975 an arrangement has been in force between the Lesotho government and the mining companies by which sums between a minimum of 60 per cent and a maximum of 90 per cent of the miner's basic wage are compulsorily deferred by the employer and paid into a special account in the Lesotho National Development Bank. Since these funds have to be realizable on demand they are lent out on the Johannesburg short-term money market rather than invested in long-term development projects. The miners receive 5 per cent interest on their deposits. There was initial resistance to this scheme on the part of Basotho miners, who distrusted their own government's disposition of the funds thus generated. Very little information has been made public about the way the scheme has worked in practice (see Rugege 1979).

The estimates of the net value to Lesotho of migrants' earnings may be compared with the country's escalating balance of payments deficit over the period 1973 to 1976 (Table 1.5). Until the mid-1970s exports were dominated by wool and mohair. Significant recent developments have been a boom in the tourist industry and the capitalization of diamond-mining by DeBeers at Letšeng-la-Terai, a remote site in the northern mountains. Diamond exports were worth R0.45 million in 1976, R1.25 million in 1977 and R16.7 million in 1978. The last figure may be compared with wool exports worth R2.9 million in 1978 and mohair exports worth R4.8 million. Thus diamonds have now overtaken the traditional exports in value. However, the industry scarcely contributes to a solution of the problem of unemployment (see Ström 1978: 132–40).

The political economy of migrant labour

The failure of peasant self-sufficiency in Lesotho – in particular the questions of land shortage, population increase and lack of access to capital – must be examined against the background of a larger system of production which demanded, not that Africans grow sufficient food to preserve their economic independence, but that they contribute their labour to the 'white' economy. So long as Basotho were making a viable livelihood off the land, they would not make their labour available to white-owned farms and industries.

For the purpose of the following analysis it is convenient to distinguish two overlapping phases in the incorporation of Basotho as wage-labourers. The first phase, lasting for about one hundred years from the 1870s to the early 1970s, was one of rapid albeit uneven industrial expansion in the core areas of South Africa, initially in mining and farming and latterly in manufacturing. Wages were poor and the conditions of migrants' residence and employment were rigidly controlled by the notorious 'pass' laws. By and large, however, employment in South Africa was readily available to Basotho migrants who needed it. The second phase is marked by the establishment of border control posts between South Africa and Lesotho in 1963, the formal proscription of all foreign migrants in sectors of employment other than mining and agriculture, and the exclusion of Basotho women from the South African labour market. This process of alienation of labour through the manipulation of political boundaries was extended and intensified in the 1970s, through the 'internalization' policy of mining recruitment (described below), the fulfilment of the Bantustan policy in respect of three African 'homelands', and through measures designed to reinforce the distinction between migrants on the one hand and Africans with rights of permanent residence in 'white' South Africa on the other hand. The effect of these measures has been to concentrate unemployment in the labour reserves. Although the number of Basotho migrants employed in the mining sector in the 1960s and 1970s steadily increased (Table 1.4), Lesotho is acutely vulnerable to the threat of mass unemployment in the 1980s. In this book I am particularly concerned with the repercussions of the second phase, which I describe as one of relative alienation.

The phase of incorporation

The story of white farming in South Africa is the story of perennial competition for labour against African self-sufficiency on the one hand

and the demands of mining and manufacturing industries, which paid higher wages, on the other hand. White farmers took the view that raising wage levels would actually reduce the supply of labour available. The empirical and theoretical invalidity of this view has been effectively demonstrated by Berg (1961), Francis Wilson (1971) and van Onselen (1975). Nevertheless, as Wilson observed (1971: 120), the belief in the backward sloping labour supply curve has had important repercussions in South African history. Instead of raising wages, farmers preferred to use alternative, coercive, means of assuring a labour supply. In the earlier period, as we have seen, these took the form of protective grain tariffs imposed against imports from Basutoland by the Transvaal and the Orange Free State. Above all, however, it was the Land Act of 1913 which deprived Africans of the capacity to compete where, initially at least, Africans were more successful than white farmers because of their lower opportunity cost of engaging in commercial agriculture. The Act stopped Africans from buying land in 'white' areas; it severely limited the independent productive activities of Africans on white-owned land, either as 'squatters' paying rent to land-owners or as entrepreneurs who owned oxen and ploughs and entered into share-cropping arrangements with land-owners. Under the latter system of 'farming-on-the-half' the African worked the land and handed over half the crops reaped to the white land-owner in return for the right to live and cultivate and graze animals on his farm. Such independent activities 'made the kaffirs too rich' and simultaneously deprived the whites of their labour supply and undermined their markets in grain (F. Wilson 1971: 126–31).

The 1913 Land Act had two indirect effects on Basutoland. Firstly, according to Plaatje (1916: 103–6), some of the 'squatters' and share-croppers who were forced off land in the Orange Free State migrated into Basutoland, exacerbating the population pressure there. Secondly, since it may be regarded as 'an act of collusion amongst the hirers of labour not to give remuneration above a certain level … the Land Act was, for farmers, what the maximum-permissible-average agreement was for the mining magnates' (F. Wilson 1971: 128). The depression of agricultural wages affected migrants from Basutoland who worked on white farms in the Free State in the same way as it affected Africans who were dispossessed. Discriminatory legislation of this kind either directly compelled these people to take up wage employment or confined them to reserves from which, unable to eke out a subsistence livelihood, they were forced to migrate and offer their labour on white farms and in industry.

The British administration in Basutoland was by no means indifferent to the question of an adequate labour supply for white farms and industry. It had been a condition of political incorporation in 1870 that the cost of annexing and administering the territory should be met out of a hut tax based on the number of huts in each family compound. The Governor's Regulations of 1871 fixed the rate at ten shillings per hut (Burman 1976: 4). British officials rationalized a policy of benign neglect by contradictory principles. On the one hand, they endorsed the philanthropists' view that 'native cultures' should not be interfered with. On the other hand, they shared Cecil Rhodes' view that Africans should learn the dignity of labour. Thus a policy that Jack Spence has described as a 'neat coincidence of interest between private altruism and public parsimony' (1968: 14) was also readily compatible with the labour requirements of South African farms and industry. The best evidence for this is the Resident Commissioner's remarks in 1899:

Though for its size and population Basutoland produces a comparatively enormous amount of grain, it has an industry of great economic value to South Africa, viz. the output of native labour. It supplies the sinews of agriculture in the Orange Free State, to a large extent it keeps going railway works, coal mining, the diamond mines at Jagersfontein and Kimberly, the gold mines of the Transvaal and furnishes, in addition, a large amount of domestic services in the surrounding territories ... To [those] who urge higher education of the natives, it may be pointed out that to educate them above labour would be a mistake. Primarily the native labour industry supplies a dominion want and secondarily it tends to fertilize native territories with cash which is at once diffused for English Goods (CAR 1898–9).

In this way the administration was sensitive to the wider interests of imperialism.

However, the process of proletarianization was undoubtedly accelerated by the existing structures of inequality within rural communities in Lesotho. As I have indicated above, there is evidence throughout the first half of the twentieth century that some chiefs enriched themselves at the expense of their subjects, by abusing the principle of equity in the administration of arable land which is inscribed in the customary law, and by exacting excessive tribute in labour from resident citizens, in fines and livestock from petty offenders, and in cash from returning migrants. Both deliberately and by default, the chiefs and the administrative officers connived in the out-migration of the country's able-bodied manpower. The colonial legislation which facilitated recruitment procedures has been reviewed by Kowet (1978) and by Rugege (1979).

Meanwhile the Chamber of Mines had begun from 1896 to consolidate a uniform strategy of recruitment and wage determination. Though it did not alleviate absolute shortages of labour, the policy of official collusion effectively limited competition for labour between companies which

24

would otherwise have forced a rise in wages (F. Wilson 1972a; Jeeves 1975). In this way the mining industry was able to maintain black wages at a very low level and to apply a uniform wage structure. The policy has survived successive shortages of labour and also, more recently, labour unrest arising from low wages, poor industrial relations and the frustrations of compound life (Leys 1975). In addition, the mining companies were able to bring pressure to bear on the South African government to pass a series of harshly refined measures to control the flow of labour. These are the 'pass' laws incorporated in the Black (Urban Areas) Act of 1923 and subsequent amendments, based on the notorious principle enunciated by the Stallard Commission in 1921: 'The native should only be allowed to enter the urban areas, which are essentially the white man's creation, when he is willing so to enter and to minister to the needs of the white man and should depart therefrom when he ceases so to minister' (cited in F. Wilson 1972b: 160).

The rights of Africans to live and work in 'white' South Africa were most rigidly circumscribed by the provisions of Section 10 (1) of the Black (Urban Areas) Consolidation Act of 1945 as amended. The relevant sub-sections of this Act provided that no African may remain for more than 72 hours in a 'proclaimed' (later 'prescribed') area without proving that he or she

    (a) has resided there continuously since birth; or

    (b) has worked there continuously for one employer for ten years; or has resided there continuously and legally for fifteen years, subject to certain other conditions; or

    (c) is a close dependent relative of, and ordinarily co-resident with, an African who qualifies under (a) or (b), provided that he or she also initially entered the area lawfully; or

    (d) has been granted special permission to be in the area.

During the 1950s all the formidable resources of the South African state were mustered to enforce the principle that Africans were redundant in 'white' South Africa in any other capacity than as units of labour. The Nationalist Government ruthlessly implemented a series of measures designed to regulate the supply of labour and to tighten control of the movement of Africans and of the conditions of their employment. All urban areas were 'proclaimed' in terms of this legislation: in practice this meant all areas where there was a significant concentration of Africans. All Africans in South Africa who had reached the age of sixteen years were required to possess a comprehensive reference book, designed to replace a number of the 'passes' which had to be carried previously. Influx control was applied to women as well as to men. Labour bureaux

Families divided

were established at which all work-seekers had to register, and the powers of local authorities to remove 'idle or undesirable' Africans were widened.[12]

In this way the pattern was established by which unskilled black workers both from foreign labour-supplying states and from the African reserve areas within South Africa spend their working lives oscillating between their rural homes and their places of employment in 'white' South Africa. The mine compound system and influx control made it impossible for migrants to bring their families to settle at the place of work. Indeed, the justification from the mining industry's point of view of a policy of paying sub-subsistence wages has always rested on two presuppositions inherent in the system of oscillating migration: firstly that migrants also derive an income from working the land in the rural areas and that the two sources of income are complementary; and secondly that wages need not be paid at a level necessary to sustain the expensive urban infrastructure and social services which would be required by a stabilized labour force of miners with their families (F. Wilson 1972a; Wolpe 1972; D. Clarke 1977a, 1977b). Further, migrant labour was much more susceptible to political control than stabilized labour, through its high annual turnover, the possibility of repatriating 'agitators' and the ability to police the mine compounds easily (F. Wilson 1976; cf. van Onselen 1976).

There are disadvantages in oscillating migration from the employers' point of view, in that a high turnover of unskilled manpower is an inefficient and wasteful method of using human capital. But the 'fine tuning' of South African labour administration has been able to overcome this disadvantage to some extent, through 'bonus' incentives to skilled migrants to return to the same employers (F. Wilson 1975) and, especially at a time of massive recession, through an effective ban on the recruitment of unskilled labour. The system has enabled employers historically to evade their responsibility to pay a living wage: Wilson has shown that the real earnings of black workers on the gold mines were no higher in 1969 than they had been in 1911 (1972a: 46, 66).

The phase of relative alienation

Until 1963, since there were no border-control posts, migrants from Basutoland were not effectively distinguished from migrants from the African reserve areas in South Africa, in terms of their access to the South African labour market. From that year, however, various pieces of legislation introduced and consolidated such a distinction, reflecting Prime Minister Verwoerd's formal acknowledgement that the British

26

High Commission Territories would not be politically incorporated into South Africa (Spence 1971: 496–503). The Aliens Control Act of 1963 made it an offence for a foreign African to enter South Africa without a travel document issued by his own country and recognized by the South African government. The Black Laws Amendment Act of 1963 required all foreign Africans entering South Africa for work, except those re-cruited to work in the mines and other specified industries, to have prior written permission to do so from the Secretary of Bantu Administration and Development (now Co-operation and Development) or an officer authorized by him. Correspondingly, a prospective employer who wished to employ foreign Africans in South Africa had to apply for a 'no-objection' certificate from a Bantu Affairs Commissioner to the effect that there was no suitable local labour available. Border control posts were established in 1963, and the travel documents of Basotho authorized to enter South Africa for work or merely to visit were endorsed accordingly, and the details of employment and conditions of entry specified. No citizen of Lesotho who was not in authorized employment in South Africa on 1 July 1963 could remain in a 'prescribed' area within the provisions of the Urban Areas Act as outlined above. In other words, it became impossible for those who joined the labour force after that date to acquire rights to continuous employment and residence in South Africa. A further, devastating, effect of these changes was that after 1963 women from Lesotho were effectively precluded from legal access to the South African labour market. This is directly reflected in the sharp reduction in the number of female 'absentees' recorded in the 1966 census, by comparison with 1956 (Table 1.1).

In 1968 further regulations were introduced which were designed to extend and entrench the system of migratory labour for all Africans. Provision was made for the establishment of labour bureaux in the Bantustans, and Africans who sought employment were allowed to take it up only on the basis of contracts signed for periods not exceeding one year. At the end of each contract a worker had to return to the labour bureau nearest to his home, and re-register as a work-seeker in a particular category of employment. Employers had to repatriate workers to their homes at the end of the period of service. In spite of a 'call-in' card system whereby a worker could return to the same employer, by definition this was on the basis of a new contract, so that workers recruited on contract after 1968 could never qualify to live and work in 'white' South Africa on a permanent basis under the provisions of Section 10 (1) of the Urban Areas Act. This is the legal framework which presently applies in South Africa.[13] Similar provisions were incorporated

27

in the specific agreements which South Africa made with each labour-supplying state in the 1960s, except that foreign Africans required special permission for any category of employment other than mining and farm labour, and that South African labour would be given preference over foreign labour. In general, if a man was qualified in 1968 to be in a 'prescribed' area under Section 10 (1) (d) of the Urban Areas Act, he could remain there subject to the continuation of his particular employment. But it must be presumed that men identified as citizens of Lesotho could not qualify in this way after 1963.

In the light of this discussion, the legal constraints which presently apply to migrants from Lesotho may be summarized as follows. They are not permitted to enter South Africa for the purpose of seeking work: they may only engage in employment in South Africa through a labour contract made in Lesotho. Otherwise, they require special permission to be so engaged, under sections of the South African legal framework which specifically discriminate against foreign Africans. Such permission has been granted from time to time in the past but, in view of the prevailing level of structural unemployment, it is quite unlikely to be granted in the future (Spiegel 1979: 24). The period for which workers are recruited may not exceed one year, and in any case they must return to Lesotho within a period of two years. A worker may not become the tenant of a house in a 'prescribed' area of South Africa; and he may not be accompanied by his wife or children to be resident with him. Labour contracts are not available to women from Lesotho.

In spite of these constraints it is clear that considerable numbers of Basotho migrants are either employed on contract in sectors other than mining or are illegally employed in South Africa. On the basis of figures extrapolated from three sample surveys of migrants in the mid-1970s, van der Wiel (1977: 22) estimated that, of 200,000 migrants regularly employed in South Africa, 81 per cent were employed in mining, 10 per cent in the manufacturing and construction industries, and 5 per cent in domestic service. Employment in agriculture, at 1 per cent, is much less significant than past estimates suggest (Leistner 1967: 49). Allowing for the fact that not all regular migrants are away at work at any one time, and for an unknown proportion of migrants who are illegally employed and whose presence may not be recorded in South Africa, the total number of migrants extrapolated from these surveys in Lesotho is approximately consistent with official South African figures for the number of Africans from Lesotho actually working in the Republic. This figure was 160,634 in February 1977 (SAIRR 1977: 223).

During the 1970s, various political and economic pressures induced the mining industry to initiate a policy of 'internalizing' mine-labour

28

recruitment, in order to reduce dependence on foreign supplies and to increase dependence on South African supplies (for a full analysis, see D. Clarke 1977b). The indispensable condition of this reversal of policy, following a long period of wage stagnation and of increasing dependence on foreign supplies, was the liberation of the international price of gold from its fixed official rate of 35 dollars an ounce. The first price boom took off in June 1972, following the international 'war over gold' described in detail by Johnson (1977). This allowed wages in the mining industry to rise in such a way as to compete with wages in the manufacturing industry for the first time, and therefore to attract black South Africans. The wage increase was in any case an immediate political necessity, in the wake firstly of the strikes which took place in Durban and elsewhere in 1972 and 1973 and secondly of widespread violence and unrest in the mining compounds themselves, attributable to low wages and poor working and living conditions.

Independently of these factors, two events in 1974 exposed the vulnerability of the mining industry to political developments outside South Africa's borders. President Banda of Malawi imposed a total ban on the recruitment of labour from Malawi, in response to a plane crash in Botswana in April 1974 in which 72 Malawi miners returning home were killed. The ban turned out to be a temporary one only: recruiting was resumed in 1977, but never reached its former level. The other event was the collapse of Portuguese colonialism in Mozambique. The new FRELIMO government was in no position economically to phase out the recruitment of Mozambique nationals for work in the South African mines. But the mining industry regarded the future supply of labour from Mozambique as uncertain for political reasons. In any case the increase in the price of gold had made Mozambican labour relatively expensive to the industry, under the provisions of the Mozambique Convention by which part of the miners' wages had been paid to the Portuguese government in gold valued at the old official price. Accordingly, the industry took unilateral steps both to phase out this agreement and to reduce its dependence on Mozambique as a source of supply.

In December 1973 foreign Africans constituted 80 per cent of the black labour force employed on mines affiliated to the South African Chamber of Mines, and South Africans constituted the remaining 20 per cent. In December 1978, the respective proportions were 45 per cent and 55 per cent (Table 1.6). These figures reflect the success of the 'internalization' policy from the mining industry's point of view. In the short term, in order to make up for the sudden reduction of labour from Malawi and Mozambique, the effect of the policy was to increase the numbers from Lesotho in employment on the mines. Thus in the short term, also,

Table 1.6. *Geographical sources of black labour distributed by TEBA, as at 31 December 1973 and 1978.*

| | 1973 | | 1978 | |
Source	Numbers	Percentage	Numbers	Percentage
SOUTH AFRICA	86,221	20.42	250,311	54.93
Lesotho	87,229	20.66	104,143	22.85
Botswana	16,811	3.98	18,129	3.95
Swaziland	4,526	1.07	8,352	1.83
Mozambique	99,424	23.55	45,168	9.91
Tropicals	127,970	30.32	29,618	6.50
FOREIGN	355,960	79.58	205,410	45.07
Total	422,181	100.00	455,721	100.00

Source: TEBA Annual Reports.
Note: Until 1975 the vast majority of miners in the category Tropicals (areas north of latitude 22°S) were from Malawi. Since 1974, however, substantial numbers have been recruited from Zimbabwe.

Basotho were able to take advantage of the substantial wage increases which accompanied the changes in the distribution of recruitment. Table 1.7 shows that the average annual cash earnings of black labourers on the gold mines increased from R257 in 1972 to R1,476 in 1978. The cost of living in Lesotho more than doubled over the same period. In real terms, therefore, average earnings in 1975 were two and a half times their value in 1972, and thereafter fluctuated in terms of their capacity to keep pace with inflation.[14]

These jobs were by no means secure, however. In April 1978 it was estimated that Lesotho would have to anticipate the loss of about 40,000 jobs in the 1980s (Lusaka 1978). This trend is clearly evident in a recent steep decline in the numbers of miners recruited: from a peak of 160,516 in 1976 to 143,204 in 1977, 115,044 in 1978 and 92,823 in 1979 (figures from Department of Labour, Maseru). Overall numbers in employment were only sustained during these years (see Table 1.4) through longer periods of service by miners already on contract. In the longer term, it has been estimated that 'the most probable outcome is a reduction of Basotho migrants to approximately 50 per cent of present numbers by the year 2000' (Eckert and Wykstra 1979: 17–18).

Most of the increase in the South African supply of mine labour during the 1970s was drawn from the Bantustans, the Transkei in particular (Fig. 1.3). Thus the 'internalization' policy has greatly

Table 1.7. *Average annual cash earnings of black labour on the gold mines, 1972–8.*

Year	Average annual cash earnings (current rands)	Cost of living index, Lesotho (Oct. 1972 = 100)	Index of real earnings (Oct. 1972 = 100)
1972	257	100.0	100
1973	350	112.8	121
1974	565	128.4	171
1975	947	146.6	251
1976	1,103	162.1	265
1977	1,224	191.0	249
1978	1,476	211.0	272

Sources: Earnings 1972–6 from Stahl (1979: 30); 1977 from SAIRR (1978: 213); 1978 from SAIRR (1979: 240). The cost of living index is Index B, Retail Price Indices, Bureau of Statistics, Maseru (all urban households with an income of less than R500 p.a. in 1972–3). In view of the cost of transport, this index probably understates the rate of inflation in the rural areas of Lesotho.

increased the employment in mining available to residents of the Bantustans, which partially mitigates the effects of an appallingly high and steadily rising level of unemployment in other sectors of the economy.[15] But the boundary between 'foreign' sources of supply and South African sources has already been re-drawn. Millions of black South Africans were defined as citizens of Transkei, Bophuthatswana and Venda on the attainment of their 'sovereign independence', respectively in 1976, 1977 and 1979. These people were summarily deprived of their South African citizenship and converted into foreigners: they are regarded as 'guest-workers' in the country of their birth; they no longer appear in South Africa's unemployment statistics; and Pretoria has effectively disclaimed responsibility for their social and economic welfare. Their 'sovereign independence' is, in fact, their compulsory political alienation. The other seven 'homelands' (Fig. 1.4) are still part of the Republic of South Africa. In official parlance they are referred to as 'Black States' and regarded as incipiently 'independent' in the same manner. There is some evidence to suggest that the elaborate infrastructure of labour bureaux throughout the country is used to distribute employment and unemployment in such a way as to bring political pressure to bear on recalcitrant Bantustan leaders, and to render relatively invisible the worst problems of poverty, hunger and ill-health by concentrating them in remote and isolated areas.[16]

The clearest evidence of the South African government's policy prior-

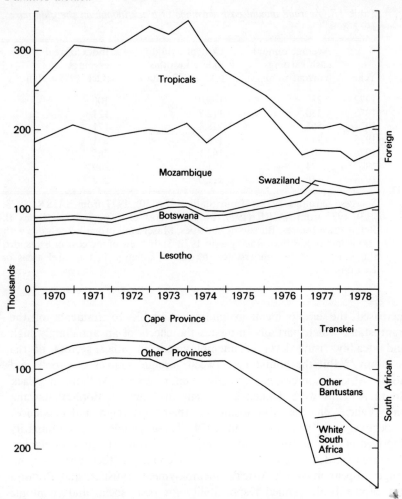

1.3 Geographical sources of black labour (TEBA), 1970–8
Source: TEBA Annual Reports
Note: Until 1976 South Africans were classified by their province of origin; from 1977 by their origin in the 'white' areas and the ten Bantustans

ities emerged in 1979 with its reaction to the reports of the Wiehahn and Riekert Commissions of Inquiry into labour relations and utilization of manpower respectively. The government initially rejected Wiehahn's recommendation that black migrant labourers and commuters should be given trade union rights, while accepting that this was desirable for Africans permanently resident in 'white' South Africa. In September 1979, however, statutory trade union rights were extended by ministerial

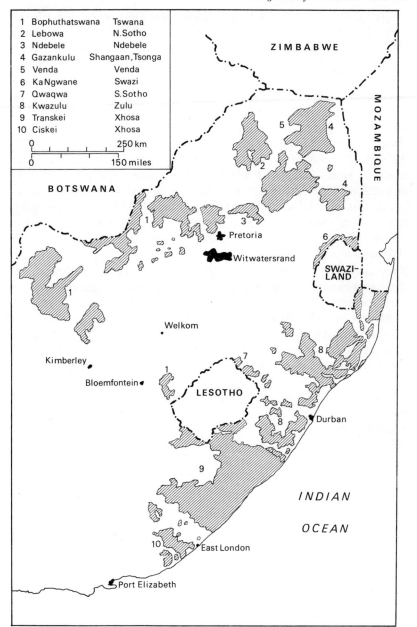

1	Bophuthatswana	Tswana
2	Lebowa	N.Sotho
3	Ndebele	Ndebele
4	Gazankulu	Shangaan,Tsonga
5	Venda	Venda
6	KaNgwane	Swazi
7	Qwaqwa	S.Sotho
8	Kwazulu	Zulu
9	Transkei	Xhosa
10	Ciskei	Xhosa

1.4 A map of the labour reserves: Lesotho and the South African Bantustans (1969).
In view of continuing changes in the consolidation plans and the elimination of 'black
spots', this map no longer accurately represents the Bantustan boundaries
Source: Horrell (1973)

33

discretion to 'all citizens of South Africa and countries which previously formed part of South Africa' (SAIRR 1979: 285). More importantly, Riekert's recommendations reflect an explicit commitment to ease restrictions on labour mobility for Africans with rights under Section10 (1), and at the same time to tighten the mechanisms of influx control applied to workers domiciled outside the 'white' areas.[17] These reports and the official response to them represent a significant change of policy. In 1968 the government's repeatedly expressed ambition was that *all* Africans should be migrant labourers (Rogers 1976: 10; Davis 1978: 5). In 1979, the Minister of Co-operation and Development Dr Piet Koornhof made a widely publicized speech in the United States in which he stressed that 'the urban black is not a transient phenomenon, but a permanent part of the South African setup'.[18] This change of policy reflects the government's anxiety to improve conditions for urban Africans in 'white' South Africa, in order to forestall future volatile outbursts of black anger such as the events of June 1976 in Soweto. On the other hand, the measures recommended by Riekert, in particular, will inevitably exacerbate the problems of poverty and unemployment in the rural periphery. Accordingly, they are an attempt to deal with the symptoms and not the underlying causes of black discontent. They are wholly consistent with the contemporary rationale of the strategy of separate development from Pretoria's point of view, which is to export the problem of unemployment while avoiding political responsibility for it.

The conclusion of this analysis is that the structures of apartheid in the late 1970s and the early 1980s are directed towards the alienation of black labour, in a literal sense, through the manipulation of political boundaries. There are two aspects of this process. One aspect is that the areas from which black labour has been drawn on a very large scale in the past may be placed at different points in a scale of relative foreignness, with respect to the access of their populations to the South African labour market. The significant boundaries on this scale may be represented as a series of concentric circles (F. Wilson 1979) which demarcate the following areas:

1. Outer foreign: Malawi, Mozambique.
2. Inner foreign: Botswana, Lesotho, Swaziland.
3. 'Independent' Bantustans: Transkei, Bophuthatswana, Venda.
4. 'Non-independent' Bantustans: KwaZulu, Ciskei, Lebowa, etc.
5. 'White' South Africa: Africans with rights of permanent residence.

In this perspective, as the poorest and most 'foreign' of the heavily dependent labour reserves, Lesotho is acutely vulnerable to the threat of mass unemployment in the 1980s.

The other aspect of the process of alienation is the institutionalization of ten different 'national' identities, which are supposed both to embrace all black South Africans and to divide them in the achievement of their political aspirations. To the extent that conflicts assume an ethnic form, consciousness along class lines is suppressed, and political control of the labour force is maintained by proxy, through the Bantustan leaders. Koornhof's claim before American audiences in 1979 that 'apartheid as you came to know it ... is dying and dead'[18] was based on the South African government's endorsement of one of the priorities explicitly avowed by Wiehahn and Riekert, that of eliminating racial discrimination. To the extent that the policy of ethnic nationalism has replaced the policy of racial discrimination as such, the claim is justified.[19] But since ethnic nationalism is a strategy by which Africans are forcibly deprived of basic political and economic rights in the country of their birth, Koornhof's claim and the sense of reform implicit in it are at best a distortion of the truth.

In the 1980s, then, the supplier states are faced with a potentially massive crisis of unemployment, through natural population growth, the extrusion of 'redundant' Africans from the South African economy, and a prospective absolute and permanent cut-back in the number of miners employed from foreign sources. One response has been a proliferation of international interest in the consequences of the supplier states' dependence on the export of labour to South Africa. This interest is reflected in the funding of a series of fact-finding missions and large-scale surveys by organizations such as the World Bank, the United States Agency for International Development (USAID) and the International Labour Office (ILO) (IBRD 1975, 1978; USAID 1978; Böhning 1977; Stahl and Böhning 1979). Another response was an international conference in Lusaka arranged by the Economic Commission for Africa in April 1978, in order to co-ordinate strategies for dealing with the potential crisis (Lusaka 1978). Participants were less than sanguine, in a period of deepening economic recession and conflict between the supplier states, about the prospects of establishing a labour-supply cartel.

Nevertheless, in 1979 the ILO took the initiative of proposing an Association of Home Countries of Migrants (AHCM), consisting of Botswana, Lesotho, Swaziland, Malawi, Mozambique and possibly Zimbabwe (Stahl and Böhning 1979). It would seek to bring pressure on South Africa to pay for the creation of alternative employment opportunities within the AHCM economies, in the context of an agreed programme for the phased withdrawal of their labour. The economic bargaining power of such an Association would be based on the threat of immediate and total withdrawal of labour from South Africa, which would impose short-term costs on the South African economy of such magnitude that the mining industry might well be prepared, especially in view of spectacular leaps in the international gold price,[20] to consider the alternative, of a levy paid per man-year of foreign labour employed. In view of the millions of man-years of labour contributed by the labour-supplying states to South Africa's economic growth, the moral case for such compensation is overwhelming (F. Wilson 1976). But the practical politics of achieving it are formidably difficult. In the first place, there are so many imponderable factors involved – the price of gold, the demand for labour, the future political complexion both of South Africa itself and of the supplier states. In the second place, the bargaining power of the AHCM countries would depend on the extent to which they are able to act together, and also on the possibility of effective collusion with the 'independent' Bantustans. But governments and international agencies are unlikely to negotiate with states whose existence they do not formally recognize. In the third place, the threat of unilateral withdrawal of labour would only be credible if a massive United Nations back-up fund were established for employment creation in the AHCM countries.[21]

This is the contemporary political and economic framework within which Basotho migrate to work in South Africa. In the following Chapters I seek to analyse the impact of oscillating migration on the lives of migrants and their families.

2

Migrant labour: a way of life

The migrants and their families with whose lives I am concerned belong to five village communities in three different areas of Lesotho. I spent a total of twenty-two months in Ha Molapo, on the edge of the Leribe plateau (Lowlands), between August 1972 and November 1974; six weeks in Ha Nkopa and Malimong, in the Makhalaneng valley (Foothills) in June and July 1974; and two weeks only in Nokaneng and Ha Pitso, in the Semonkong area (Mountains), in September and October 1974 (see Fig. 1.1). The names of all five villages are pseudonymous, as are the names of their inhabitants.[1] The detailed case studies used in this and other Chapters are drawn from Ha Molapo, because my fieldwork was overwhelmingly concentrated there. But I draw on work in the other two areas for comparison of basic demographic data.

The village of Ha Molapo is perched on a ridge on the north-eastern side of the Leribe plateau, overlooking the Hlotse river valley and opposite Moshoeshoe I's birthplace of Menkhoaneng. It is only a few miles east of the main road between the towns of Hlotse (Leribe 'camp' in Fig. 1.1) and Butha Buthe. The area chief, who resides in Ha Molapo, is subordinate to the principal chief of Leribe, whose home is at Leribe village some miles from Hlotse. The original inhabitants of Ha Molapo were followers of Molapo, second son of Moshoeshoe I. Shortly before the Gun War of 1880, Molapo sent Letlala, of the Sia clan, to settle there in order to serve as the 'eye of the chief'. Some years later, probably about 1890, Molapo's son Jonathan placed one of his own sons, also called Molapo (a pseudonym) over Letlala's area and the outlying villages. Letlala became a subordinate headman but the family retained its influential position through its established prerogative that the family head act as principal adviser (*letona*) to the chief. Many of the present inhabitants of Ha Molapo are descendants of various branches of the Letlala family. Appendix 3 contains an extended account of the factional conflicts between them. There are two other large agnatic families strongly represented in the village: brief biographical details of one of them, the Thapelo family of the Fokeng clan, are given in Appendix 1. Otherwise the community is very diverse in respect of its clan affiliations.

Since there are today two contiguous named settlements to the west and east of Ha Molapo, respectively, the boundaries of the population surveyed were somewhat arbitrarily defined by the physical features of a ridge and a road. The 73 households which constitute this population are not identifiable as a clear-cut administrative entity. Until his death in 1978, Morero Letlala, the senior member of the founding family, had been trying to establish the right to be 'gazetted', i.e. to be listed on the official gazette of recognized headmen. One of the issues at stake was the precise extent of his informally acknowledged administrative authority. Since he was known as a prominent supporter of the opposition BCP, the resolution of the issue was complicated, as such issues almost invariably are, both by dissensions within the family and by party-political factionalism (for details see Appendix 3). In 1972–4 public affairs were dominated by a small BNP clique, but the majority of the local population were supporters of the BCP. This was clear despite the fact that, both before and after a brief period of 'open' politics in 1973, party affiliations were seldom publicly advertised.

The two villages of Ha Nkopa and Malimong lie on opposite slopes of the Makhalaneng valley in the Maseru district. Although less than two miles apart, and overlooked by the twin peaks of Thabana li'Mele, the villages are separately administered because the Makhalaneng river is the boundary, at this point, between the principal chieftainships of Rothe and Matsieng. Nearby, at a bend of the river, is situated the Thabana li'Mele Handicraft centre, which in June 1974 employed 52 people, most of them women from villages in the valley. The history of this craft centre is bound up with that of local political alignments. Designed as a labour-intensive project, it was set up in 1968 and managed by an expatriate Swede who is remembered for his excellent work and good relations with the employees. But he was alleged in 1970, at the time of Qomatsi (the Emergency which followed the election), to have been gun-running on behalf of the opposition. I was told that one of Chief Jonathan's cabinet ministers, a former teacher whose home was in Ha Nkopa, had been besieged in his house by armed members of the BCP. The Swedish manager was expelled and the project was shut down.

The centre was re-opened in 1973 with many of the former employees, but by the following year it had not yet established a viable outlet for its craft products and its future was in some jeopardy, not least because of a prolonged and unhappy dispute between the two expatriates who had taken over management. At the time of my fieldwork there were a number of recurrent tensions: over wages, which were at the flat rate of R0.70

per day for most employees instead of the previous piece-work rates; over the earnings discrepancy between the ordinary employees, for whom a wage rise was conditional on sales turnover, and two supervisory and clerical staff, who had just been awarded a wage increase out of the project grant made by a Swedish development agency (SIDA) through the International Labour Office; and over alleged favouritism in the allocation of jobs to residents of particular villages and members of particular families. It was clear that 52 jobs distributed between women from many villages and at a monthly wage amounting to R14 were a welcome source of pocket-money for many households. It was equally clear that they could never offset the need for an income from migrant labour. Two male apprentice potters had already abandoned the project in favour of mine contracts, as mine wages began to rise in 1973 and 1974 (Table 1.7).

In 1974 the majority of the household heads in Ha Nkopa (15 out of 23) could be placed on one of two agnatic genealogies, comprising families of the Koena and Kholokoe clans respectively. Almost all household heads were identified as BNP supporters. Thirteen of the 34 household heads in Malimong could be placed on the genealogy of the headman's family, of the Hlakoana clan, a branch of the Koena. There were a number of smaller families; otherwise clan affiliations were diverse.

The villages of Nokaneng and Ha Pitso lie on the isolated upland plateau of Semonkong, at a height of about 2,200 m in the Thaba Putsoa range. Nearby are the spectacular LeBihan falls (192m) over the Maletsunyane river, which were vividly described by the missionary Hermann Dieterlen on a visit in 1884 (CB: 499–501) and are a considerable tourist attraction today. In the second half of the nineteenth century this area had been in regular use as a summer grazing ground, with established cattle-posts (*metebo*), but there were no permanent settlements until after the Gun War of 1880, when refugees moved in from elsewhere. The then Paramount Chief Lerotholi's son Leloko was placed as chief over the area in about 1913, and in 1974 the villages of Nokaneng and Ha Pitso were under the authority of his son Manama Leloko Lerotholi. Semonkong as a whole is subordinate to the principal chieftainship of Matsieng. Most settlements in this area are small, Nokaneng and Ha Pitso having only ten households each. The economic regime is somewhat different from that of the Lowlands: wheat, maize and peas are the most important crops – wheat even displaces maize as a regular element in the daily diet – while sorghum does not ripen at this height. Most Mountain households have many more livestock than Lowland households (see Chapter 4). In spite of this, there seems to be little difference in the extent of dependence on migrant labour (Table 2.1).

The migrant career

The histogram in Fig. 2.1 is a demographic profile of Lesotho's population aged between 15 and 59 in 1966, by sex, 5-year age cohorts and residential status. It represents, in other words, the population identified as 'economically active' for the purpose of defining Dependency Ratio 1 in Table 2.4 below. The skewed age and sex distribution of absentees reflects the mining industry's preference for younger men and the fact that labour contracts are not available to women. The census figures from which the histogram is derived indicate that 42 per cent of males aged 20 to 59, and 51 per cent of males aged 20 to 39, were absent from Lesotho at that time (FFYDP: 245, 247). The corresponding figures from the 1976 census were 44 per cent and 52 per cent respectively (preliminary results, Bureau of Statistics). Specific studies in the 1970s suggest a rather higher incidence of absence than recorded in either census. For example, a survey of 1,286 households in the Phuthiatsana Irrigation Project area (Lowlands and Foothills) and the Thaba Tseka Livestock Project area (Mountains) in 1976 revealed that 62 per cent of all males aged 18 to 59 and 77 per cent of males aged 20 to 39 were absent migrant labourers (van der Wiel 1977: 32). A survey of 442 households in the Tsa Kholo area of Mafeteng district (Lowlands) in 1976 recorded 61 per cent of all males aged 18 to 60 as wage earners

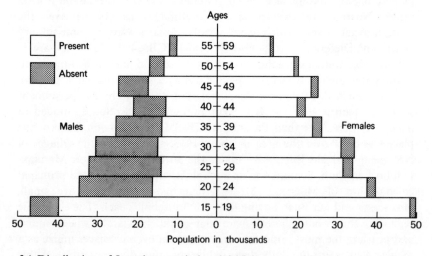

2.1 Distribution of Lesotho population (1966) by sex, residential status and age cohorts 15–59
Source: FFYDP

(Feachem *et al.* 1978: 18). The latter figure, it should be noted, includes a number of people in paid employment within Lesotho, but the large majority were in South Africa. The question of how absentees are defined is discussed fully below.

In his survey van der Wiel found an 'inverse relationship between the rate of external labour migration and the level of education' (1977: 35). But this is true only of the higher levels of education, since there are so few employment opportunities available within Lesotho, and people with some years of secondary schooling must still go to South Africa for work. Moreover, the increase in mine wages in the 1970s led some primary school teachers in Lesotho to abandon the profession in favour of mine contracts. Thus Spiegel (1979: 69–72) found that differences in level of educational attainment were more significant in the allocation of individuals to different occupational grades within the mining sector than in distributing individuals between mining and non-mining sectors.

The large majority of migrants are employed as contract labourers who return for varying periods of 'rest' between contracts. The mean length of service of Basotho labourers in the gold mines over the period 1970–6 varied between a maximum of 14.4 months in 1974 and a minimum of 10.6 months in 1976. During these years more than two-thirds of mine workers consistently took up a further contract within six months of returning home at the end of the previous contract. On the basis of a survey of Basotho who had completed their migratory careers, van der Wiel reached the conclusion that 'the real average length of his working life that a migrant worker spends outside Lesotho is estimated to be 16 years for those coming from the lowlands and 13 years for those coming from the mountain zone' (1977: 43, 47, 52).[2] These years of absence are concentrated in early manhood and middle age.

Individual labour histories are variations on a single basic theme: the repetitive movement between a rural home in Lesotho and an industrial centre in South Africa. The paradigm of the successful migrant career for a man is to establish his own household and to build up a capital base, through the acquisition of land, livestock and equipment, to enable him to retire from migrant labour and to maintain an independent livelihood at home. Few men achieve independence in this way. Most must commit themselves in their declining years to dependence on the remittances of sons or of other junior kin who in their turn engage in the oscillating pattern. The stories of five men from Ha Molapo – an elderly man, two middle-aged men and two young men – illustrate characteristic variations on the basic theme. Some of the experiences of female migrants are described in Chapter 7.

41

Destitution in old age Levi (Household <u>118</u>)[3] was born in 1897 at Leribe, the village of the second most powerful chiefly family in Lesotho. As a child he was taken to his mother's natal home at Pitseng, and then to Ha Molapo. He went to the circumcision lodge (*mophato*) in 1914 with the Tlokoa near Sani Pass, on the eastern border with Natal, where he was a hired herdboy, and where he earned twenty small stock which later helped him to marry. After the 'flu epidemic of 1918 which Basotho remember as *Mokakallane*, he had to support himself owing to the loss of many of his family, and he went to work for a brief spell in Durban (Natal). He came home in 1921 and then left to work for the Milling Company, Vereeniging (Transvaal), where he was employed continuously for seventeen years at £3 per month. He married in 1922 with cattle which he had bought entirely with his own earnings, and in due course he had three sons and a daughter. In 1933, during short annual leaves spent in Lesotho, he started to work for the chief of Ha Molapo in an unpaid official capacity as a writer of *bewys* (stock transfer authority).

When war broke out in 1939 Levi took up a job at Victoria Falls Power Station, Vereeniging, at £6 per month, rather than enlist in Lesotho at £3 per month. In 1948 he left that job and came home, only to go out once again to seek work. He found no vacancy at the Power Station, so he started a different job at Vanderbijlpark (Transvaal), but only worked there one month before falling ill and returning home. He did not go out to work again. He ceased working for the chief in 1951 and was effectively retired since that year. His wife died in 1969 and in 1972–4 he was living with his youngest son and his family in his own household. He was stricken with gout and 'bad feet' but his sons did not support him in the way that kinship morality would demand because, I was told, he himself had philandered in his youth and frequently neglected their mother. The village boys even stole his garden peaches, the one resource he could call his own. Levi died at the end of 1978.

The wages of enterprise: (1) a clothes salesman Moeketsi (Household <u>129</u>), born in 1936, had been a regular migrant for twenty years by 1974. He used to work on the gold mines, and also sell clothes in the mine compound in his off-time. He then took up this side-line on a full-time itinerant basis, and he now sells clothes all over the black townships of the Rand. He carries a certificate of *bona fide* employment, on a commission basis, with City Clothing Manufacturers (Johannesburg). This does not qualify him to work in South Africa and he is subject to perpetual harassment under the pass laws. In commenting on this, neighbours from Ha Molapo remarked that he and others in the same position had to live on open hillsides and skulk in water conduits. During his visit home in 1974, the police checks at the border posts became even more stringent than previously. In order to avoid the difficulties of crossing the Caledon river (in flood) undetected, Moeketsi signed on for a mine contract but escaped from the train in transit and made his own way to Johannesburg where he resumed his relatively lucrative form of self-employment. Despite his illegal status he was able to make regular remittances to his wife in the village and she was in the unusual position of being able to plan ahead for the ploughing season. They cultivate one field belonging to his wife's family and also have a regular share-cropping arrangement with his mother 'MaLebelo (Household 115) in respect of one of her fields (see Chapter 3 for details). He also assists his mother to buy fertilizer and seed; and one of his daughters by his first wife, who died in 1969, lives with 'MaLebelo to give her domestic help. Moeketsi and his second wife have a smartly painted house on the ridge which overlooks the rest of the village.

Desertion in middle age Molefi (Household 170) was born in 1931. He took his first mine contract in 1951 and worked sporadically thereafter, completing four contracts, each of about two years' service, at three different mines, before he was repatriated in 1969 after a medical examination for an unpleasant infectious rash. He was instructed not to return for another contract until this disability had healed. An occasional carpenter and mason, he claimed in 1973–4 to make a living by undertaking building work for other people, but he was never in regular work and his wife, particularly, was unable to make ends meet, having to beg small jobs, such as washing clothes and drawing water, in order to make a few shillings to feed her children. In 1974 he deserted her and went to live nearby with his cross-cousin by whom he had already begotten a child. An adolescent son had been hired out to a neighbouring family (Household 135) as a herdboy. Molefi tried without avail to get access to this boy's post office savings book, in which his employer had placed his annual wages in order to stop Molefi from taking the money and drinking it. The crop return from cultivation of his one field in the 1972–3 season failed to cover the cash investment he had made.

The wages of enterprise: (2) a successful miner Masopha (Household 112) was born in 1941. He took his first mine contract in 1961 and by 1973 he had completed six contracts totalling a period of 9 years and 7 months, distributed as follows: 1 year and 6 months at Randfontein; and then five separate contracts at East Daggafontein, of 1 year and 11 months, 1 year and 8 months, 2 years and 2 months, 1 year and 2 months, and 1 year and 2 months. He built up a steady record of continuous employment at East Daggafontein; he successfully passed the 'boss-boy' course in November 1972, and was employed for the last three months of his contract ending in early 1973 as a 'boss-boy' at a rate of R1.25 per shift. Owing to the imminent closure of the mine, Masopha decided to leave in good time and establish a secure base for the future elsewhere, since he anticipated competition at other mines from many others with 'boss-boy' certificates similarly discharged on closure. He was given a discharge card from East Daggafontein which specified his last recorded wages and guaranteed that provided he took his next contract before mid-November 1973 he would be taken on at an equivalent or higher rate of pay at another mine of the Anglo American group. In August 1973 he took a new contract to Vaal Reefs South but did not exploit his 'boss-boy' certificate immediately because, he said, it is important for a man to take time to size up the situation when he newly arrives at a mine. 'If you show them certificates etc. as soon as you start, the Boers are rough, they make it tough for you, so you lie low for a while until you see what they're like.' After two months at Vaal Reefs he showed them his 'boss-boy' certificate and was immediately placed on a new scale. The remaining part of the contract shows the spectacular rise in wages and also his own rise in the labour hierarchy in the mine. In December 1973 Masopha was earning R1.70 per shift; he was placed on a new scale during December at R2.20 per shift and, including a general rise on the group mines of 10 cents per shift in January 1974, ended that month at a rate of R2.30 per shift. He ended his contract in August 1974 being paid at a rate of R4.50, which was then the top rate applying in the Anglo American group of mines.

Meanwhile, during his leave in 1973, he had established domestic independence by building a new stone house in Ha Molapo, and he worked hard to clear the ground around it. His wife had a new baby in April 1974 and in August he returned home with a radiogram and records. The place became the centre of attraction for the 'young set' on leave from the mines, displaying their shoes, urban panache and new dancing styles. Masopha has no land: 'we live by buying'. By 1978 two more children had been born to them and, in Masopha's absence, his wife told me that since 1974 he had not returned to the mines at all but had been a self-employed carpenter in Butha Buthe, six miles away. He came home at week-ends. In this way he was able to exploit the new opportunities for investment in homestead-building which arose out of a substantially higher level of miners' remittances in the mid-1970s.

Towards structural unemployment Thabo (Household 172) was born in 1954 and began his migrant career in 1970. In a period of nine years he completed nine separate mine contracts, distributed as follows:

Mine (and approx. location)	Recruiting Agency	From	To
1. Western Areas: gold (Johannesburg, Transvaal)	NRC (TEBA)	Feb 1970	Sept 1970
2. Freddies Consolidated: gold (Odendaalsrus, Orange Free State)	NRC (TEBA)	Oct 1970	Aug 1971
3. Kilbarchan Colliery: coal (Newcastle, Natal)	NCOLA	Sept 1971	Sept 1972
4. Springfield Colliery: coal (Vereeniging, Transvaal)	ACROL	Sept 1972	Aug 1973
5. Arnot Colliery: coal (Middelburg, Transvaal)	ACROL	Jan 1974	Oct 1974
6. Arnot	ACROL	Mar 1975	Dec 1975
7. Arnot	ACROL	June 1976	Dec 1976
8. Kriel Colliery: coal (Witbank, Transvaal)	ACROL	June 1977	Feb 1978
9. Cornelia Colliery: coal (Vereeniging, Transvaal)	ACROL	Apr 1978	Nov 1978

Thabo came home in November 1978 with a re-engagement certificate dated 16 November 1978 to the effect that 'Should he return to this colliery (Cornelia) by 9 January 1979 he will be guaranteed re-employment and will on engagement receive his original rate of pay', which was R5.87 per shift at the time of discharge. 'Should he overstay the condoned period of absence he will be returned to the issuing colliery only if vacancies exist ...' and paid at the slightly lower rate of R5.64 per shift. Thabo reported at his district recruitment office in Lesotho on 5 January 1979, but was told the mine was closed, and his re-engagement certificate was endorsed accordingly. Despite two certificates of competence which he had acquired at Kriel – as a coal-cutter operator and a coal-buggy driver – he was again refused employment on 26 April 1979. He spent a year thereafter just 'sitting' at home, picking up various odd jobs, while he and his family became increasingly desperate about the prospect of his return to the mines.

In April 1980 Thabo heard from a friend with whom he had worked at Arnot in 1975 that the manager there was looking for men who had worked there previously. He set off immediately on the long journey to the Transvaal in the hope of obtaining a letter from the mine manager which would instruct the recruiting office in Lesotho to give him a new contract. He spent over a week moving from one mine to another, only to be told they were all full up. Eventually he heard of one coal mine that was still looking for labour, but he did not have time to go there to try to obtain a letter because the eleven days he had been allowed at the border post had elapsed and he risked arrest by remaining in South Africa. He came home in a state of depression, intending to set off again in a few weeks' time. He had spent R18 on the return rail fare and more than R30 on other essential expenses, to no avail. Having no money for the journey himself, he had been given R10 by his brother-in-law in Lesotho, R3 by his elder brother working at Springfield colliery, and a sum of R35 by various friends. Thabo's ambition was to acquire a heavy-duty driving licence, with which he hoped to obtain employment in Lesotho. He had failed the test in 1977, and needed money before he could undertake the necessary training.

Ironically, the theme of the TEBA calendar for 1980, widely distributed in Lesotho, was 'Modern Mining Means Secure Living'. It advertised (1) Security of work through your TEBA Bonus Certificate, (2) Security in your old age, (3) Security for your family and (4) Security with good pay. In reality, modern mining represents security only for 'stabilized' professionals, an increasing proportion of a labour force whose overall numbers are rapidly diminishing (see p. 30). In 1976 just over 30 per cent of TEBA mine recruits from Lesotho were 'Specials', i.e. holders of re-engagement guarantee certificates; in 1979 the proportion of 'Specials' was 60 per cent (personal communication from M. Hobson, TEBA office, Maseru). The corollary of this changing proportion is obvious: Thabo's experience of redundancy at the age of 25, after nine of his best years spent working underground, is increasingly typical. Many men and their families now face a desolate future. Thus 'stabilization' of mine labour and structural unemployment are two sides of the same coin.

Village and household demography: a synchronic view

The *de jure* and *de facto* populations of the five villages as recorded in surveys in 1974 are shown in Table 2.1. The surveys were conducted at slightly different times of the year: Ha Nkopa and Malimong (Foothills) in July 1974; Nokaneng and Ha Pitso (Mountains) in September–October 1974; and Ha Molapo (Lowlands) in October 1974. Nevertheless, differences in the proportion of absentees were found not between zones but between villages within zones. Aggregation of the data on a zonal basis shows that 18.6 per cent were absent from the Lowlands, 17.8 per cent from the Foothills and 18.1 per cent from the Mountains. The presentation in Table 2.1 begs an immediate question:

46

Table 2.1. *Resident and absent populations, by village, 1974.*

Village	Zone	Number of households	Population de jure	de facto	Absentees No.	%
1. Ha Molapo	L	73	361	294	67	18.6
2. Ha Nkopa	F	23	116	100	16	13.8
3. Malimong	F	34	171	136	35	20.5
4. Nokaneng	M	10	54	46	8	14.8
5. Ha Pitso	M	10	62	49	13	21.0
All villages		150	764	625	139	18.2

L = Lowlands; F = Foothills; M = Mountains.

what is the definition of an absentee? It is easy enough to record persons who are physically present. But the sociology of absenteeism is vital to an understanding of life in a community deprived of its most vigorous members. The most obvious manifestation of the problem of definition is the fact that survey results do not consistently refer to the same phenomena. In comparing the results of different studies and in assessing the impact of out-migration on particular communities it is necessary firstly to explore the problem of defining the household and secondly to distinguish the following categories: absentees, migrant labourers and paid employees.

The definition of the household

Almost all men and a few women spend most of their middle years absent from their rural homes. Yet, when their working lives are over, or when they have reached a stage in the life cycle when they can depend on the support of children or of other kin, the large majority return home to settle permanently. From the perspective of individual migrants it is clear that in spite of prolonged periods of absence from home they continue to 'belong' in some sense to Lesotho. One aspect of this belonging is citizenship of a local area defined in terms of allegiance to its chief. I discuss this aspect in Chapter 3. Here I am concerned with the more prosaic sense in which individual migrants continue to belong: their earnings as absentees constitute a large part of the livelihood of the village. Their membership of a particular household is expressed in terms of a continuing responsibility to contribute towards its maintenance.

By what criteria, then, is the household defined? It is not a co-residential group: the energies and resources of its members are divided

47

between a variety of activities both in Lesotho and in South Africa. Nor can it be defined by criteria of kinship for, although its members are almost invariably kin of one sort or another, there is striking variation in actual kinship composition both between households and within households over time.

The Basotho themselves have no precise way of talking about the household. The terms *ntlo* and *lelapa* both have physical referents, respectively to the hut and to the yard – the enclosed domestic space outside the hut. But both these words are also used to refer to the 'house' of the house–property complex. In addition, *lelapa* may refer both to the nuclear family as the basic form of domestic association and to the wider agnatic family (see Chapter 5). Despite this flexibility of terms of reference, the physical parameters of the homestead are easily defined. The homestead is the area occupied by those members of the household who are resident in the reference community. It consists of one or two or several huts, often forming the apices of a small enclosure which affords some domestic privacy, bounded by mud-brick walls or a high reed fence known as *seotloana*. Many homesteads incorporate both the traditional thatched *mohlongoafatse*, a round domed hut with a low entrance passage, and a hut of modern rectangular design with a thatched or corrugated sheeting roof. Building materials vary with the local environment. In the Lowlands, huts are built either of mud-brick or, most attractively, of cut sandstone blocks. The first method is considerably cheaper but much less durable; whereas stone-built huts have a much longer life and constitute a valuable investment. In the Mountains, the most common material is black volcanic dolerite.

Most households, then, comprise resident members who occupy a homestead in a Lesotho village and one or more absent members who may be contributing to its income. One problem is to distinguish clearly between its tangible manifestation as a partially co-residential group – the unit of observation in the village – and its overall functional manifestation in terms of income-generating activities. It is helpful to retain the term household when referring to both these aspects of its identity, because the household remains the unit of economic viability whether or not its members are physically dispersed at any one time. The rate of turnover in membership present and absent, respectively, would render it absurd to refer to a household by one term when it has absentees and another term when it has not. Villagers themselves of course make no such distinction, although they may loosely refer to actual residents as 'those we live with' (*bao re lulang le bona*) or 'those who eat from one pot' (*ba jang potong e le'ngoe*); and to absent migrants as 'those who make us live' (*ba re phelisang*). Collectively, they may be known as 'people of our place' (*ba h'eso*) but this term also refers to close relatives irrespective of household membership.

Absentees, migrant labourers and paid employees

Nevertheless it is clearly important, in assessing the sociological implications of oscillating migration, to understand whether a household is discussed in the sense that includes absent members or in the sense that excludes absent members. *De jure* household membership includes temporary absentees, while *de facto* household membership refers only to those persons actually resident in the village homestead at any one time. The use of *de jure* in this sense implies no normative statement about who ought to belong to a household. It is merely a convention which I have adopted from census practice and which allows the inclusion in the reference population of those who are judged as belonging to particular households but who happen to be absent at the time of enumeration. In view of the fact that absence can be prolonged and the difficulty of deciding at what point prolonged absence becomes permanent emigration, the criterion for defining *de jure* membership, and thence the category *absentee*, is necessarily arbitrary. But it must be made explicit in each case. For the purpose of the 1966 census, a person had to have been home within the previous five years to be included among the *de jure* population. I used a stricter criterion to define the limits of enumeration in my village surveys. Each person recorded as a *de jure* household member should have spent some time in the household, however brief, during the fieldwork period from August 1972 to November 1974. This seemed a reasonable condition in view of the South African legal requirement that migrants should return to Lesotho within two years of the date of entry into the Republic. If, in lieu of such a visit home, there was nevertheless convincing evidence that the absentee made some contribution to the income of the household during that time, I included him or her on those grounds. The reasons for the absence of individuals are, of course, diverse: employment in South Africa is by far the most important but there are a variety of others such as schooling, 'visiting' and so on. The distinction must also be made between absence in South Africa and absence from the reference community elsewhere in Lesotho.

We are now in a position to distinguish in principle two ways of assessing the demographic impact on sending communities of dependence on the export of labour. One index is the *incidence of absenteeism*, that is, the number of absentees from a given population at any one time, distributed for example by sex and age cohorts. The other index is the *rate of labour migration*, that is, the temporal distribution of migrant labourers' departures from a given population in a specified time period. Even on the unjustified assumption that all absentees are migrant labourers and that all migrant labourers are absentees, the incidence of absenteeism at a given time and the rate of migration per annum would only coincide under two conditions, neither of which holds in practice, namely that the mean period of absence is one year and that departures are evenly distributed throughout the year. The incidence of absenteeism may be readily established through census data, subject to satisfactory criteria for identifying 'absentees'. But the rate of migration cannot be established unless departures are observed continuously over the time period in question. Otherwise, the only source of information, inevitably partial, is labour recruitment agencies which record the numbers of contracting labourers from specified areas during the period in question.[4]

The category *migrant labourers* includes both wage labourers who are absent in South Africa at the time of enumeration and people who are 'resting' at home but are classified as still engaged in a migratory career. Criteria for identifying the latter are inevitably arbitrary and, again, must be made explicit in each case. For example, van der Wiel included in his estimate of the total migrant labour force persons who had worked in South Africa for at least one month in the twelve months prior to the date of enumeration (1977: 16). On this basis he found that about 20 per cent of the active migrant labour force was at home in Lesotho during the period of his surveys. The ILO study in Lesotho in 1977 selected its sample of migrants from those who had worked in South Africa for at least three months within the period of three years prior to the date the survey was conducted (Sebatane 1979: 6). I found that, having conducted three separate censuses in Ha Molapo over a fieldwork period of two years, it was not difficult in practice to identify those who were still engaged in a migratory career, by reference to their past labour history, their age, household circumstances and expressed intentions.

The category *paid employees* includes both migrant labourers and people in paid employment within Lesotho. It may seem perverse to include migrant labourers who are temporarily unemployed within the category of paid employees. But it is essential to take account of the fact that more households are directly dependent on an income from migrant earnings than exhibit the absence of a migrant labourer at any one time. It is also important to recognize that the proportion of migrant labourers who are recorded as resident in the reference community is susceptible to variation as a result of contingent alterations in the shift system on the mines and improved transport arrangements which allow rather more frequent visiting home by miners in mid-contract,[5] and also as a result of relative distance between the reference community and the place of employment. Therefore the number of migrant labourers, identified by specified criteria such as those above, is a better index of aggregate dependence on the export of labour than the number of migrants who are actually absent at any one time. On the other hand, changing recruitment policies in recent years have made it considerably more difficult than it used to be for Basotho to take up mine contracts at will. Therefore criteria used in the future to identify those still engaged in a migratory career must take account of prevailing levels of structural unemployment.

The differences between the three categories (absentees, migrant labourers and paid employees) are schematically represented in Fig. 2.2, together with an exemplary distribution from Ha Molapo in October 1974. This diagram may be used to clarify comparison of the following findings:

1. 61 per cent of three samples of 1,759 households had migrant labourers actually employed in South Africa at the times the surveys were conducted in 1974 and 1976 (van der Wiel 1977: 18) (Box 5);

2. 56 per cent of 125 households in the Mokhotlong district (Mountains) and 65 per cent of 442 households in the Mafeteng district (Lowlands) had members actually in paid employment at the time of the surveys in 1976 (Feachem et al. 1978: 18) (Boxes 2 + 3 + 5);

3. 66 per cent of 73 households in Ha Molapo (Lowlands) had paid employees, in the sense defined in Fig. 2.2, in October 1974 (Boxes 2 + 3 + 4 + 5).

It may be inferred that wage labourers are distributed between nearly two-thirds of rural households, and that the remaining third of households are relatively disadvantaged in respect of an income from wage labour. The relevance of this finding is that it undermines the assumption that the past availability of employment in South Africa to most able-bodied Basotho males implies an equitable distribution of income between rural households. For households vary significantly in their demographic composition, and the actual distribution of wage labourers between households is the most important single variable which determines particular households' income and also their capacity to invest in agriculture and other economic activities.

The spatial and occupational distribution of paid employees from Ha Molapo in October 1974 is shown in Table 2.2 The proportions of female migrants and of migrants employed in sectors other than mining are both substantially higher than van der Wiel's estimates for the country as a whole (see Chapter 1). There were 15 absentees not in paid employment

In Lesotho at time of census				In South Africa at time of census	
ABSENTEES elsewhere in Lesotho		Present in reference community		A B S E N T E E S	
1	2	3	4	5	6
Absent for reasons other than paid employment			Resting at home	Currently employed	Absent for reasons other than paid employment
				M I G R A N T L A B O U R E R S	
		P A I D E M P L O Y E E S			

Box	Definition	Absentees	Migrant labourers	Paid employees	Ha Molapo, Oct. 1974 Male	Female
1.	Persons elsewhere in Lesotho for reasons other than paid employment	+			8	3
2.	Persons in paid employment elsewhere in Lesotho	+		+	1	—
3.	Persons in paid employment in reference community			+	2	2
4.	Migrant labourers temporarily 'resting' at home		+	+	7	2
5.	Migrant labourers currently employed in South Africa	+	+	+	40	11
6.	Persons in South Africa for reasons other than paid employment	+			1	3
	Ha Molapo, October 1974	67	60	65	N = 73 households	

2.2 Schematic representation of absentees, migrant labourers and paid employees identified as *de jure* members of a reference rural community in Lesotho, together with an exemplary distribution from Ha Molapo, October 1974 (see Table 2.2)

Table 2.2. *Distribution of paid employees from Ha Molapo, by sex, country of employment, occupational category and presence in or absence from the reference community, October 1974.*

Country of employment	Occupational category	Males		Females		Total
		Present	Absent	Present	Absent	
	Mining	6	21			27
	Manufacturing	1	4	1		6
	Construction		3			3
SOUTH	Sales/clerical		4			4
AFRICA	Domestic service			1	7	8
	Medical service				1	1
	Unknown		8		3	11
	sub-total	7	40	2	11	60
	Sales/clerical		1			1
LESOTHO	Building blocks	1				1
	Café employees			2		2
	Area chief	1				1
	sub-total	2	1	2	–	5
TOTAL (N = 73 households)		9	41	4	11	65

(Fig. 2.2, Boxes 1 + 6), comprised as follows: three wives resident in South Africa with their husbands, one of whom had an infant son; four herdboys hired out elsewhere in Lesotho; two adolescent girls in boarding school; two adolescent boys in the initiation lodge (*mophato*); one man in hospital; one man was an itinerant pedlar; and one woman was 'visiting' elsewhere at the time of the census.

Dependency ratios

One way of amplifying the point about demographic composition is to compare rural households with respect to two other variables: *de jure* household size, and sex of household head.

It may be inferred from Table 2.1 that mean *de jure* household size varies between zones: 4.95 persons in the Lowlands, 5.04 in the Foothills and 5.80 in the Mountains. But the three largest villages, taken separately, all exhibit two distinct modes in the frequency distribution of *de jure* household sizes, respectively at two and six persons per household. The other two villages are too small to analyse independently. It seems justifiable therefore to treat the five villages together for the purpose of investigating variation in household size. The histogram in Fig. 2.3

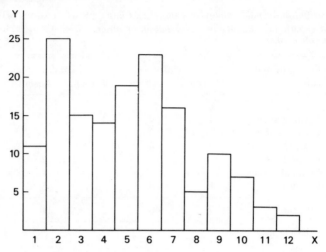

2.3 A histogram showing the frequency distribution of 150 households (Y-axis) by number of *de jure* household members (X-axis)

shows the frequency distribution of *de jure* household sizes for all 150 households. On the basis of this distribution I would justify a crude distinction between 'small' households, containing one to four persons, and 'large' households, containing more than four persons.[6]

Most demographic surveys in Lesotho indicate a relatively large proportion of female-headed households. For example, John Gay (1977: 59) found 29 per cent and 27 per cent, respectively, in the Foothills and Mountain areas covered by the Senqu Project. Van der Wiel (1977: 37) found 34 per cent overall in the Phuthiatsana and Thaba Tseka project areas. In Ha Molapo there were 32 female-headed households (44 per cent) both in October 1974 and in October 1978. However, comparison of these results is difficult because the criteria used to identify the household head are neither uniform nor self-evident. Spiegel (1979: 54) found that 28 out of 83 households (34 per cent) in the community he studied in Qacha's Nek had female heads. But he explicitly acknowledged the possibility of classifying 10 of the 55 'male-headed' households as 'female-headed' instead, depending on the relative weights attached to Sesotho customary identification, titles to arable land and prominence in household decision-taking. In that case his sample would contain 45 male-headed households (54 per cent) and 38 female-headed (46 per cent). It is often difficult in practice to decide whether a senior resident widow or her junior (unmarried) migrant son ought to be regarded as the household head. It is possible that the proportion of female-headed households identified varies inversely with the scale and

Table 2.3. *Distribution of households by* de jure *household size and sex of household head, Ha Molapo, October 1978.*

De jure household size	Sex of household head		All households
	Male	Female	
Small (1 to 4)	15	19	34
Large (> 4)	26	13	39
All households	41	32	73

directly with the intensiveness of the fieldwork on which the results are based.

Table 2.3 shows the 73 households of Ha Molapo classified by *de jure* household size and sex of household head. For the following analysis I have used survey data from October 1978 rather than from October 1974 because information on the age distribution of the population in the earlier survey was incomplete.[7] These categories of household may be compared with respect to their *dependency ratios*. The dependency ratio is conventionally defined as the ratio of 'dependants' to people who are 'economically active' within a given population: for example, the sum of children (aged less than 15 years) and the elderly (aged 60 or over), expressed as a ratio of other adults (aged 15 to 59). In Lesotho, as in the other labour reserves in the rural periphery of southern Africa, very many adults are either unemployed or underemployed in respect of their involvement in income-generating activities. Therefore an alternative, which I call Dependency Ratio 2, could be worked out as the number of *de facto* household members (rural consumers) expressed as a ratio of paid employees who are *de jure* household members. The results of this exercise applied to the Ha Molapo population of October 1978 are shown in Table 2.4. The numbers involved (Table 2.3) are perhaps too small for statistical generalization. But the results are suggestive of a consistent gradation along a continuum of relative advantage and disadvantage, viz. small male-headed, large male-headed, large female-headed and small female-headed. In particular, there is a striking disparity between small male-headed and small female-headed households. The significance of this disparity is elaborated in Chapter 7.

This sort of exercise is necessarily crude, carried out in default of a more sophisticated approach. It is enough to establish that wage earning capacity varies significantly with the demography of household composition. Any inferences about income distribution must, however, be qualified with respect to the following points: firstly, there is of course

Table 2.4. *Alternative dependency ratios, Ha Molapo, October 1978.*

De jure household size	Dependency Ratio 1 Sex of head			Dependency Ratio 2 Sex of head		
	Male	Female	All	Male	Female	All
Small	0.59	1.39	0.91	3.18	6.33	4.29
Large	1.13	1.20	1.15	4.79	5.40	4.98
All households	1.00	1.26	1.09	4.39	5.67	4.80
Definitions	Children + Elderly			*De facto* household members		
	Adults			Paid employees		

Note: Children (< 15 years); Elderly (60 + years); Adults (15–59 years).

a considerable range in the earning capacity of migrants in different occupations and in different categories of underground work in the mines; secondly, there is considerable variation in the regularity and reliability of remittances sent by migrants, on which it is extremely difficult to obtain accurate and reliable information; and thirdly, a comparison of earning capacity in terms of the distribution of migrants between households alone does not take account of income transfers that may be taking place between households, either regressively, in terms of opportunities for accumulation at the expense of the poor, or progressively, in terms of networks of extra-household diffusion of cash which serve to mitigate inequalities in the distribution of able-bodied manpower. This is why work on inter-household income transfers is so important (see pp. 157–8 below).

Residential turnover: a diachronic view

The above results illustrate some significant aspects of demographic variation between households at any one time. They do not illustrate another extremely important aspect of household demography under conditions of oscillating migration: the instability of residential associations through time. Diachronic variability in the composition of particular households emerges only from similar surveys conducted at different points in time. I was able to carry out four such surveys in Ha Molapo: in May 1973, December 1973 and October 1974 during the main period of fieldwork, and in October 1978 during a brief re-visit. Over this period I found that small households either disappeared, amalgamated with other households or remained relatively stable: typical of the latter are households consisting of widows living on their own or with a young companion, or of nuclear families in which the husband/father was consistently absent. Larger households, on the other hand, particularly three generational complex households, exhibited such regular and unpredictable residential turnover as to make it very difficult, in some cases, to identify *de jure* household membership with any confidence. Three detailed examples of this 'perpetual state of flux' are given here. They may be compared with similar findings in the Keiskammahoek district in 1948–50 (Houghton and Walton 1952: 53–4, 64).

Household 172

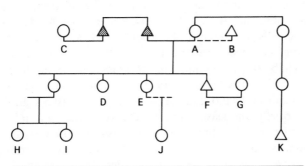

Reference		Date of birth*	May 1973	Dec 1973	Oct 1974	Oct 1978
'MaMorena	A	1914	+	+	+	+
Hendrik	B		−	+	−	
	C		+			
	D	1948	−	−	−	−
	E	1950	−	−	+	+
Thabo	F	1954	−	+	−	−
	G	1958				+
	H	1966	−	−	+	−
	I	1968	−	−	−	+
	J	1973		−	+	+
	K		−	+	−	−
de facto members			2	4	4	5

* where known
+ indicates presence
− indicates absence

2.4 Household 172

'MaMorena (A) is a widow. In 1973–4 she maintained an irregular relationship with Hendrik (B), a man of 'coloured' origin and polyglot resources, who was reputed to get his living by 'the tricks of a jackal', in particular by the illicit peddling of diamonds and dagga (cannabis). He would stay in the household for a while and then disappear for months on end. In 1973 he contributed his labour to the ploughing of 'MaMorena's three fields, but by 1978 the relationship had come to an end. Together with her husband's younger brother's widow (C), who has a large household nearby, 'MaMorena spent the month of May–June 1973 in the yard adjoining her own two huts, because they were in mourning for their mother-in-law who had just died. 'MaMorena has six surviving children. Her eldest daughter is married nearby in Ha Molapo; her eldest son has his own household elsewhere in the village and has not supported his mother at all since his marriage. In 1973–4 'MaMorena depended principally on remittances from the elder (D) of her two unmarried daughters, who was working in Pretoria, and from her youngest son Thabo (F), a coal miner in the Transvaal earning R1.84 per daily shift in 1973. At Christmas 1973 the household consisted of 'MaMorena, Hendrik, Thabo and 'MaMorena's elder sister's grandson (K) who was briefly on leave from a relatively well-paid job in a Transvaal printing company but who did not visit or write thereafter. In 1974 'MaMorena's youngest daughter (E), who had been working in Alberton (Transvaal) and had been 'spoilt' there by a Tswana youth, came home with her year-old baby (J), apparently to stay indefinitely. She and her mother were daily customers in the village beer-houses. Meanwhile 'MaMorena's eldest grand-daughter (H) had also come to live in the household, partly to help with the domestic chores and partly to have easier access to her school than from her parents' village five miles away. By 1978 her younger sister (I) had taken over this role.

Thabo suffered severely crushed ribs in a coal-mine accident in August 1974. He spent two months in hospital and came home to convalesce at the end of October 1974. He had received R600 in compensation for the injury, from which sum he bought a blanket and household goods for his mother, a radiogram (R95) and records for himself, and three sheep for ritual purposes at R15, R15 and R16 respectively. One of these animals was used in a ritual to cleanse his eldest sister's child of *seqoma* pollution;[9] another was killed to 'give a little food' to his deceased father, in other words to provide a feast for the ancestors (*balimo*); and the third he had bought in anticipation of performing the *koae* rite (see Chapter 6) which follows an elopement – he had already asked his mother and sister (E) to look out for a suitable girl, 'one who knows how to cook and grind'. In 1975 they found one (G), and Thabo and his mother transferred a sum of R276 in two instalments of bridewealth amounting to eight head of 'cattle' (Appendix 2, No. 22). In September 1978

'MaMorena told me that she had contributed substantially to these payments through a little private enterprise of her own: she turned a sum of R30 which Thabo had given her into a sum of R118 through engaging herself in the illicit dagga traffic. In 1976 Thabo's wife gave birth to their son, who in 1978 had been weaned and was living at her mother's village.

Household 117

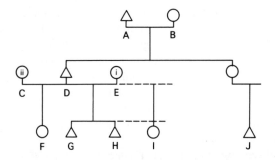

Reference		Date of birth	May 1973	Dec 1973	Oct 1974	Oct 1978	Oct 1978
Malefetsane	A	1914	−	−	+	+	
	B	1919	+	+	+	+	
	C	1957					+
Tšoene	D	1941	−	+	−		−
	E		+				
	F	1976					+
	G	1966	+	−	+	+	
	H	1969	+	−	+	+	
	I	1972	+	−	−	+	
	J	1968	+	−	+	−	
de facto members			6	2	5	5	2

2.5 Household 117

Malefetsane (A) was born in 1914 at Matsieng, the King's village. His family moved repeatedly until they settled in Ha Molapo in 1934, having lost all their livestock. Malefetsane took his first mine contract in 1934 and retired from an active migrant career in 1963. He had accumulated a number of animals and his eldest son Tšoene (D) had just embarked on his migrant career. By the early 1970s, however, bridewealth payments on behalf of his two sons had deprived the household of all its livestock, and Malefetsane took up a further gold-mine contract at Marievale

(Transvaal) in January 1973, from which he returned home in August 1974. His wife (B) is permanently resident in the household. She received irregular remittances from Malefetsane during 1973–4 and also occasional help from her two sons, both married migrants. One of them, Tšoene (D), employed in a Natal coal mine, had not yet built his own homestead. Tšoene's wife (E) was resident in the household in May 1973 together with her three children, of whom the two eldest (G and H) were Tšoene's but the third (I), as her mother-in-law put it, 'she had simply made in the veld' during Tšoene's absence. She disappeared with all three children in June 1973, after eight years of marriage. In 1974 she was reputed to be 'just roaming about' in Virginia (Orange Free State) and there was little the family could do to bring her back. However, more than sufficient bridewealth transfers had taken place to secure Tšoene's paternity of all her children, and in 1974, following negotiations with E's parents, the two boys G and H, aged eight and five respectively, were returned to their grandparents in Ha Molapo, though not the youngest child (I) who had not yet been weaned.

Not long after, between mine contracts, Tšoene found himself another young wife (C), who bore him a daughter (F) in 1976. He finished building his own homestead next to his parents' yard, and installed his new wife there, so that by 1978 there were two separate households. His young wife told me in September 1978 that he had already transferred nine head of bridewealth 'cattle' in cash to her parents. She also described a stereotypical pattern of migration as a means to establishing domestic autonomy, in terms which may be quoted in full.

On your first trip to the place of the whites (*makhooeng*), you support those who brought you up (*u phelisa ba u holisitseng*). On your second trip, you take out money that counts as cattle for marrying a wife (*u ntša chelete e nyalang mosali, e balang likhomo*). On your third trip, you look after everything in your own homestead (*u lokisa ntho e'ngoe le e'ngoe lapeng la hao*).

Meanwhile Tšoene's errant first wife (E) had produced another child 'in the veld' in the Free State, and taken it to her natal village six miles from Ha Molapo. In September 1978 Malefetsane's wife expressed her determination to bring that child, too, into her own household: 'I'll fetch it at Christmas. We *married* that woman, after all. The law is with us.'

Household 130

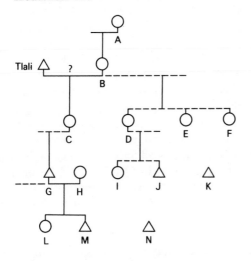

Reference		Date of birth	May 1973	Dec 1973	Oct 1974	Oct 1978	Oct 1978
'MaNtsoaki	A	1897	+	+	+	+	
Ntsoaki	B	1916	−	−	+	−	
Lydia	C	1934	−	−	−		+
	D		−	−	−	−	
	E					+	
Martha	F	1955	−	+	−	+	
Teboho	G	1951	−	+	−		
'MaMohlaoli	H		−	+	+		
	I	1967	−	−	+	+	
	J	1970	−	−	+	+	
	K		−	−	−	−	
	L	1971	−	+	+		
	M	1973	−	+	+		
	N	1971			+		+
de facto members			1	6	8	5	2

2.6 Household 130

'MaNtsoaki (A) is an elderly widow. She holds two fields which she cultivated assiduously in the 1972–3 and 1973–4 seasons through remittances derived mainly from the earnings of her grand-daughter Lydia (C). 'MaNtsoaki was the sole permanently resident member of the household throughout the period 1972–8. Her daughter Ntsoaki (B) 'retired' to Lesotho in early 1974 after spending most of her adult life in Middelburg (Transvaal). She had been 'married' to Tlali, also a resident of Ha Molapo, and borne one child Lydia (C) by him. Subsequently he contracted leprosy, and Ntsoaki went to the Republic to seek work to support herself. There she bore three other daughters (D, E and F). They grew up partly in Middelburg and partly in her mother's household in Ha Molapo. Ntsoaki's relationship with Tlali was the subject of sporadic and bitter recriminations in 1972–4. Ntsoaki and her mother vigorously rejected Tlali's claim to paternity rights over all Ntsoaki's offspring, on the grounds that Tlali had never transferred enough bridewealth cattle to justify this claim and that in any case he had forfeited any claim he might have had through having ill-treated her. In October 1978 Ntsoaki was reported to be back in South Africa, staying with another daughter at Alberton (Transvaal), in order to get medical treatment for a recurrent but unspecified illness.

In 1973–4 Lydia was running a successful medical practice in Middelburg. She claimed apprenticeship in Lourenço Marques (now Maputo) and she had a certificate of membership of the African Dingaka (Doctors) Association dated 1965. She made an extended visit to 'MaNtsoaki's household in July 1974, bringing back large items of furniture and a kitchen suite – accumulated on hire purchase and incongruous among Sesotho household equipment – in preparation for her own imminent 'retirement' to the village. She built herself an adjoining shack with corrugated iron roof and elaborate interior furnishings, and by 1978 she was settled in the village, constituting together with the boy N a household independent of her grandmother's by the criterion of separate cooking arrangements. She apparently supported 'MaNtsoaki to a considerable extent through her earnings in the informal sector – her continuing medical practice and her regular trade in Sesotho beer and in hard liquor such as brandy. Lydia has no husband and has never been married. The boy N, of unknown parentage, had been 'given' to Lydia by his mother who lived next door in Middelburg. He was brought to Lesotho in July 1974 to be reared in 'MaNtsoaki's household, and in 1978 was living with Lydia in her separate household. Having had an operation on his back, this child was described as a *sehole* (cripple) by Ntsoaki, who regarded him as a bad deal for this reason. He was also listless and withdrawn, probably due to infant malnutrition.

Lydia's eldest half-sister (D), having been 'married' by a Pedi man in Middelburg, sent her two young children (I and J, by other men) to be brought up in Lesotho. They came with Lydia in July 1974 and remained in the household after the latter's departure. They both attend one of the local primary schools. Their mother does not come to visit them. Her sister (E) had been married since 1971 in a village some miles distant from Ha Molapo. Throughout 1972–4 she was not regarded as a member of the household, but in September 1978 she had taken refuge there after being beaten by her husband. She has no children. Martha (F) had been brought up in the household and was resident with 'MaNtsoaki until December 1972 when she eloped to a village six miles away. She made an extended visit home at Christmas 1973, and she was ritually 'washed' early in 1974 following symptoms of pseudocyesis. There were signs of a conjugal rift throughout the rest of that year. In September 1978 she told me that she and her 'husband' had long since split up – anyway he had never transferred any bridewealth – and she was preparing to return to work in domestic service at Newcastle (Natal) which she found much more lively than Ha Molapo. As she put it, 'the life here is very boring' (*bophelo ba mona bo-boring haholo*). She had not yet conceived a child and was resigning herself to a fate of barrenness.

Lydia had been 'spoilt' either in Botswana or South Africa. Her son Teboho (G) has a South African passport but this does not qualify him to reside in a 'prescribed' area with his family. In 1973 he had a relatively good job in a Johannesburg construction company. He was home for a few weeks at Christmas 1973, during which visit he caused resentment in the household by spending a considerable amount of time with his maternal grandfather Tlali, who lived alone elsewhere in the village (Household 156) and who wished to recognize Teboho as his effective heir. Teboho had married 'MaMohlaoli (H) in 1971. She had spent a short time with him in Johannesburg, where she bore two children by him (L and M), and settled in 'MaNtsoaki's household with them in the latter part of 1973. Separate bridewealth transactions took place in 1972 and 1973 which together wholly fulfilled the Sesotho customary expectation of 20 cattle, 10 small stock and a horse (Appendix 2, No. 18). Nevertheless in 1978 there was no sign of her or of her (by then three) children. I was told that some time previously she had gone off with the children to Johannesburg, where her father was a teacher, apparently because Teboho had another liaison in Johannesburg and was no longer adequately supporting her. Teboho then established his 'other woman' in Tlali's old homestead – he had died in 1976 – together with one of her own two children and one of the two she subsequently bore to Teboho. The old woman 'MaNtsoaki was very bitter about these developments, remarking that in any case since Teboho had first got married she had never seen anything of his money. In September 1978 she said they would take steps to recover 'MaMohlaoli's children on account of all the bridewealth cattle that had been paid to her father, and Martha (F) told

63

me that she and her sister (E) would shortly be going to Johannesburg for the purpose.

While Ntsoaki was living at Middelburg, many years ago, she had 'bought' a boy of Xhosa origin (K), unwanted by his mother, because she had no sons of her own. K was an absent migrant throughout 1972–4. However, Ntsoaki insisted that he made regular remittances in support of the household. By 1978 he had married; his wife had been briefly resident in the household but had then gone to join him at work in the Transvaal. 'MaNtsoaki told me that he still sent her money occasionally – R10 or so at a time.

These detailed examples illustrate two very general points about the structure of community in the labour reserve. One is the sheet-anchor role of a permanently resident senior wife or widow, while the boundaries of the *de facto* household perpetually ebb and flow around her. The other is the dialectical interplay of two temporal processes: the oscillation of wage labour and the cycle of human reproduction. For much of the residential turnover can be attributed to the contradictory exigencies of conjugal association. On the one hand, the economic viability of a conjugal relationship in practice requires the separation of spouses. On the other hand, the prolonged separation of spouses is most conducive to the destruction of the conjugal relationship. This theme is developed in Chapters 5 and 6.

3

Managing the land

The principle that all land is vested in the nation (*sechaba*) is fundamental to concepts of land tenure in Lesotho. Individual rights of access to land are a prerogative of citizenship, and land cannot be bought and sold. In the nineteenth century Moshoeshoe I granted sites to European missionaries and traders only on the express understanding that such grants did not alienate the land from the Basotho (*Basutoland Records* II: 536–7). Since the settlement of the present boundaries of the country in 1869, insistence on the principle that land could not be alienated has been the best defence against further foreign encroachment and also the most effective way of assuring the basic means of livelihood to all those who recognized the authority of Moshoeshoe and his descendants. Basotho today defend the traditional system on these grounds; and critics of the system have often failed to acknowledge their importance.

However, productive activities on the land have long ceased to provide an adequate livelihood for the large majority of Basotho. Contrary to the Prime Minister's assertion in the Second Five Year Development Plan, agriculture does not 'support 80 per cent of the population' (SFYDP: xi). It is the 'backbone of the economy' (Lesotho 1972: 6) only in the residual sense that there are very few other employment prospects within the country. For the most part, individual land holdings today are small, fragmented, eroded and exhausted. An increasing proportion of the population has no lands at all (see Chapter 4).

It has long been argued that greater security of tenure is a condition of more effective use of the arable land that is available in Lesotho (Cowen 1967; Williams 1972; but cf. Nobe and Seckler 1979). It is less clear what form specific changes should take. Opposition to various reform proposals has been consistent. Commoners are well aware that recognition of permanent individual titles would prejudice the principle that all citizens are entitled to land. The chiefs are well aware that the most important prerogative of chiefly office – the right to administer land – would be irretrievably eroded. After years of prevarication on the issue,

Chief Jonathan's government introduced legislation in 1979 involving long-term leases of certain categories of land for public and commercial uses, and individual licences to cultivate surveyed plots of land which will be heritable over specified periods of time. Ownership will remain vested in the nation. It will be many years, however, before such a scheme can be fully implemented in the rural areas. Meanwhile the population is rapidly increasing and the land itself continues to deteriorate. The political framework within which rights to land are presently administered will be subject to increasing strain. In the following sections I first describe this political framework and then distinguish the sets of rights which Sheddick (1954) defined as administrative and usufructuary rights.

The chieftainship

Every village or village section has a headman (*ramotse*) who belongs to the lowest stratum in the chiefly hierarchy. He may or may not be 'gazetted' – officially recognized by the government – depending on the number of tax-payers for whom he is responsible. He is politically subordinate to the area chief (*morena*) within whose area of jurisdiction his village lies. This chief in turn owes allegiance to one of twenty-two Principal and Ward Chiefs who constitute the upper stratum of the chieftainship. Nineteen of these senior chieftainships are held by descendants of Moshoeshoe I and of two of his brothers. The other three chiefs represent communities of Tlokoa, Khoakhoa and Taung respectively. The apex of the hierarchy is the present King Moshoeshoe II, the senior representative of the Sons of Moshoeshoe. The traditional prerogatives of his office are strictly circumscribed by the limitations inherent in his modern role of constitutional monarch.

The hierarchy of traditional authority is much more complex than this simple model would suggest. This is due to the historical quirks of the 'placing' system. In the past senior chiefs used to 'place' their sons and other junior relatives in charge of sub-divisions of their territory. The widespread practice of polygyny meant that there were many junior sons and junior collaterals (brothers, cousins and their descendants) with political aspirations to be placed in this way. Each new placing created an additional level in the hierarchy which the descendants of each incumbent expected to be maintained in perpetuity. This worked in such a way as to consolidate the power of the Koena aristocracy, at the expense of the chiefs and headmen of other clans. It also worked progressively in favour of the descendants of the first 'house' of Moshoeshoe as against those belonging to junior lines of descent. But the placing system was consistent only with an expanding polity. When there were no new areas to settle, a new placing could only be made at the expense of existing placings.[1] In the first decades of this century, under conditions of increasingly acute land shortage, the continuing pro-liferation of chiefs and sub-chiefs reached absurd proportions. I have already quoted, in Chapter 1, the remark of a member of the National Council in the early 1930s that 'there are now as many chiefs in Basutoland as there are stars in the heavens' (Pim 1935: 48).

Reforms were therefore introduced in 1938. Their effect was to 'freeze' the system to some extent and to curtail the discretion of chiefs in making subordinate appointments. From that date, every placing had to be approved by the central government and an official gazette of recognized chiefs and headmen was established. Steps were taken simul-taneously to reduce the number of chiefs' courts, whose operation was cumbersome and inefficient, and thereby to curtail the judicial functions of chiefs. When the Basuto National Treasury was set up in 1946, the recognized chiefs were paid salaries or tax gratuities, partly in com-pensation for their loss of income from court fines and stray livestock (Basutoland 1958).

These reforms induced widespread insecurity in the lower levels of the chiefly hierarchy. In the first place, senior chiefs were no longer able to accommodate the political aspirations of junior kinsmen. And the estab-lishment of an official gazette led to a scramble for recognition in which many lower chiefs and headmen were displaced altogether. In the second place, the tax gratuities received by those who were gazetted were quite arbitrarily assessed, and did not compensate them for the loss of previous revenues (Jones 1951: 48–51). Many politically sensitive Basotho realized that the substitution of one form of income for the other would under-mine the accountability of chiefs and headmen to their subjects which was expressed in the Sesotho maxim 'a chief is a chief through the people' (*morena ke morena ka batho*) (Jingoes 1975: chapter 6). The wave of 'medicine' (*liretlo*) murders that swept Basutoland in the late 1940s was attributed largely to the insecurity induced by the reforms. Lesser chiefs invoked sinister ways of resisting their official eclipse (Jones 1951).

The ramifications of the placing system and the rigid constraints which were imposed as a result of the 1938 reforms are highly significant in the internal politics of the Koena aristocracy. Each incumbent of the para-mountcy was able to place his own sons and brothers in senior positions, with the result that twelve of the senior chieftainships are held by members of the house of Letsie I alone (see Figure 3.1). Relative seniority within the house of Moshoeshoe involves competitive principles of reckoning: men either look 'round about them' vis-à-vis the incumbent

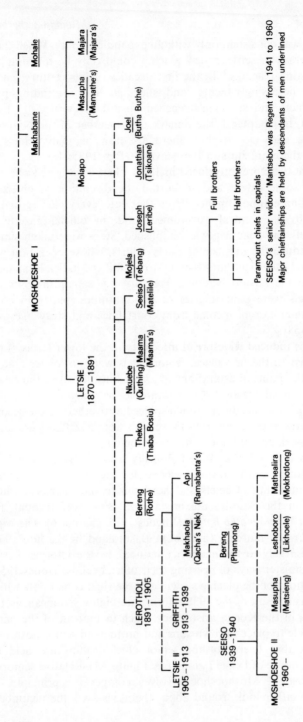

3.1 The nineteen principal and ward chieftainships held by the 'Sons of Moshoeshoe'

MOSHOESHOE I

Makhabane

Mohale

Masupha ('Mamathe's)

Majara (Majara's)

Molapo

Joseph (Leribe)

Jonathan (Tsikoane)

Joel (Butha Buthe)

LETSIE I 1870–1891

Nkuebe (Quthing)

Maama (Maama's)

Seeiso (Matelile)

Mojela (Tebang)

Full brothers

Half brothers

Paramount chiefs in capitals
SEEISO's senior widow 'Mantsebo was Regent from 1941 to 1960
Major chieftainships are held by descendants of men underlined

Theko (Thaba Bosiu)

Bereng (Rothe)

Makhaola (Qacha's Nek)

Api (Ramabanta's)

LEROTHOLI 1891–1905

GRIFFITH 1913–1939

LETSIE II 1905–1913

SEEISO 1939–1940

Bereng (Phamong)

Masupha (Matsieng)

MOSHOESHOE II 1960–

Leshoboro (Likhoele)

Mathealira (Mokhotlong)

68

paramount; or they look 'backwards' vis-à-vis the four cardinal lines of descent in Moshoeshoe's first house, those of Letsie, Molapo, Masupha and Majara. Ian Hamnett has called these the circumspective and retrospective principles of seniority, respectively. In his very interesting book *Chieftainship and Legitimacy* (1975) he has shown how conflicts of precedence derive directly from the inconsistencies inherent in a system in which junior collaterals of a chief belonging to a senior cardinal line compete for seniority with senior representatives of junior cardinal lines. There is some doubt, for example, whether the second chief in Lesotho is the junior brother of the present King or the senior descendant of Molapo, the second son of Moshoeshoe I. The complexities of the present administrative structure may be attributed in part to the unregulated proliferation of placings before 1938; and in part to the differential reckoning of seniority by junior agnates anxious to avoid progressive displacement from the centres of power.

Despite conflict and inconsistency within the chieftainship hierarchy, the structure of authority relations from the point of view of commoner villagers is relatively uncomplicated. A man owes allegiance to a chief by virtue of his residence in that chief's area. And the formal expression of allegiance implies the right to reside. Conversely, a chief's authority is defined by his sovereignty over residents of a particular territory. Such authority is unambiguous except, in the past, with respect to *paballo* rights,[2] and except that, because of the variable number of levels in the hierarchy, the structure may not be symmetrical for two different villages subordinate to the same chief. For example, a chief may exercise authority over outlying villages through subordinate village headmen, whereas he may exercise direct and exclusive authority in the village where he himself resides.

The boundaries of a chief's area are usually marked by physical features such as a mountain peak, a ridge, a stream or a donga (erosion gully). It is made up of villages with their respective arable lands and other lands set aside for grazing and other public purposes. The boundaries of each administrative sub-division should be publicly known, and old men are often called to testify orally to a grant of land, or a pacing of the boundaries, that took place many years before. Old men recall with pride and some nostalgia the days when herdboys' squabbles with sticks and stones over prize grazing turned into full-scale battles between their elders, the subjects of different chiefs (see Jingoes 1975: 19–55). In this sense the old political loyalties survive.

In the years since independence in 1966, the substance of chiefly power has been steadily eroded. Party political structures have proliferated both at the district level and at the village level (Breytenbach 1975; Feachem *et al.* 1978: 65–72), and the district administrative offices are now the most important conduits of executive authority. However, chiefs retain a formal role in the way that this authority is transmitted from central government to villagers. The public gathering or *pitso* convened by a chief at the appropriate level in the hierarchy remains the proper instrument of all official communication, though it is often clumsy and inefficient in practice. Disputes, tax matters, court summons and statutory requirements of all kinds must pass up and down the chieftainship hierarchy, irrespective of individual chiefs' competence or otherwise in particular matters. Subject to conflicting pressures from above and below, chiefs today tend either to relapse into inertia, as the least offensive course of action, or to align themselves overtly with the most convenient political faction. In these circumstances political middlemen may exploit their resources of literacy or judicial expertise in order to articulate the channels of communication between the different levels in the chieftainship hierarchy or between the chieftainship and local administration as parallel and potentially conflicting structures of authority (Perry 1973, 1977). Only one man in Ha Molapo, the head of the Letlala family, knew English at all well. He had learned the importance of written evidence both through his experience of family succession disputes in the village (see Appendix 3) and through his migrant career in a clothing factory in Germiston (Transvaal). He had inherited and carefully preserved papers relating to a boundary dispute which had taken place in the 1920s, and he was of invaluable service to the area chief when the issue flared up again in 1974. In 1972–4 a resident of the settlement adjoining Ha Molapo was drawing a small monthly allowance from the Principal Chief's office at Leribe village, ten miles away, in his capacity as the latter's 'eye' in Ha Molapo. Described by villagers as an informer (*mpimpi*), he also took it upon himself to organize an *ad hoc* group of vigilantes on behalf of the ruling party during the political crisis of January 1974.

Administrative and usufructuary title

The most politically sensitive aspect of the chief's remaining prerogatives is the right to administer titles to arable land. A chief holds *administrative* title to land in the area of his jurisdiction. He is responsible for allocating arable lands in an equitable manner to persons who qualify for such allocation and who thereby hold *usufructuary* title: that is, the right to cultivate and to dispose of the product. The criteria nominally applied to assess an individual's claim for an allocation of land are citizenship, sex and marital status. An indispensable first condition is membership of the political community defined by reference to the chief's area of jurisdiction. A second condition is that the applicant be male. Women do not normally hold usufructuary titles in their own right, though married women and widows have clearly defined rights to maintenance from the product of their husbands' fields; while an unmarried daughter cannot in general expect a personal allocation of land at her own natal place. A third condition is that the applicant be married. Thus, a married man domiciled in the chief's area is in principle entitled to an allocation of three lands (*tšimo*, plural *masimo*), for cultivation of maize, sorghum and wheat respectively. Allocations should be made impartially on the basis of need but, as will be seen below, the available land is quite inadequate for this provision to be met in practice. The chief is subject to various political pressures to favour particular applicants at the expense of others. In any case 'need' is properly interpreted as relative to household demography, which would in theory require constant adjustments in the distribution of land. Such adjustments are impracticable and the inequities of distribution that result both from demographic accident and from political manipulation are a source of acute resentment.

Security of usufructuary title is normally granted for the holder's life but is subject to two provisions in the *Laws of Lerotholi* which allow the chief, on inspection, to re-allocate the land to someone else. These are (1) where a field has been uncultivated for a period of two successive years, and (2) where a land-holder has more fields than are judged necessary by the chief to provide subsistence for himself and his family.[3] Although these provisions are seldom invoked they represent a degree of insecurity of tenure since they afford grounds for argument in a dispute whose origin may lie elsewhere.

Prior to the Land Act of 1979 (p. 66), there were two major pieces of legislation affecting the administration of arable land in Lesotho. The Land (Procedure) Act of 1967 provided that each area chief had to convene a *pitso* for the election of a Land Committee (*komiti ea mobu*), consisting of five people resident in his area of jurisdiction; such committee to be re-elected every three years. The Land Act of 1973 replaced the Land Committee with a Development Committee (*komiti ea ntlafatso*) which would consist of seven members – four to be elected at a *pitso* convened by the area chief and three to be appointed by the Minister of the Interior. The formal intention was that every chief should carry out his administrative duties in consultation with an elected advisory body which would also maintain a written record of all applications for and allocations of land made within his area. Both in the manner of their election and in the practical interpretation of their terms of reference, these committees have often worked as party political organs.

Litigation over usufructuary title to land is second only in frequency and vituperation to litigation over bridewealth (Chapter 6). Disputes commonly arise through overlap between the limits of chiefly prerogative, on the one hand, and expectations of inter-generational transmission within a family, on the other hand. Implicit in the foregoing discussion of land tenure is the principle fundamental (in its generality) to Sesotho land law, namely '(arable) land is not an inheritance' (*mobu ha se lefa*). But a son may legitimately claim, as an immanent aspect of the jural relationship of filiation, the right to cultivate his father's lands. As Hamnett has put it, 'The difficulty here is that it is true *both* that land is not an inheritance but reverts to the chief for re-allocation, *and* that a son has a legitimate expectation to be given his father's lands (or some of them, or equivalent lands), and this expectation, moreover, is recognized in customary law' (1975: 78, his emphasis). In exemplifying an attractive general argument about the nature of customary law, Hamnett contends that a logical contradiction obtains only when such principles are regarded independently of particular sets of circumstances; and that, this being so, both principles remain inviolate outside the context of litigation. The impasse, then, is only an apparent one: 'over the whole area of land law there is a play of norms, general in character, potentially inconsistent in their implications, and ... it is in the specifications and application of these norms in particular cases that decisions are reached which are at once *unconstrained* and at the same time *lawful*' (Hamnett 1975: 82, his emphasis). It follows that the resolution of a particular dispute is not simply predictable by applying one of these principles of customary law. Were its application to particular circumstances not in question, there would be no dispute.

Since, in law, 'land is not an inheritance', there is inherent uncertainty in the testamentary disposition of usufructuary title after the holder's death. Rather than risk this uncertainty, many men prefer to arrange the inter-generational transmission of title during their own lifetime. This is often an effective device, subject of course to the chief's approval, of ensuring the retention of 'family' lands. Such an arrangement can usually be made only after the marriage of a son, and typically occurs at a stage in the developmental cycle when the father has ceased to migrate himself. In view of the fact that successful cultivation requires considerable cash investment (see below), a man can exert little 'pull' over the junior generation by merely retaining his lands, despite the acute shortage of arable land, if he does not also have an independent source of income. In these circumstances, he may prefer to transfer nominal title in the lands in good time to his sons and commit himself to dependence on them after his own retirement from migratory labour. At the same time, some provision must be made for his wife, for a widow is entitled to retain two lands following her husband's death and these only become liable for re-allocation after her own death. These arrangements sometimes create conflict between siblings who, in competition for their father's lands, also share responsibility for the maintenance of their mother. In exceptional circumstances a widow can manage on her own, without the support of her sons, but only if she has a large holding of land and can make share-cropping contracts so that she herself is not required to find the substantial cash inputs necessary for cultivation. But a woman in this position is seldom able to exert the political patronage necessary to retain a large holding; and most widows must depend to a considerable extent on their children for support.

The ambivalence of these conflicting principles emerges clearly from two cases of litigation which took place in Ha Molapo in 1973. Both arose out of an accusation by a senior son against a parent for the latter's failure to consult him in the disposition of family lands.

The tactics of case management. Mafa, of the Letlala family (Appendix 3, S24), brought a case against his mother for unilaterally disposing of her field to his younger brother, her second son Tebang, who had no field. The family council (*khotla la lelapa*) upheld the widow's right to dispose of her field in the manner she thought best. The field had remained uncultivated, owing to default by the other party to a regular share-cropping arrangement, since the death of her husband a few years previously. Mafa held title to one field, quite inadequate to provide for his own large family. As eldest son and heir to his father, Mafa insisted on his right to be consulted in the matter and appealed against the decision of the family council. So the case came before the area chief. The chief wanted 'clarification' of the letter written by Morero Letlala, the family head, setting out the grounds of the council's decision. The family council met again to reconsider the terms of the decision and, following some devious lobbying, this time the reverse decision was reached — that Mafa should cultivate the field himself and maintain his mother out of the yield therefrom. This despite the strenuous objection of the old woman who made it clear that she wanted the field to go to Tebang precisely because he was the more reliable of the two. So she appealed against the decision in her turn, and the chief's court reviewed the matter from the beginning. The court deferred a decision pending an inspection of the field, and in the meantime, constitutionally weakened by tuberculosis, Tebang died.

Here no clear resolution was reached because of the adventitious death of one party to the dispute. But the different tactics employed by the protagonists reflect the conflicting norms involved. Before the chief's court Mafa presented his case firmly in terms of the eldest son's claim to be consulted in the disposal of his widowed mother's usufructuary title and his reciprocal filial obligation to look after her interests. His mother also wished to ensure retention of the field within the family but, in order to arrange that her second son, not her eldest, should take over usufructuary title, she had gone with Tebang before the chief and announced her restoration of the field to the chief as a public gesture of generosity, in view of the fact that it had not been cultivated for a number of years and in view of the principle that arable land is not heritable. At the same time she appealed to the chief's generalized obligation to provide land for those without it. She explicitly repudiated any claim to transmit the field to her son, and instead invoked the chief's duty to find a field for his landless subject.

The land committee's dirty linen Early in 1973 a new land committee was elected in Ha Molapo in accordance with the provisions of the 1967 Land (Procedure) Act. Its five members, all supporters of the ruling BNP, included both Khomo and his senior daughter-in-law 'MaNapo. Khomo had five fields and three sons. His eldest son Stephen, 'MaNapo's husband, had been given two fields held by Khomo's father on the latter's death, but his other two sons held no land in their own right. On her election 'MaNapo inspected the records of the previous land committee, which had been dominated by supporters of the opposition BCP. She discovered that Khomo had arranged officially, albeit unknown to Stephen and herself, for four of his five fields to be allocated to his other two sons (two each), himself retaining a single field for his own use. Stephen took his father to court not so much to challenge the fairness of the distribution but to charge him for his failure to consult his eldest son in the matter. The court upheld Khomo's right to dispose of his fields in the manner that he saw fit, subject only to the approval of the chief-in-land-committee, and remarked incidentally that it was difficult, without new evidence, to justify merely reversing the decision of the previous land committee which had approved the allocation. There was some discussion of criteria for identifying the limits of Khomo's obligation to consult his eldest son in the disposal of property, which included the question, flippant but not rhetorical, put to 'MaNapo by a member of the court: 'Must your father-in-law consult you when he disposes of his trousers?' The unrepentant daughter-in-law averred that he must. The main issue, however, was whether Khomo had formally called a family council to announce his intention of disposing of his fields to his sons, or whether he had made a private arrangement in collusion with officials who were not personally involved. There was conflicting evidence on this point, some of the family witnesses insisting for Khomo that he had called a family meeting but that Stephen had refused to attend, others insisting for Stephen that Khomo had refused outright to discuss the matter with 'this glutton of mine' (referring to his son).

Had the court not decided in favour of Khomo on the administrative ground noted above, the most important pointer to a resolution of the dispute would have been the court's assessment of whether it was Khomo or Stephen who had behaved rudely and aggressively in respect of failure to discuss the matter in family council. In comment on the case the chairman of the previous land committee, Morero Letlala, took some ironic satisfaction in the unedifying spectacle of father-in-law and daughter-in-law confronting one another in court over a squabble within the family, although they were both members of the new land committee and of the same political faction.

In both these cases the tension between parent and eldest son reflected a degree of ambiguity inherent in the generality of conflicting norms of Sesotho customary law relating to the transmission of arable land. By contrast with the provisions in the *Laws of Lerotholi* which allow re-allocation but are seldom invoked, this area of practical uncertainty is a frequent source of litigation. I have cited two examples of disputes, both within families, but problems also arise between unrelated individuals over the criteria for and validity of re-allocations of land which do not represent *de facto* inheritance of usufructuary title. People who are tactically inept in the management of the judicial process, or who are otherwise unable to defend themselves, are sometimes exposed to unscrupulous manipulation by witnesses with a grudge or by political middlemen on the land committee. Similarly, individuals who aspire to receive an allocation of land must be prepared to invest considerable time and effort and even, more crudely, cash bribes, in order to build up the social and political credit necessary for favourable consideration by the chief-in-land-committee. This is not easy for young migrants who spend most of their time abroad.

Agricultural operations

Crop production in the Lowlands of Lesotho is dominated by the staples maize (*poone*) and sorghum (*mabele*). Winter wheat (*koro*) and pulses – peas and beans – are also common. Sorghum does not ripen well in the Mountains, where the most important crops are maize, summer wheat and peas. Depending on their zonal distribution these crops require slightly different seasonal adjustments (Ashton 1952: 122ff; Sheddick

75

1954: 73ff; Lesotho 1972: 16, 71–6; Turner 1978). However, the important constraints may be described in relatively general terms. Climatic and environmental vicissitudes – drought, hail, frost, bird and insect damage – are notoriously unpredictable. The ploughing and planting season is short, being contingent at one end on the early summer rains and at the other end on the risk of frost as the crops are ripening. Germination is often poor, and the young shoots may be destroyed either by lack of moisture or by cut-worm. These factors together imply a high risk of crop failure.

Land-holding households are seldom self-sufficient in respect of the resources they must muster for effective cultivation. The principal operations of the agricultural season – ploughing, planting, weeding and harvesting – are dependent on the availability of oxen, plough, planter, labour and cash. Ploughing is the most critical of these operations. It is heavy work on hard and arid soils and it places optimum demand on male labour during a period of unpredictable brevity in October and November. Some indication of an absolute scarcity of male labour may be derived from the fact that in October 1974, when households had to concentrate their resources to make ploughing arrangements, 46 out of 73 households in Ha Molapo (63 per cent) had no adult male present (17 years or older). Wykstra (1978) estimated the labour time required for effective cultivation at the peak load times of ploughing and weeding. His conclusion was that, while there is aggregate under-employment in agriculture on a year-round basis, there is probably an absolute shortage of male and female labour, respectively, at these peak times.

According to the 1970 agricultural census, 35 per cent of Lowlands households owned a plough; more than half owned no livestock at all; and more than 70 per cent of cattle were owned in herds of ten head or fewer (Lesotho 1972). In view of the sex and age distribution of animals per holding household, and the poor condition of oxen in the ploughing season after inadequate winter grazing, the majority of livestock-holding households are unable to constitute a ploughing team from their own resources. Only two households in Ha Molapo, for example, were able to put together a team of six beasts from their own livestock resources in the 1972–3 season. Most households must either pool their resources with those of other households or they must hire draught power directly from a ploughing contractor – a tractor-owner or the manager of a cattle-team. In addition to the expenses involved in this, optimum crop yields also depend on the use of selected hybrid seeds and nitrogenous or phosphatic fertilizers.[4] Successful farming therefore requires investments which are expensive in terms of cash, labour time and social organization. In view of the high risk of crop failure the investment is not necessarily worthwhile.

Land itself is so scarce that a deliberate decision to let a field lie fallow is an unusual indulgence, although Basotho are of course aware of the need for regeneration. There is no obvious way of interrupting the spiral of decreasing returns in which, the lower the crop yield, the less people can afford to let the land rest and recover. Thus failure to cultivate is generally attributed to a variety of circumstances: lack of money, lack of labour, lack of cattle, absence of the holder in South Africa. Often an answer is in the form of a listless shrug accompanied by the poignant recitation: 'I haven't ploughed, we lack life (health), oxen, we lack money.' If the rains are late, as they were in 1972, failure to plough, due to inability to make the necessary *ad hoc* arrangements, may be vaguely rationalized as 'the sun'. Apart from the practical deficiencies of labour, capital equipment and cash, many people see themselves, rightly, as prey to climatic vicissitudes over which they have no control. Thus the specific technical inadequacies are set within a framework of lack of expectation (see Westcott 1977).

Ashton remarked in the 1930s on 'the absence of any driving incentive to the Basotho to develop their lands and improve their agriculture' (1939: 155). He attributed this to the fact that the income that could be derived from migrant labour exceeded the income that could be derived from working the land. Such a disincentive is much stronger today, in view of the continuing decline in agricultural productivity, the increasing shortage of land and the wage increases of the 1970s (Chapter 1). Rising industrial wage levels in South Africa have contradictory implications in this respect. On the one hand, they have greatly enhanced most households' capacity to invest in agriculture. On the other hand, they have greatly increased its opportunity cost. Thus one effect of recent substantial wage increases is to expose the relative futility of engaging in agriculture at all, at a point where migrants find it more sensible to buy food directly than to undertake the uncertain effort of growing it at home. In the circumstances it is perhaps surprising that so many people do continue to engage in agriculture. Spiegel (1979) has stressed the importance of a residual security function, such that migrants still aspire to be allocated land and continue to invest in agriculture and livestock, even when they cannot ensure a worthwhile return in the short term, in order to demonstrate their long-term commitment to the rural social system. In view of this aspiration and in view of the fact that migrant earnings are the primary source of agricultural capital, it may be more sensible to redistribute management functions than to encourage a small number of progressive farmers *at the expense of* professional migrants' access to land and livestock.[5] This point is taken up in Chapter 4.

The variety of inter-household contractual arrangements that Basotho farmers commonly make may be summarized as follows:[6]

1. A land-holder hires the tractor belonging to an entrepreneur. The tractor-owner is almost invariably an outsider and operates on a wholly commercial basis.

2. A land-holder hires the team of animals managed by an entrepreneur. The parties may or may not be related. For this type of contract, however, payment of cash for ploughing or planting services is the rule rather than the exception even between kin.

3. Several households pool their resources in order to constitute a ploughing team. Particular contributions may be in the form of labour, animals or equipment such as a plough or planter. The arrangement is based on mutual convenience and no cash passes. There is likely to be a greater degree of friendship/equality between the parties concerned than in any other form of contractual relationship. However, some arrangements of this kind involve a clear distinction between senior partners and junior partners.

4. A land-holder makes a share-cropping arrangement with a contractor who undertakes the task of ploughing in return for a half-share of the crop. If the contractor is also an entrepreneur he ploughs the land himself with his tractor or team of animals. If he is not an agricultural entrepreneur in this sense he independently hires an entrepreneur to do the ploughing. In either case the land-holder and the share-cropping contractor, who are often kin, are jointly responsible for seed and fertilizer and for the labour of weeding and reaping. The crop is divided equally between them.

5. There is occasional variation on this pattern, where the contractor has full private use of part of the land-holder's land in exchange for his ploughing services. In this case land-holder and contractor are independently responsible for the seed, labour etc. on their respective portions of the land-holder's land.

6. Labour for weeding and reaping commonly assumes two forms: (a) hired labour which is paid for either at the standard daily wage rate ('two shillings' or R0.20 in 1972–4) or in kind, in a measure of grain; and (b) reciprocal labour in which two women undertake to assist each other in their respective fields. Otherwise, occasionally for weeding and reaping and often for threshing, work-parties (*matsema*) may be called which involve the provision of food and beer by the land-holder for a group of people gathered for work on a particular day.[7]

In 1973 the 73 households of Ha Molapo held 113 fields altogether, from which it is clear that the mean holding per household was no more

78

than half the traditional entitlement of three fields per land-holder. They were not evenly distributed between households, however: 10 households held no land at all; 30 households held one field; 20 held two fields; 11 held three fields and the remaining two households held four and six fields respectively. The fields themselves were not surveyed, and the number of fields is only an approximate indication of the relative acreage held (see Table 4.2), since fields are notoriously variable in size and quality of land.

In the 1972–3 season, 25 out of the 113 fields in Ha Molapo (22 per cent) were not cultivated at all, a proportion which is probably typical even of relatively good seasons. Of the 88 fields which were cultivated, 16 were share-cropped, and 72 worked by the holding household under a variety of other contractual and co-operative arrangements. The fact that land-holders often make two separate contracts for ploughing and planting, in respect of each field they hold, renders it very difficult to classify all the contractual arrangements made, either by household or by field. The following case studies are intended to exemplify the range and diversity of such arrangements. That they are crudely representative may be inferred from the distribution of plough traction in respect of the 72 fields worked by the holding household in 1972–3: 28 of these were ploughed by hired tractor; 6 by cattle belonging to the land-holding household; a further 10 by cattle belonging to kinsmen of the land-holder; 17 by cattle belonging to unrelated contractors; and 5 by a team made up from the combined resources of several households (113, 117 and 120), a co-operative network which is described below. I was unable to record the necessary information in respect of the remaining 6 fields.

The most common form of share-cropping arrangement is as follows. A land-holder who lacks capital resources will make an arrangement with another party, who may or may not hold land himself but who either has funds to hire the necessary equipment or has direct access to oxen, plough and labour. A land-holder seldom regards as satisfactory an arrangement in which the price of being able to cultivate at all is the loss of half the crop. But many land-holders have little choice. An elderly widow, for example, who holds land but has few cash resources may find it to her advantage to share-crop with an active migrant kinsman who has no land but has the capacity to hire the capital inputs.

Double share-cropping 'MaLebelo (Household 115) is a widow, aged 62 in 1973. She has no migrant support within her household, but she retains the two fields held by her husband. In 1972–3 she made share-cropping arrangements, respectively, with her own second son

79

Moeketsi (Household 129) and a distant classificatory son, both of whom are migrants with their own families and independent households.

In the first case, her son Moeketsi supplied cash to hire a tractor; she planted at no cash cost by combining her own planter with a neighbour's cattle (enabling him to plant his own land also), while Moeketsi paid for seed and fertilizer; the labour of weeding was shared between herself and her daughter-in-law Mavis, Moeketsi's wife, and they split the cash cost of hiring two other women, one of whom was 'MaLebelo's daughter resident nearby (Household 103); for reaping they were assisted by an elderly neighbour who was rewarded with a standard measure of grain. Otherwise, they divided the yield equally between them.

In the second case, her classificatory son Sebakeng supplied cash to hire a tractor; they shared the cash costs of seed and fertilizer and of planting; the labour of weeding and reaping was undertaken by 'MaLebelo and Sebakeng's wife. 'MaLebelo met her own cash commitments through her regular brewing turnover and also through remittances from her eldest son Lebelo (Household 114) whose homestead adjoins her own. She made the same arrangements in 1973–4 except that the second field was ploughed by a local entrepreneur's cattle team and not by tractor.

A senior wife's dilemma 'MaPeete (Household 106), born in 1914, is the senior wife of a polygynist, Serjeant (Household 105). She holds one field. In the seasons 1972–3 and 1973–4 she made a share-cropping contract with 'MaRosa, the wife of her junior co-wife's younger brother (Household 123). 'MaRosa and her husband have no land, and he is a regular migrant on the coal mines. 'MaRosa paid for a tractor to plough, while the costs of hiring cattle with planter and of buying seed – half maize, half sorghum – were shared between the parties. During the weeding season 'MaRosa was ill so she paid for the help, in her name, of an adolescent girl then resident with 'MaPeete, and they jointly hired two other women; harvesting was done by 'MaPeete and 'MaRosa, each recruiting voluntary assistance from among their respective close kin. The yield was shared equally between them but, at market prices prevailing in 1973, they did not recover the cash investment made. The arrangement was suspended in the 1974–5 season, because 'MaPeete had at the age of 60 gone off to Lenasia (Johannesburg) to seek work as a domestic servant. Her husband having no regular income, and having to support a large family by his second wife, 'MaPeete was unable to make ends meet at home. She returned in 1975, and by 1978 her husband's two eldest sons were both away on mine contracts. One was sending her remittances specifically to cultivate her field, and she no longer had to resort to the share-cropping arrangement. She brewed beer regularly in order to supplement this income.

An inter-household co-operative network   Three neighbouring households (113, 117 and 120) pooled their resources in the seasons 1972–3 and 1973–4. Tsoeu (120) and Malefetsane (117) each held two fields; and Malefetsane's elder brother's widow 'MaFetang (113) held three. In October 1972 Tsoeu possessed three beasts fit for yoking to 'MaFetang's plough. Together with three beasts belonging to Malefetsane these made up a full ploughing team of six animals. With this team, and the labour of Malefetsane and of his elder son Tšoene, they cultivated one of Tsoeu's fields, both of Malefetsane's and two of 'MaFetang's. They also used the team to plough for Malefetsane's younger son, an absent migrant, who had his own household elsewhere; and for a distant kinsman of Tsoeu with whom Tsoeu had made a share-cropping contract. For the other of his own two fields Tsoeu had made a share-cropping contract in reverse with one of his sons-in-law who provided cash for hiring a tractor to plough it. Tsoeu was able to borrow a planter from a friend of his, whereas Malefetsane had to hire a planter from another neighbour. Otherwise the same co-operative arrangement applied to planting of the lands.

In October 1973 Malefetsane no longer owned any cattle, having transferred his three animals in an instalment of bridewealth for his son Tšoene's marriage (see Chapter 2); and both he and his son were absent migrants during the ploughing season. However, Tsoeu's sister's son Renang, domiciled in Household 120, was home from a mine contract at Welkom (Orange Free State), and the labour for ploughing was provided by Renang and by Tsoeu's adolescent son Ntholi. The widow 'MaFetang had two beasts which the previous year had been herded out elsewhere because she had no herdboy, but which she brought back home in 1973. Tsoeu was able to borrow a beast from someone else 'through friendship' and once again they were able to make up a ploughing team. They ploughed the same fields as above, and Tsoeu repeated both his share-cropping contracts, with his son-in-law on his own field and his distant kinsman on the latter's field. His son-in-law hired a tractor to plough the former, and Tsoeu ploughed the latter with his team.

The respective contributions to the ploughing operations made by the three households in the network are summarized on page 82. It may be seen that Household 117 made no contribution to the inputs in the second year, but was nevertheless able to draw on credit in the co-operative network established through the previous year's arrangements, since Malefetsane and Tšoene (117) had provided the labour then. In October 1974 it became

season	cattle		plough	labour
1972–3	3 from (120)		(113)	2 men from
	3 from (117)			(117)
1973–4	3 from (120)		(113)	1 man, 1 boy
	2 from (113)			from (120)
	1 from Tsoeu's friend			

apparent that the network was going to break down. 'MaFetang no longer kept her animals in Ha Molapo, because her younger sister's son who had been herding them had returned to his own home. In November 1973, at the end of the ploughing season, Tsoeu had slaughtered an ox to make a marriage feast for his daughter's husband's people, and the households were thus quite unable to constitute a ploughing team. Renang was absent on another mine contract, and Ntholi was in initiation school. Malefetsane and his son were both absent, and Tsoeu himself was in no physical condition for holding the plough. It seemed likely that they would have to abandon the co-operative effort and each household would have to make its own contractual arrangements for 1974–5. When I left Ha Molapo in mid-November 1974 Tsoeu had still not made arrangements to plough and it was not clear where the money to hire a tractor would come from. He died in mid-1975.

The most expensive items in the farming budget are the costs of hiring plough traction and buying fertilizer. Hiring a planter and team is also expensive. It is not essential since it is always possible to broadcast the seed by hand (*ka Sesotho*), but this method is recognized as relatively inefficient. The household which hires a tractor to plough the land and hires oxen for planting selected hybrid seed bought at government-subsidized rates at the co-operative store, and which also applies artificial fertilizer, is likely to achieve a substantially better yield than the household which has an arable holding of comparable size but has ploughed with a neighbour's tired oxen, late in the season, having hand-broadcast seed set aside from the previous year's crop, without using fertilizer. Results from the seasons 1972–3 and 1973–4 show a significant correlation between levels of cash investment in intensive techniques and average yields. The 1972–3 season was generally a poor one, owing to very late rains, and many households were unable to recover the value of their cash investment let alone begin to meet their 'subsistence' requirements.[8] Most did rather better in the 1973–4 season. There were thirty-six households in Ha Molapo in that year of whose agricultural operations I was able to obtain reasonably complete records. Mean yield per household of the staple grains maize and sorghum together was 7.2 bags.

Four households reaped negligible amounts of less than 1 bag; thirteen reaped between 1 and 5 bags; eleven between 6 and 10 bags; and eight achieved more than 10 bags.[9] The net value of crop yields may be judged from the fact that after the harvest of 1973 the average price at which Lowland traders would buy grain from villagers was about R4.30 per bag of maize and R6.10 per bag of sorghum (ASB 1973). However, the cost to villagers of purchasing the equivalent quantities of maize flour later in the year was rather higher than this.

Household 135 'MaFako's husband Polao, born in 1935, is employed at Sasol, the South African plant for extraction of oil from coal, in the Orange Free State. He sends her regular remittances and comes home as often as he can obtain short leave from work – two or three times a year. They work two fields which are nominally held by Polao's elderly father, a widower who eats his meals from his daughter-in-law's 'pot' but sleeps in his own hut elsewhere. In 1974 their livestock holdings were one bull, two cows, three calves and two donkeys. In 1972–3 the household's agricultural operations were as follows:

Field A	ploughing:	hire of tractor	R11.00
	planting:	hire of neighbour's cattle and planter....	R 3.00
	seed:	maize bought from co-operative store ...	R 4.90
	fertilizer:	3 bags at R2.50 each.........................	R 7.50
	weeding:	'MaFako, Polao's mother's brother's wife	—
	reaping:	'MaFako, Polao's MBW and 'MaFako's BW	—
	yield:	13 bags maize	
		cash outlay	R26.40
Field B	ploughing:	hire of cattle belonging to Polao's mother's sister................................	R8.00
	planting:	hand-broadcast................................	—
	seed:	sorghum from previous year's crop.......	—
	fertilizer:	none...	—
	weeding:	(as above)	
	reaping:	(as above)	
	yield:	1 bag sorghum	
		cash outlay	R8.00

The total cash outlay was R34.40 and the crop yield was 13 bags of maize and 1 bag of sorghum, of which 1 bag of maize was given to 'MaFako's brother's wife and 1 basket of sorghum (there are 5 to 6 baskets per bag) to Polao's mother's brother's wife for their assistance. In the season 1973–4 'MaFako made similar arrangements, involving greater expense, but they reaped 23 bags of maize and 2 of sorghum. This was

83

the outstandingly successful marital partnership in Ha Molapo in respect of regular migrant remittances combined with domestic enterprise.

Household 129 Moeketsi is a commission clothes salesman for a Johannesburg company. He has no land in his own name but his wife Mavis has the use of a field belonging to her own family in the next village. They supplement cultivation of this field (A) through a regular share-cropping contract with Moeketsi's mother 'MaLebelo on one of her fields (B). In 1973–4 their operations were as follows:

Field A	ploughing:	hire of tractor....................................	R 7.50
	planting:	hire of neighbour's cattle........................	R 2.00
	seed:	maize bought	R 2.20
	fertilizer:	3 bags (including 1 of Super)	R 6.80
	weeding:	Mavis and a neighbour (help reciprocated).	—
	reaping:	Mavis and a neighbour (help reciprocated).	—
	yield:	6 bags maize	
		cash outlay	R 18.50
Field B	ploughing:	hire of tractor....................................	R 12.00
	planting:	hire of neighbour's cattle for R3........each	R 1.50
	seed:	maize bought for R4.40...................each	R 2.20
	fertilizer:	4 bags, all bought by Moeketsi's wife.......	R 8.00
	weeding:	Mavis, 'MaLebelo	
	reaping:	Mavis, 'MaLebelo	
	yield:	8 bags maize, i.e. 4 bags each	
		cash outlay	R 23.70

The total cash outlay was R42.20 and the yield which accrued to them was 10 bags of maize. There were no payments in cash or kind for labour independent of the cost of ploughing and planting.

Household 137 'MaPuleng's husband Motlalepula is a coal miner in Natal and sends irregular remittances. Their economic circumstances are fully described in Chapter 7. They hold one field, and in both seasons 1972–3 and 1973–4 their agricultural operations were markedly unsuccessful.

1972–3	ploughing:	hire of cattle..	R 5.00
	planting:	hand-broadcast.....................................	—
	seed:	sorghum bought from Motlalepula's kinsman	R 0.75
	fertilizer:	none	—
	weeding:	'MaPuleng (but germination very poor)	
	reaping:	'MaPuleng	
	yield:	negligible (less than 1 bag sorghum)	
		cash outlay	R 5.75

84

1973–4	ploughing } planting }	hire of cattle from Motlalepula's mother's brother's daughter, single charge for both.	R 5.00
	seed:	maize bought from neighbour	R 1.50
	fertilizer:	none	—
	weeding:	'MaPuleng	
	reaping:	'MaPuleng	
	yield:	2 bags maize	
		cash outlay	R 6.50

The total cash outlay was just under R6 in one season and just over R6 in the next, and the yields were very low.

Access to arable land, either directly in the form of usufructuary title or indirectly through a share-cropping contract, is of course a *sine qua non* of the rural household's agricultural enterprise. But these farming budgets suggest that agriculture in Lesotho seldom provides even minimal security to the household without regular access to cash earnings. Above all, it must be understood that inflation strikes at the heart of agricultural operations. In 1972 ploughing charges in the Leribe district varied between R0.80 and R1.00 per Sesotho acre;[10] two years later they were approximately R1.50 per acre. I estimate that tractor-hire rates in October 1974 were at least 25 per cent higher than those prevailing in 1973, as a direct result of the Yom Kippur war and the oil embargo which followed it; while the price of fertilizer was about 50 per cent higher than in the previous year. Both these items are more or less directly related to the price of oil. It is the 'peasants' in Lesotho and the other labour reserves who, far from being cushioned by a 'subsistence' livelihood from the rise in the cost of living, suffer the full effects of the international crisis of capital.

4

Differentiation, poverty and class formation

In Chapters 2 and 3 I discussed household strategies of participation in wage labour and domestic agriculture, respectively, with reference to detailed examples from one village community. We are now in a position to stand back and assess the available evidence on the relationship between migrant labour and domestic agriculture, with reference to Lesotho as a whole.

A misplaced orthodoxy

It is commonly taken for granted that there is a 'remarkably equitable' distribution of income in rural communities in Lesotho, and a relative absence of differentiation. This is attributed both to a relatively even distribution of productive assets within the country and to the fact that most rural households depend on the export of labour to South Africa (IBRD 1975: 21; SFYDP: 3; cf. also Ström 1978: 30). The 'generalization' of poverty in Lesotho is undeniable. But the received view is expressed in a variety of more specific propositions which, being officially endorsed in the Second Five Year Development Plan, have presumably influenced the making of policy. These propositions are misleading in two respects. Firstly, they distort our understanding of the patterns of differentiation that it is possible to identify. Secondly, they misconceive the relationship between income that accrues from domestic sources and income derived from migrant earnings. My purpose in this Chapter is to substantiate these criticisms and to propose a more realistic perspective within which to understand the empirical evidence on rural household income distribution. Further, I argue that the 'generalization' of poverty does not preclude significant rural differentiation; and that increasing dependence on migrant labour tends to exacerbate rather than to inhibit the process of differentiation.

The specific propositions whose validity I question are as follows.

1. 'The incidence of migrant labour is higher among poorer families than among the richer. Therefore the farm incomes of the poorer rural households are supplemented by income from migrant labour to a greater extent than those of the relatively richer households' (IBRD 1975: 21).
2. The incidence of migrant labour varies inversely with the size of land holding: 'thus families with no land, or below average quantities of land, and therefore lower incomes from agricultural activities, tend to have a higher probability of any given number of household members working in the Republic of South Africa, and thus a higher income from remittances' (Cobbe 1976: 78).
3. A preference by migrant miners for investing their deferred pay in livestock tends to 'increase the incomes from livestock of families with below-average land holdings' (Cobbe 1976: 78); and, since Basotho have access to similar external employment opportunities, the ownership of livestock is relatively evenly distributed throughout the population (IBRD 1975: 21; SFYDP: 3).

These propositions are subject to a number of objections, both logical and substantive. Firstly, propositions 1 and 2 are formulated with primary reference to the distribution of assets in the rural economy, such that households which are poorer in this respect are presumed to exhibit a higher rate of migration, and to derive a higher level of income therefrom, than households which are better off in respect of their domestic assets. However, farm income is partly derived from the investment of migrants' earnings, and households with an income from wage labour are better able to invest than households without such an income. This is admitted in respect of livestock (proposition 3) but implicitly denied in respect of crop production (all three propositions). This apparent contradiction is only resolved through the wholly implausible suggestion (proposition 3) that households with little or no land are compensated by an income from livestock.

Secondly, it is not possible to decide which households are 'richer' or 'poorer' overall in default of further information on the proportional contributions to total household income of employment in South Africa and of productive assets in land and livestock in Lesotho. A 'levelling' effect of the kind implicit in all three propositions cannot simply be assumed. It must be demonstrated. It is important in particular to recognize that variables of household size and demographic composition affect both consumption requirements and migrant earning capacity. For example, if households of six persons have access to the same amount of land and the same number of livestock as households of three persons, then assets are evenly distributed between households but not between persons. Conversely, larger households on average obviously have a larger migrant earning capacity and therefore a greater potential income from the export of labour than smaller households; and this difference is likely to be far more important than the difference between their respective consumption requirements, especially in view of the fact that approximately one third of rural households derive negligible income from migrant earnings (see Chapter 2).

Thirdly, even if the two variables of size of land holding and incidence of migrant labour do vary inversely, it does not follow that there is a direct causal relationship, such that individuals migrate *because* they do not have access to land. There is a more plausible explanation of inverse variation between the two variables: that it is due to the differential distribution of land holding and migrant labour, respectively, between households at different stages of the developmental cycle. For example, a male household head aged 50 or 60 years is more likely to hold arable land than a male household head aged 35. But migrants predominate in the younger age range. And an elderly widow who has retained usufructuary title to her husband's lands often has no migrant support within the household. In other words, it is not necessary to assume a cause and effect relationship as the natural explanation of the observation that households with land send out fewer migrants than households without land. A more realistic view is that almost all men have to migrate for economic reasons but that, because of the prevailing shortage of land, men often acquire title to land subsequently and not alternatively to undertaking a migrant career.

Fourthly, and perhaps most fundamentally, the assumption that migrant earnings *supplement* farm incomes is a distortion of relationships at the micro-economic level. At the macro-level, the failure of agricultural output to meet subsistence needs, in Lesotho as elsewhere in the periphery of southern Africa, is a reasonable index of aggregate dependence on the export of labour. However, as was clearly demonstrated in Chapter 3, successful farming is not conducted independently of a regular cash income. Migrants invest both in arable crop production and in livestock as well as, even more importantly, in the building of a 'house' with all that this implies in material and ideological terms (Chapters 5 and 6). Investments in agriculture and livestock are interdependent because, as we have seen, the economic value of bovines derives largely from their use as draught animals. The capacity of particular households to invest in the domestic economy is thus largely determined by their wage-earning capacity in the South African industrial sector.

Two inferences may be drawn from the above discussion which are fundamental to an understanding of rural differentiation in Lesotho. The first is that migrant wage-earning capacity, rather than farm income, must be viewed as the independent variable in assessing the manner in which individual households dispose their resources. The second is that the developmental cycle of the household – the way in which its size and composition change through time – must be built into any explanation of observed differences in wealth and income between rural households. With these points in mind we can proceed to evaluate the available evidence on differentiation, to identify the poor and to analyse the class positions of villagers in Lesotho.

Some evidence on land, livestock and income distribution

Any investigation of differentiation requires criteria for distinguishing 'richer' and 'poorer' households. One method of doing this is to compare households by reference to the sum of their material and non-material assets at a given point in time (the stock approach). Another method is to compare households by reference to their total income over a given period of time (the flow approach). Using first one method and then the other, I will briefly review the evidence on differentiation in rural communities which emerges from various survey results.

The principal productive assets in the domestic economy are land and livestock. Most surveys conducted in Lesotho show a relatively equitable distribution of land. This is plausibly attributed to a system of land tenure which recognizes the right of every married male tax-payer to usufructuary title in some arable land, and theoretically allows re-allocation of land in accordance with the demography of household needs. However, over the period 1950 to 1970, the proportion of landless households reported in three agricultural censuses increased from 7 per cent in 1950 to 9 per cent in 1960 and 13 per cent in 1970 (Douglas and Tennant 1952; Morojele 1962 etc.; Lesotho 1972). Other surveys conducted during the 1970s have revealed even higher proportions of landless households – 19 per cent in Qacha's Nek district (Spiegel 1979: 59) and 23 per cent in a small national sample (Lesotho 1975: 19).

The squeeze on land is also reflected in the fact that, while the number of land-holdings increased over the period 1950 to 1970 (Table 4.1), this increase overwhelmingly predominated in small holdings of less than 4 acres, suggesting the increasing use of marginal land. Table 4.1 shows that 36 per cent of holdings in 1950 were smaller than 4 acres; 44 per cent in 1960; and 50 per cent in 1970. Table 4.2 shows that, in 1970, 13 per cent of households held no land; 43 per cent of households held less than

Table 4.1. *Distribution of land holdings by farm size, Lesotho, 1950–70.*

Percentage of holdings in each size class

Size of holding (acres)		1950	1960	1970
Small	(0.01–3.99)	36	44	50
Medium	(4.00–7.99)	40	36	34
Large	(8.00–14.99)	20	16	13
Very large	(15 plus)	4	4	3
Number of holdings		149,800	155,287	185,076

Source: IBRD (1975: 93).

Table 4.2. *Distribution of land, Lesotho, 1970.*

		Households	Acreage	Fields
Size of holding (acres)			(percentages)	
No land		13	—	—
Small	(0.01–3.99)	43	23	39
Medium	(4.00–7.99)	30	39	38
Large	(8.00–14.99)	12	28	18
Very large	(15 plus)	2	10	5
Total numbers		212,228	909,788	402,220

Source: Lesotho (1972).

4 acres; and 14 per cent of households had holdings of 8 acres or more, constituting 38 per cent of all arable acreage. Table 4.2 also shows that the number of fields per holding is an accurate guide to relative acreage only for the medium size of land-holding. The smallest fields are found in holdings of less than 4 acres and the largest in holdings of 8 acres or more. Therefore an assessment of the distribution of land-holdings by reference to number of fields held is an understatement of inequalities in the distribution of actual acreage between households. On the other hand, the 1970 census results broadly endorse Hamnett's finding from the 1960 census that 'there is a strong positive correlation between size of household and size of holding, a circumstance which lends support to the view that the large holdings do not usually represent an inequitable distribution of land resources; rather, the holdings tend to be large because the households attached to them are large' (Hamnett 1973: 43).

Holdings of livestock may be assessed in two ways: firstly by reference to the way the livestock ratio (the number of stock units per head of the human population) has changed over time; and secondly by reference to the distribution of livestock between households at any one time. Census

Table 4.3. *Livestock and human populations in Lesotho, 1921–76.*

Year	Large stock	Small stock	Stock units	De jure population	Livestock ratio
1921	726,740	2,748,643	1,276,476	544,147	2.35
1931			1,629,031		2.75
1936	499,522	1,674,964	834,515	661,809	1.26
1946	537,442	2,349,990	1,007,440	689,919	1.46
1956	510,145	1,993,819	908,909	794,253	1.14
1966	436,567	2,343,176	905,202	965,913	0.94
1976	589,600	1,745,500	938,700	1,216,815	0.77

Note: Stock units were calculated at the rates of 1 unit = 1 large stock (cattle and horses) = 5 small stock (sheep and goats).
Sources: Livestock figures for 1921 and 1936 to 1966 from CARs; for 1976 from ASB (1977). The estimate of stock units for 1931 is taken from Pim (1935: 33), and that of the livestock ratio for 1931 from Poulter (1973: 60). *De jure* population figures from Table 1.1 above.

figures on stock holdings are available from the Colonial Annual Reports (Table 4.3), but in view of the fact that conditions for pastoralism in Lesotho are notoriously variable from season to season, the only inference that can safely be made is of a general decline since the 1930s in the number of livestock relative to the human population. A striking example of short term fluctuation in absolute numbers was the devastating loss of livestock which occurred between 1931 and 1934 owing to the combination of an exceptional drought with massive recession in world trade (Pim 1935: 147). Table 4.3 shows that the mean livestock holding per head of the *de jure* human population has approximately halved since the Second World War. Irrespective of changes over time in the concentration of livestock holdings, therefore, it may be inferred that livestock today contribute a much smaller proportion of mean household income than they did in the past.

Some indication of the contemporary distribution of livestock between rural households is given in Table 4.4. This distribution suggests that livestock are much more unevenly distributed than is land. Almost half the households in 1976 owned no livestock at all, while 10 per cent of households controlled nearly 60 per cent of all livestock. The ownership of livestock is also correlated with the size of household, so that the distribution of livestock per head of the human population is less inequitable than the distribution per household.

It is difficult to determine to what extent this concentration of livestock is a recent phenomenon. In the past, chiefs' holdings were very much larger than commoners', but comparison is complicated by the fact that *mafisa* arrangements were very widespread, as a means by which

Table 4.4. *Distribution of livestock, Phuthiatsana and Thaba Tseka, 1976.*

Livestock units	Households %	Livestock %	Mean household size
None	48	—	4.4
0.1–4.9	27	16	5.2
5.0–9.9	15	26	6.1
10.0–19.9	6	21	7.1
20.0 plus	4	37	7.8

Note: 1 livestock unit = 1 bovine/equine = 5 sheep/goats.
Source: Van der Wiel (1977: 86). Number of households = 1,286.

chiefs attracted political clients. *Mafisa* is 'the practice whereby a stock owner entrusts a portion of his stock to the care of another who, while he is in no way a hired employee, acts as caretaker of that stock in return for certain rights of usufruct over the stock' (Sheddick 1954: 109). The caretaker may use the animals for milking or draught purposes and he is also entitled to annual wool and mohair clippings. All natural increase, however, belongs to the owner. Thus the management of livestock does not necessarily coincide with its ownership.

Despite this difficulty, which applies both in the past and the present, it will be helpful to compare the available evidence on differentiation in the 1930s with survey evidence from the 1970s. In 1934 some evidence from the Qacha's Nek district was submitted to Sir Alan Pim, which revealed a striking positive correlation between an individual's age and his holdings in land and livestock, and an inverse relationship between such assets and participation in wage labour (Table 4.5). This evidence is not very surprising in view of the facts that employment in the gold mines has always been concentrated in the earlier phases of the individual's life span, and that maximum holdings in land and livestock are characteristically attained in the later phases. But Table 4.5 tells us nothing about differences within age cohorts, approximately defined as they are. And it is differences of this kind between households rather than between individuals that are of importance in analysing differentiation within rural communities.

In the 1930s Ashton was able to compare 66 households in or near the chief's place at Mokhotlong (Mountains). Using stock ownership as the principal criterion of economic status, he judged this sample to be somewhat wealthier than the average in the Mountain zone. He found that 6 households (9 per cent) were 'wealthy', having about 20 cattle and 50 sheep; 19 (29 per cent) were 'less wealthy', having less than 20 cattle, etc.; 19 (29 per cent) were 'middling', having less than 10 cattle; 9 (13 per

Table 4.5. *Economic profile of three groups of tax-payers, Qacha's Nek, 1934.*

100 tax-payers	of less than 5 years' standing	of 5 to 9 years' standing	of more than 9 years' standing
At home	32	40	70
Absent	68	60	30
at gold mines	55	15	17
Number with no stock	80	32	17
Number with no land	84	30	9
Average number of cattle owned	0.27	1.67	5.93
Average number of lands	0.22	1.25	3.12
Average number of dependants	0.67	2.93	5.86

Source: Pim (1935: 41).

cent) were 'poor', having little or no stock, but being helped by wealthy friends and relations; and 13 (20 per cent) were 'very poor', having little or no stock and no wealthy friends (Ashton 1939: 167). Ashton's general comment was as follows:

the position is not as good as it was, so that the children of today are not as favourably placed as were their fathers. Eighty years ago when the Highlands were first populated, the people had more meat and milk than they have now, and except during the early years of their settlement when their crops failed regularly, they even had more grain. Hunting used to be excellent, but today practically every sort of game has been exterminated. Almost everyone had cattle and small stock, but today many have none... Finally, each household used to have as much ground as it wanted to till, whereas they are now being restricted (1939: 169).

He went on to contrast the Lowlands with the Mountains:

In the Lowlands ... wealth is somewhat differently distributed... The gaps between the 'Wealthy' and the 'Very Poor' is [sic] greater, for on the one hand there are chiefs who have an income of several hundred pounds a year ... coupled with a substantial revenue from their flocks, lands and courts, while on the other hand there are peasants who have neither stock nor land (1939: 169).

He estimated that the proportion of 'wealthy' and 'less wealthy' households was lower in the Lowlands than the Mountains, and this is consistent with the fact that livestock holdings have always been larger in the Mountains than in the Lowlands.

These findings may be compared with those of two recent surveys. One was conducted in 1976 in the districts of Mokhotlong (Mountains) and Mafeteng (Lowlands) by members of a team whose terms of reference

93

were to evaluate the benefits derived from piped water supplies (Feachem *et al.* 1978). The other was conducted in 1975–6 in the Phuthiatsana Project area and the Thaba Tseka Project area (van der Wiel 1977).

The water team found the following results. The pattern of labour migration was broadly similar in the Mountains and the Lowlands, in terms of both the mean number of wage earners per household and the overall percentage of absent household heads. There was a much higher level of stock holdings in the Mountains than in the Lowlands, and half the Lowland households had no stock at all. The households wealthier in livestock also produced more grain, whereas 8 per cent of households had neither grain nor stock. There was a concentration of successful agricultural activities within relatively few households, but a wide distribution both of paid employment and commercial beer brewing amongst all households. However, there was a tendency for households with particularly large stock holdings to have more paid employees, probably because these households also tended to be larger. The presence or absence of the household head was a good general index of relative wealth; and the poorest households were small and all-female.

Van der Wiel's survey of 1,286 households revealed marked differences in rural household income and also marked variation, between different income strata, in household size and proportional contributions to household income from crops, livestock and migrant labour. He noted a 'rather weak negative correlation' between household assets, defined in land and livestock, and participation in wage labour; but went on to demonstrate a difference between the rate of migration for household heads, negatively correlated with household wealth, and the rate of migration for other household members, positively correlated with household wealth. The explanation of this is probably that younger household heads, less likely than older men to have acquired title to land or to have established a herd of animals, are sole breadwinners; whereas older household heads retire to preside over larger households containing subordinate younger migrants, and have established title to land. A few older men are also likely to have acquired some livestock. It is unlikely therefore that livestock ownership compensates for deficiency in land, as suggested in proposition 3 at the beginning of this Chapter. Van der Wiel confirmed the importance of variables of demographic composition:

The age and sex composition of the household is an important factor determining a household's position on the income distribution scale. The degree to which a household receives cash from off-farm earnings depends almost entirely on the presence of an able-bodied male among the household members... The majority of households in the low-income group consists of widows living with little children, thereby lacking a potential wage-earner (van der Wiel 1977: 88).

Table 4.6. *Distribution of rural household income in rands per annum (R), by source of income, income strata and mean household size, Phuthiatsana and Thaba Tseka, 1975–6*

Category	Income strata									
	0–199 very low		200–599 low		600–999 medium		1,000 plus high		All strata	
Source	R	%	R	%	R	%	R	%	R	%
crops	26	(39)	66	(16)	30	(3)	75	(4)	47	(6)
livestock	20	(30)	85	(21)	51	(6)	204	(12)	90	(11)
FARM	46	(70)	151	(37)	81	(9)	279	(16)	137	(17)
migrant labour	5	(8)	215	(53)	698	(81)	1,238	(71)	554	(71)
other (Lesotho)	15	(23)	42	(10)	80	(9)	222	(13)	92	(12)
OFF-FARM	20	(30)	257	(63)	778	(91)	1,460	(84)	646	(83)
domestic income	61	(92)	193	(47)	161	(19)	501	(29)	229	(29)
migrant labour	5	(8)	215	53)	698	(81)	1,238	(71)	554	(71)
TOTAL	66	(100)	408	(100)	859	(100)	1,739	(100)	783	(100)
households No	347		257		347		335		1,286	
%	(27)		(20)		(27)		(26)		(100)	
mean household size	3.1		4.9		5.1		7.7		5.2	

Source: Van der Wiel (1977: 88).
Note: All figures in brackets are percentages.

Data on sources of income for this sample of 1,286 households in the year 1975–6, by income strata, are set out in Table 4.6. The method of imputing a cash value to all forms of income inevitably introduces a number of biases, and for this reason the figures in the table should be interpreted with caution.[1] Several conclusions may nevertheless be drawn from them. Firstly, the proportion of overall household income derived from migrant earnings was 71 per cent in 1976. This may be compared with estimates of 59 per cent in 1974 and 43 per cent in 1970.[2] The trend is clearly an increasing dependence on the export of labour. Secondly, the poorest households, the 27 per cent in the 'very low' income category, derive only 8 per cent of their income from migrant earnings, and 70 per cent from farming. But their farm income is still absolutely lower than that for all other income strata, which exhibit a clear reversal of the proportional contributions of farm income and migrant labour, respectively. This suggests that approximately one quarter of rural households have meagre domestic resources and very little

95

access to migrant earnings. They are also the smallest households, on average. But the difference in mean household size between these income strata does not compensate for the absolute difference between them in mean household income. The inference is probably justified that households identified as very poor in terms of their annual flow of income are so principally because they have a much lower able-bodied earning capacity than richer households.

The Poverty Datum Line (PDL) for an average rural household of 5.2 persons in July 1976 was R1,152 per annum (van der Wiel 1977: 89).[3] It may be inferred from Table 4.6 that at least three quarters of rural households had an income below the PDL. Allowing for variation in mean household size between income strata and in particular for the fact that households in the 'very low' income category are less than half the size on average of households in the 'high' income category, it may be estimated that in 1976 at least two thirds of the rural population were living at a level below that specified in the PDL as necessary to maintain a minimum level of health and decency.

In summary of the various sources of evidence discussed I reach the following conclusions, presented in the form of propositions alternative to those listed at the beginning of this Chapter.

1. Access to land as a productive asset is relatively evenly distributed amongst the rural population, except that (a) about one fifth of all households have no land at all, (b) most land-holdings are steadily decreasing in size, and (c) there are still a small number of households with large holdings.

2. But inferences about household productive capacity cannot be made directly from size of land-holding, owing to (a) the frequency of share-cropping arrangements, which distribute yields between land-holding and non-land-holding households, (b) wide variation in yields per unit area through differential use of intensive methods, and (c) the fact that each season, for one reason or another, up to one quarter of the arable lands available are not cultivated.

3. To a large extent successful farming activities depend directly on investment derived from cash earnings. Therefore farm income is supplementary to an income from migrant labour rather than the other way around.

4. A policy of investment in livestock by migrants has probably been a rational one, by comparison with alternative possibilities, despite the risks involved. From the evidence available, however, it cannot be argued with conviction either (a) that the distribution of livestock complements the distribution of land, such

that households with less income from agriculture have more income from livestock; or (b) that the distribution of livestock is relatively even amongst the rural population.

5. The evidence suggests, rather, an approximate correlation between household size, domestic productive capacity (crops and livestock) and migrant earning capacity. Small female-headed households are particularly disadvantaged in respect both of their migrant earning capacity (see Chapter 2) and of their domestic productive capacity; and it seems legitimate to single out such households as the proper focus of any programme designed to relieve absolute poverty in Lesotho. They constitute perhaps a quarter of all households, though a rather lower proportion of the population as a whole.

Class formation and the developmental cycle

The evidence reveals considerable differences between richer households and poorer households. Are these differences attributable to the demography of household development and dissolution? Or are they attributable to processes of class formation in the periphery? Posed as alternatives in this way, these questions evoke an old issue: that which divided Chayanov and the Organization of Production school on the one hand from orthodox marxists on the other. Chayanov argued that differences in agricultural output between Russian peasant households were attributable to their differential labour capacity relative to their consumption requirements. 'Inequalities of income and of land per head depended on the changing family composition, measured by the dependency ratio (the ratio of consumers to workers) which rose and fell through the family life cycle. In consequence, inequality itself was neither reversible nor irreversible but cyclical' (Harrison 1975: 309). Accordingly, Chayanov defended the persisting viability of a specifically peasant economy. The marxists, by contrast, argued that the Russian peasant economy was breaking up in the latter half of the nineteenth century, through monetization, the growth of the international and domestic trade in grain, and through industrialization; and that a rural bourgeoisie and a rural proletariat were emerging with opposed class interests. With the collapse of the New Economic Policy in the later 1920s and Stalin's drive to industrialization, Chayanov was identified as an apologist for the kulaks and his views were officially discredited. However, there is evidence of a resurgence of interest in his ideas since their first publication in English in 1966 (see Kerblay 1971; Sahlins 1974: 87–123; Harrison 1975).

For the purpose of explaining inequalities of income distribution between rural households in Lesotho it is helpful to invoke the idea of a dependency ratio which is defined in the circumstances as the ratio of dependants to paid employees (see Chapter 2). This ratio varies both between households at any one time and within households through time. But a peasantry defined by the absence of wage labour, which Chayanov was writing about, is obviously very different from an industrial proletariat based on the land and partly engaged in farming, which is characteristic of the periphery of southern Africa. Wage labour is the relationship through which Basotho participate in a larger system of production, and through which rural households have been partly 'freed' from the land over time. Therefore it is wrong to counterpose an explanation in terms of the developmental cycle of the household to an explanation in terms of class formation. The questions raised at the beginning of this section are falsely antithetical. They must be answered within a single frame of reference. Differentiation in Lesotho must be analysed with reference both to the developmental cycle of the rural household and to the contradictory forces of capitalist accumulation as they apply to the labour reserve.

Such an analysis may be summed up in these terms. The inequalities of income distribution in Lesotho reflect the exigencies of the developmental cycle under conditions peculiar to the labour reserve. These conditions are: (1) the concentration of earning capacity in the middle age-ranges of able-bodied manpower; (2) the absence of developed state mechanisms (such as progressive taxation, unemployment benefit and pension schemes) for effecting transfers of income between households at different stages of the developmental cycle; and (3) certain demographic features of the system of oscillating migration: notably, a high proportion of widows and of female-headed households (see Chapter 7), a distorted sex ratio in the middle age-ranges through the absence of male migrants, and a numerical preponderance in villages of the young, the female and the elderly.

But these conditions themselves can only be understood with reference to processes of transformation in the larger economy. An initially successful peasantry in Lesotho was suppressed and partly 'freed' from the land. A small proportion of the population managed to sustain a livelihood on the land, but the large majority came to depend increasingly on the export of labour. Most inhabitants of the periphery today are no longer peasants nor yet 'free' labour: landlessness is partly a function of phase in the developmental cycle and partly the result of an absolute squeeze on the arable land available to a rapidly increasing population. Most Basotho men must commit themselves to a working life in South African industry. At the same time they strive to establish land rights at home; and they are better placed to invest in agricultural activities than those without an income from migrant labour. A few agricultural entrepreneurs have been able to take advantage of share-cropping arrangements and multiple ploughing contracts to gain access to far more land than they themselves are nominally entitled to, but there is little evidence that they have yet established a profitable pattern of accumulation, because they carry the risk of the investment (cf. Helman 1973). A successful migrant career remains a pre-condition of investment on the necessary scale. Meanwhile wage increases during the 1970s have had contradictory effects. On the one hand, they have increased general dependence on the export of labour, and stimulated a variety of informal mechanisms through which migrants' earnings are redistributed within the rural community (cf. Spiegel 1979). On the other hand, they have exacerbated existing differentials both between wage-earners themselves and between households with and without direct access, respectively, to migrants' earnings. In the 1980s an increasing number of Basotho, both in absolute and in relative terms, will join the ranks of the structurally unemployed, unable to obtain employment either at home or abroad and unable to eke out a livelihood at home. The consequences of this are likely to be devastating.

Villagers in Lesotho, therefore, occupy different class positions both simultaneously and serially.[4] They do so simultaneously because rural household members distribute their energies and resources between (a) employment in the formal sector, mainly outside Lesotho; (b) the informal sector at home; (c) the domestic economy based on agriculture and livestock; and (d) unemployment at home, on account of the 'natural' surplus of labour and also the systematic extrusion of large numbers of 'redundant' Africans from the South African economy in a time of severe economic recession. They occupy different class positions serially because constraints and opportunities vary with phase in the temporal processes of household aggregation and dissolution.

5

Changing family structure

The study of changing family structure is properly the study of social process. In default of adequate evidence to reconstruct the process of change in the rural periphery of southern Africa we are often reduced to a comparison between the 'past' and the 'present'. The past in this sense is a more or less hypothetical base-line, a reconstruction of traditional society which is contingent on our relative ignorance of pre-colonial conditions and which is largely derived from ethnographies conceived within a synchronic and functionalist paradigm. Such reconstruction is therefore undertaken with reluctance and with uneasy awareness that any simple periodization of pre-colonial and colonial society or of pre-capitalist and capitalist social formations can seldom accommodate the complexities with which we have to deal.

My purpose in this Chapter is firstly to question the usefulness of well-known descriptive stereotypes such as the extended family and the nuclear family; secondly to clarify the empirical evidence relating to diverse temporal processes of family constitution in Lesotho; and thirdly to resolve some ambiguities in the ethnographic literature concerning Sesotho kinship structure.

The extended family and the nuclear family

The complex changes in family life that have taken place in Lesotho over the last hundred years have been recently subsumed under the notion of a 'movement' from the extended family to the nuclear family (Poulter 1976: 327–30). It is important to examine the validity of such a notion because this study is centrally concerned with the effects of oscillating migration on family structure.

In the less narrowly anthropological literature on southern Africa, the phrase 'extended family' is used variously and without precision to refer to any of the following: (1) the agnatic lineage, comprising the descendants in the male line of an ancestor about three generations above

100

the senior living generation; (2) an aggregate of people, variously related to a particular individual, who gather on occasions such as ancestor rituals, marriage feasts and funerals; and who may participate in processes of dispute resolution or form a pool of co-operative labour; and (3) a loosely defined network of relationships outside those of immediate kinship, upon which an individual can rely if he requires hospitality or assistance or if he is in trouble of some kind. The following quotation, from Anthony Barker's moving denunciation of oscillating migration, exemplifies this latter sense of the phrase:

It is at family level that the most pain is felt, and we cannot forget that the African cultural heritage enshrines a broader, more noble concept of family than that of the West. The extended family has proved a marvellous security for those for whom, otherwise, there was no security at all. The extended family is a net wide enough to gather the child who falls from the feeble control of neglectful parents, it receives the widow, tolerates the batty, gives status to grannies. Migratory labour destroys this ... (Barker 1973: 492).

More narrowly, much of the most principled opposition to the system of oscillating migration is based on the Christian premise that 'those whom God hath joined together, let no man put asunder' (M. Wilson 1973: 468–71; F. Wilson 1972b: 191). A man and his wife should have the right to live together and to rear their children in a stable social environment. These two strands of criticism are of course complementary. But their rationale is subtly different. In the quotation from Anthony Barker we have the idea that 'African family life' is different from that of the West and that it is undermined by migrant labour, to the detriment of African humanity. In the other argument cited, relating to the sanctity of marriage, we have the idea that the nuclear-family form represents both a natural human right and a universal aspiration, and that it is undermined by migrant labour, to the detriment of humanity. I have stressed this subtle difference of rationale not because there is any substantive disagreement between the authors concerned but in order to draw attention to the fact that powerful and pervasive ideological stereotypes of the family lie behind their arguments. It is necessary to acknowledge these explicitly in order to forestall the possibility that sociological consensus about the destructive consequences of migrant labour should be vitiated, in the first place by potentially competitive fallacies of essentialism ('the nuclear family is the basis of our civilization'; 'the extended family is the basis of African culture'); and in the second place, paradoxically, by gratuitous criticism of the imposition of western categories. What follows is an attempt to explain what I mean by this possibility.

The respective fallacies of essentialism are potentially competitive because a 'movement' from the extended family to the nuclear family is commonly alleged to accompany the transition from a 'traditional subsistence economy' to a 'western-oriented cash economy', with the further implication that this is either inevitable or desirable or both. An abstract formulation of this kind begs the question of the meaning and existence of either entity, by confounding the discrete functional criteria – co-residence, consumption, reproduction, co-operative labour, distribution of earnings, etc. – by which it is necessary to distinguish observations of family life. It also ignores the temporal process known to anthropologists as the developmental cycle of the domestic group, which manifests itself in a statistical diversity of types of household composition at any one time. There is little point in identifying the nuclear family as the basic unit of analysis in circumstances where thousands of husbands and wives are forced to live apart; where frequency distributions of household sizes commonly exhibit several distinct modes (see Fig. 2.3); where the boundaries of the *de jure* household coincide with those of the nuclear family (husband, wife and their children) in only a small minority of households – 18 per cent of my sample of 150 households (cf. Murray 1976: 146, 165) and 16 per cent of Spiegel's sample of 83 households (1979: 53); where a significant number of women bear children but remain unmarried; where many households are headed by widows; and where many children are reared by grandparents in multi-generation households because their parents are absent migrants. In these circumstances a contradiction inheres in the attempt to maintain nuclear-family integrity. A man's absence as a migrant labourer is a condition of his family's survival. But his absence also undermines the conjugal stability from which his family derives its identity.

Nevertheless, there is a well-established methodological tradition in southern African studies which, implicitly rather than explicitly, takes the nuclear family for granted as a unit of analysis. The *fons et origo* of this tradition appears to be Schapera's work in Bechuanaland (1935). He encouraged comparative studies elsewhere in southern Africa and Ashton's (1946) and Sheddick's (1948) surveys in Basutoland both directly reflect this influence. The tradition is further exemplified in the report on the Keiskammahoek Rural Survey, Volume III, in which the assumption of the analytical priority of the nuclear family renders it difficult to interpret the table on Kinship Composition of Homesteads (M. Wilson et al. 1952: 52–3, 56; see Murray 1976: 147–8). The fallacy of this assumption and its misleading practical implications are also evident from Morojele's analysis (1962 etc.) of the 1960 Agricultural Census in Basutoland. He distinguished between households and families for the purpose of identifying stock-owning and land-owning corporations, and presented separate tables for the proportions of households and families with and without land and livestock. Yet nowhere in his analysis was there any clear criterion for distinguishing between them. It can only be assumed that the number of (implicitly nuclear) families was adduced from the number of separate marital relationships, extant or otherwise, that existed within the households. This, in turn, begs the question of what is a marital relationship. Especially in the circumstances of the southern African periphery, a particular conjugal union does not fall readily into a classificatory typology of the married and the unmarried but must be understood as a temporal process during which its status is constantly susceptible to redefinition (see Chapter 6).

Thus there is some substance to criticism of kinship analyses based on the imposition of western categories such as that of the nuclear family. But such criticism is quite gratuitous if it leads the critic either to insist by contrast but without appropriate evidence on the importance of the 'extended family', or to undermine the credibility of evidence – now surely overwhelming – that the enforced separation of spouses generates acute anxiety, insecurity and conflict.[1] The latter tendency implies an alternative, distinctively African view of marriage and the family which does not presuppose intimacy between husband and wife and which is not therefore undermined by the separation of spouses. That such criticism has some influence I infer from a recent ILO report on migrants' wives in Lesotho, which the author introduced by counterposing two conflicting hypotheses: (1) that migrant labour has disastrous effects on family life, a view attributed to various published sources; and (2) that 'labour migration has been a fact of life for so long in Lesotho, and is so widespread, that it has become the normal course and families have adjusted to it ... Wives function normally in their husbands' absence ... Kinsmen take over the responsibilities of the absent migrant ...' (Gordon 1978: 7). She attributed the latter view to 'discussions with colleagues' and not to published sources, but since the (unnamed) colleagues in question were responsible for planning and conducting a large research project on migrant labour, funded by the ILO, this view cannot be dismissed as insignificant. The danger is that it effectively endorses the habit of capitalist employers and others who use the phrase 'extended family' in a residual sense to refer to something that allegedly accommodates everyone (the sick, the unemployed, the elderly) in default of decent wages or adequate social security arrangements. There is, as the quotation from Anthony Barker suggests, very little evidence to support such a view. The lesson is that an anthropological investigation of the extended family in the periphery must be undertaken within the framework of an analysis, whether in terms of income distribution or of class formation, of the structural differentiation that has been taking place in rural communities.

Such an investigation would establish that the processes of change are rather more complicated than might be implied in the notion of a 'movement' from one family form to another. Firstly, the nuclear-family form of household can be identified as one typical phase of the developmental cycle. But statistical surveys exhibit a great diversity of household composition, from widows living on their own to complex three- (or n-) generational households which reflect the centrifugal distribution of children between households rather than their centripetal concentration within the households of their parents. Secondly, the evidence from Lesotho suggests that the earnings of migrant labourers are increasingly concentrated within their own households and that households without direct access to an income from wage labour are severely disadvantaged (Chapters 2 and 4 above; Chapter 7 below). At the same time there is ample evidence relating to 'family' gatherings, court cases, co-operative labour, visiting and mutual support, to identify significant aggregations of kin outside those incorporated within the household. Thirdly, those networks of kin which are tactically articulated, normatively reinforced and susceptible to observation by the anthropologist are functionally related to constraints and opportunities which vary with phase in the developmental cycle and also with changes at the macro-economic level, for example in prevailing wage levels, the recruitment policy of the mining industry and the effective export of unemployment (see Chapter 1).

The notion of 'family structure' must therefore encapsulate diverse temporal processes. It is the exigencies of the mobility of labour operating within the temporal framework of household development and dissolution that explain observed patterns of family structure in the labour reserve.

Mobility and the developmental cycle

A man is a citizen of the area in which he was born and brought up. Alternatively, he may establish himself later in life as a citizen of a different area through formal introduction to the chief. There are three criteria indispensable to the validation of local citizenship: allegiance to a chief; domicile (but not necessarily *de facto* residence) in his area; and, on attaining the age of 21 or from the date of the first mine contract, annual payment of government tax. Most migrants, unless established as 'lost' in the Republic or as having otherwise opted out of the rural social system, may be regarded as *de jure* members of households in their area of local citizenship. South African influx control, as we have seen, prevents a man from emigrating with his family, so that almost all men envisage eventual retirement to a rural household. Accordingly they seek access to arable land as a provision for some marginal security in old age.

The life histories of older men and of their fathers reveal considerable geographical mobility within Lesotho in the late nineteenth and early twentieth centuries. This mobility took the form of steady expansion of settlement into sparsely populated areas of the country. During the first quarter of the twentieth century population growth exhausted further possibilities of expansion, and increasing concentration of numbers has brought stabilization in space (cf. Smits 1968). General shortage of arable land means that the possibility of an improved rural livelihood is no longer likely to constitute a motive for 'removal' (*ho falla*) from one area to another. 'Removal' is, in fact, likely to prejudice a man's chances of being allocated adequate land, for he is best placed to obtain access to land in the area where he and his family are well known, specifically but not necessarily in the area where his father resides. Thus, although 'removal' may still occur as a result of family quarrels, there is an ecological brake on the process of agnatic dispersion which would otherwise take place in response to increased pressure on land.

A man expects to set up an independent household as soon as he establishes a conjugal relationship. Often, however, it is some years before he is able to invest in building a stone hut of his own. If he is unlikely to inherit his parents' homestead he usually chooses an empty site not far away and seeks permission from the chief to build there. If he expects to inherit the old homestead he is likely to build a new hut as an adjunct of his parents' yard. In the latter case his minimal obligation from the outset is to provide some domestic privacy for his wife, although she undertakes household duties in co-operation with and under the eye of her mother-in-law. If a man's father is still alive following his own marriage they seldom continue to reside in the same household: the circumstances in which this does occur generally involve elderly or disabled widowers who are no longer effective household heads, being unable to manage domestic independence. But a man does not have to move far away in order to escape paternal authority, for his own earning capacity already ensures his effective independence. He has a greater chance of acquiring land by remaining within the area where he grew up than by moving elsewhere.

Thus a period of virilocal residence in marriage for both men and women is a characteristic feature of the developmental cycle irrespective of subsequent default by either partner. The *de jure* household typically assumes the structural form of the nuclear family after a man has set up a conjugal relationship in his own household and it may last until his children are old enough to reproduce in their turn. But the *de facto* nuclear family unit – a man and his wife and their children actually living together – is an irregular and transient phenomenon. Without a cash income from migrant earnings such a household ceases to be viable. There are few exceptions to this prevailing rule. The household similarly ceases to be viable if the conjugal relationship which is sustained by the man's earnings collapses through death or default. If the husband defaults, a woman must go to work herself to support her children, who often go to reside with her parents or, more likely, her widowed mother. If a wife defaults, she either takes her children with her, in which case the household ceases to exist (in the reference community), or she leaves them behind, in which case the hapless husband is in no position to support them *and* remain at home. Hence, again, recourse to grandparents. The empirical frequency of rearing by grandparents (see below) cannot be attributed merely, as one writer has suggested, to a customary claim inherent in the marriage transaction.[2] Such rearing arrangements very often reflect the exigencies of economic circumstance, in the absence of the middle generation.

The following story illustrates the centrifugal redistribution of children that commonly takes place as a result of conjugal dissolution. Koali (Household 101), aged about 30 in 1972, lived with his wife and three young children, independently of his father's household nearby (Household 104), which consisted of his father, his mother and their unmarried youngest son (see Appendix 1). Koali had worked several mine contracts in South Africa but during the year 1972–3 he was making an approximate livelihood in Lesotho by exploiting the relativities of supply and demand in small stock: he used to buy sheep and goats cheaply in the Mountains and sell them in the Lowlands at considerably higher prices. In July 1973 Koali died at home following a sudden and mysterious collapse. His wife had to go to South Africa to seek work in order to support the three young children, two of whom went to stay with her own parents in her natal village some miles away, and the third went to reside in her father-in-law's household nearby. Meanwhile Koali's younger brother left his parents' home on his first mine contract.

Thus within the Ha Molapo sample, from what had been two independent households before July 1973, each of nuclear-family form and containing three and five *de facto* members respectively, after July 1973 there emerged a single three-generational household containing five *de jure* and three *de facto* members, from which the middle generation was absent. Redistribution of the junior generation here was initiated by a death which may be considered exceptional to the natural course of a son surviving his father. But conjugal dissociation would have precipitated a similar redistribution. The example illustrates the vulnerability of the nuclear-family form of household to the short-term changes induced by dependence on the export of labour.

The ideal pattern of mobility for a woman is simply a single transfer of residence on marriage from her natal home to her husband's home. There is indeed a phase in almost every woman's life when she is virilocally resident. But actual patterns of mobility are much more complex: some detailed examples are given in Chapter 7. They are best understood in terms of a triangular set of possibilities within which the incidence of particular movements depends on the conjugal and jural components of the marital relation (Chapter 6). The apices of the triangle are a natal home in Lesotho, an affinal home in Lesotho and a workplace in South Africa. The same movements may occur in different temporal sequence in the lives of different women. For example, a woman may bear a pre-marital child and, after weaning, may leave home to work in the Republic for a period before returning to her natal home and, perhaps, subsequent marriage elsewhere. Or a woman's initial move may be the assumption of virilocal residence on marriage, followed some years later by conjugal dissociation and return to her natal home, when she may set off on a migrant career to contribute to the maintenance of her own kin including, probably, her own children. Or a woman's virilocal residence may persist throughout the years of her husband's absence until she emerges as a widow with a considerable degree of autonomy and discretion in the management of her family's affairs.

Those women recorded in the census as absent on migrant labour are predominantly those who have dependants to support but no extant conjugal association and so must rely on their own earning capacity. Such circumstances apply both to young women who engage in periods of migrant labour prior to marriage and to older women whose conjugal ties are dissolved. A girl may be 'spoilt in the yard' (*ho senyehela lapeng*) either at home in Lesotho or in the disorderly and squalid environment of township life in the Republic. A high incidence of pre-marital and extra-marital births is both cause and effect of women's entering the labour market in South Africa.

Temporal processes: the constitution of the family

One notion of family structure which purports to encapsulate the diverse temporal processes to which I have referred is the 'dissolution/ conservation contradiction'. As applied in southern Africa, this contradiction refers to the dual role of the labour reserve. It had to supply labour and it also had to provide part of the means of subsistence. At different periods in different areas, capital required the penetration of pre-capitalist social formations in such a way as partially to 'free' labour from the land but at the same time to sustain their ability to reproduce the labour force (Wolpe 1972; D. Clarke 1977a; Cliffe 1978). Hence kinship relations were both 'dissolved', in some sense, and 'conserved', in some sense. This was ensured by state policies, or rather the lack of them, relating to social security, retirement, the bringing up of the next generation and so on, responsibility for which continued to be vested in social relations in the labour reserve. Wolpe expressed it in this way: 'Accesssibility to the migrant-worker of the product (and of the "social services") of the Reserves depends upon the *conservation*, albeit in a restructured form, of the reciprocal obligations of the family' (Wolpe 1972: 435, his emphasis).

It is difficult to make sense of such a paradoxical formulation. How can relations be simultaneously restructured (i.e. transformed) and conserved? Is it not simpler to acknowledge that a certain pattern of reciprocal obligations has broken down, and that the onus placed on certain relationships – particularly the conjugal one – has intensified? I adduce evidence below to show that processes of 'dissolution' and 'conservation' are simultaneously at work in rural communities of the periphery. In Chapter 8 I also suggest that, since they are both rooted in the political economy of the labour reserve, identifying them as 'contradictory' perhaps serves a merely rhetorical purpose.

In order to introduce the argument it will be helpful to refer to two studies of a small community in Botswana. In 1934 and 1935 Schapera (1935) pioneered a method of describing the residential structure of the Tswana ward, the minimal political community. He chose two for the purpose: one in Mochudi, the principal settlement of the Kgatla tribe; the other in Serowe, the principal settlement of the Ngwato tribe. These wards had 106 and 95 inhabitants respectively. Twelve out of the sixteen household heads in Rampedi ward, in Mochudi, belonged to segments of an agnatic 'core' lineage. They were all related in the male line to the founder of the ward, one of the senior men who accompanied Chief Kgamanyane in 1871 when the Kgatla migrated from the Transvaal and established a settlement at Mochudi. Contrary to expressed Tswana norms, three out of those twelve were women. Of the four remaining household heads, one was a 'sister's son' to the core lineage, who had been adopted by his mother's brother as a child; two were men who had established their homesteads, again contrary to the norm, in the ward of their wives, i.e. they had married women belonging to the core lineage; and one was a 'stranger'. Mean household size was 6.6 persons. But the households varied considerably in size and composition: they included basic nuclear families, single-parent families, families with children from various marriages, and more complex three-generation families.

Schapera used these studies to establish the characteristic structure of the Tswana ward. It contains households belonging to segments of one or more agnatic lineages, whose constituent families are either closely related to the headman or otherwise related. There may also be 'strangers' who, over time, develop ties of kinship and marriage with the original ward members. The contemporary interest of his investigations lies in two points. Firstly, he established a method by which such basic units of social structure could be compared with those characteristic of other southern African peoples (cf. Ashton 1946; Sheddick 1948). Secondly, he provided a base-line of reliable information on particular communities from which subsequent developments could be traced in detail. A time-depth of this sort is invaluable but very seldom available to anthropologists. The opportunity to trace subsequent developments was taken up in this case by Simon Roberts of the London School of Economics, who carried out a second survey of the Mochudi ward in 1973, nearly forty years after Schapera's original work (Schapera and Roberts 1975).

Roberts found that Rampedi ward had expanded considerably in size. In 1973 there were thirty-three households, with a population of approximately 300 people. No fewer than twenty-six household heads, of whom two were women, belonged to the same agnatic core lineage. Its original structure was still discernible through the relationships between these household heads, and a number of marriages had taken place between different branches of this large family. The comparison showed that most men still set up homesteads in their own ward; that women move to their husband's ward on marriage; and that many marriages are still contracted locally. These observations led to the conclusion that 'the basic agnatic character of the grouping has proved durable over time' (Schapera and Roberts 1975: 267).

Yet Roberts also found the following features: firstly, a high rate of individual mobility, in the sense that many people who nominally belonged to the ward were absent, mostly as temporary labour migrants to South Africa – so that a survey undertaken at a slightly different time would have revealed a somewhat different resident population; secondly, a high proportion of adult women (40 out of 73) who had never married; and, thirdly, a high proportion of children (65 out of 162) born to such women. Schapera had found in 1934 that four out of six unmarried women (out of a total of 26 women of marriageable age) had borne illegitimate children. He regarded this as a 'striking illustration of the extent to which premarital sexual relations are practised' (Schapera 1935: 212). Much more striking to the modern observer is the substantial increase between the years 1934 and 1973 both in the number of unmarried women and in the number of children born to such women. These results are broadly consistent with the findings of the Botswana National Census of 1971 which revealed that, of all women aged 15 or over who had children, 43 per cent were married, 36 per cent were single, 7 per cent were divorced or separated, and 14 per cent were widows (calculated from Cooper 1979a: 11).

The trend in Mochudi is reflected in a form of household composition that is also reported to be common in other parts of Botswana, in Lesotho and in the Bantustans: the three-generational household which includes an unmarried daughter with her children.[3] For example, 75 out of my sample of 150 households in Lesotho in 1974 were found to comprise three or more generations, which gives an indication of the extent to which children are brought up in the households of their grandparents or other senior kin. More particularly, more than half of the linking parents in the middle generation were women; less than half were men. But this high incidence of intra-household links between alternate generations which are traced through women does not qualify the persistence of the predominantly agnatic structure of inter-household residential alignments reflected by the genealogical ties between household heads. In the Lesotho sample, the same high proportion of inter-generational links through women (81 per cent) and links through men (82 per cent) was traced by reference to *virilocally* resident parent(s) in the senior generation (Murray 1976: 172–3). This is so partly because, characteristically, neither an unmarried woman nor a woman who returns to her natal home following conjugal failure sets up an independent household; and partly because of the rule that a married woman should reside virilocally, which almost invariably applies in the first phase of conjugal association. The heads of large and complex households are likely both to belong to an agnatic 'core' lineage in the way that custom expects, and to preside over a domestic aggregate which includes 'women's children'. The heads of two-generational households, many of which comprise nuclear families, are also likely to belong to an agnatic core lineage in the way that custom expects, but statistical deviation from the normative rule of patrifiliation is not apparent, by definition, because there are no lineal links between alternate generations.

Household 140 'MaBereng is a virilocally resident widow whose husband died in 1948. She has seven children (all of whom are indicated in Fig.

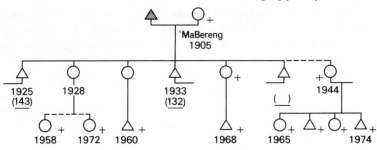

5.1 Household 140

Key: + indicates *de facto* residence in Household 140 in October 1974; (143) indicates headship of another household within Ha Molapo; (—) indicates headship of another household outside Ha Molapo; dates of birth are given where known.

5.1) and twenty grandchildren (eight of whom are indicated in Fig. 5.1). Each of her three sons has married and established an independent household: the two older sons are heads of other households within Ha Molapo; the youngest has built on a ridge of new settlement just outside the village area, about half a mile away from this brothers. All three are regular migrants. The senior son has a permanent job, with annual leave, at Stewart and Lloyds in Vereeniging (Transvaal); the second son left construction work in Johannesburg to take up a gold-mine contract at Welkom (Orange Free State) in August 1974; the third son was said to be working at Vierfontein colliery (Orange Free State).

In October 1974 'MaBereng presided over a household of 11 *de facto* residents (indicated with a plus sign in the diagram). Members of the junior generation were exclusively her daughters' children. The conjugal careers of herself and of her four daughters were the subject of considerable interest and gossip in Ha Molapo, not least on account of a series of adulterous indiscretions with members of a family of mixed blood, descendants of an Indian who had settled locally, as a doctor, at the turn of the century. 'MaBereng herself had had an affair with one of them, in the absence of her husband, which resulted in the birth of her last child, named 'MaEgypt because she was born at the time Basotho soldiers returned from the North African campaign. At least two of 'MaBereng's grandchildren were the offspring of her daughters' liaisons with various members of the same large 'Indian' (*Makula*) family; their distinctive features reflected the wisdom of the Sesotho proverb *kholu e tsoa mokopung*, 'pumpkin broth comes from the pumpkin'.

'MaBereng's eldest daughter had never been properly married but

111

simply eloped to Johannesburg many years ago, where she works as a domestic servant and from where she repatriated her children in due course. The marriages of 'MaBereng's second and third daughters appear to have been validated in jural terms, through transfer of sufficient bridewealth 'cattle' (see Chapter 6); but the whereabouts of one of these women were uncertain in 1974 and the other, whose marriage had failed in conjugal terms, had just come home from working in a Johannesburg clothing factory. Only the marriage of the youngest daughter, 'MaEgypt, was demonstrably extant in both conjugal and jural terms. However, her four children were all resident in 'MaBereng's household, since her husband had not yet built a house in Lesotho and they lacked adequate accommodation in the Johannesburg area where they normally lived. She herself was visiting in October 1974.

Thus the internal structure of 'MaBereng's three-generational household was four lineal links between alternate generations traced through women. Her three sons were all independent heads of their own households and the household structure in each case was that of a two-generational nuclear family. Relations between the four household heads concerned are defined exclusively in the agnatic idiom. This example clearly demonstrates that a high incidence of intra-household links between alternate generations traced through women is by no means incompatible with the persistence of the predominantly agnatic structure of inter-household residential alignments.

In summary, then, studies of small communities in Botswana and Lesotho illustrate processes both of conservation and of change. On the one hand, we have evidence of a relatively stable agnatic structure which endures through several generations. On the other hand, we have evidence of high rates of individual mobility, conjugal instability, illegitimacy, desertion and the break-up of families. The significant inference to be drawn from this is that study of the structure of small communities, defined in terms of the relationship between household heads, does not of itself indicate the qualitative disruption of family life that takes place over time. For the changes in kinship relations that I have described are quite consistent with the persistence of the agnatic structure of small communities as assessed in terms of genealogical relations between household heads. Indeed, far from being contradictory in their implications, both the conservation and the change are rooted in the political economy of the labour reserve. The stability of residential alignments in many areas of the periphery is directly related to the severity of South African influx control and of land shortage. A man does not have the effective option either to move with his family outside the labour reserve,

112

or to move away from his home area within the labour reserve, since he is even less likely to be allocated land elsewhere. On the other hand, the instability of conjugal relationships, the haphazard patterns of socialization and the high rates of illegitimacy are all largely attributable to the circumstances of migrant labour.

I have broadly identified two processes of 'family' constitution. One is the replication of inter-household residential alignments in terms of the prevailing agnatic idiom. The other is rapid turnover in household membership as a result of the movement of migrants, the instability of conjugal unions and the dispersion of children to be reared by their grandparents. These social processes are complex. On the one hand, as the evidence shows, they transcend ethnic or cultural boundaries. On the other hand, their impact varies between particular communities. I have suggested that the appropriate analytical framework within which to comprehend them is the political economy of migrant labour. But such a framework must be developed with full acknowledgement, firstly, that each part of the periphery has its own particular history (cf. Ranger 1978); and secondly, that the inhabitants of Lesotho, for example, construct their own experience with reference to the indigenous categories of Sesotho kinship. The issue for investigation is not, however, the accuracy with which the anthropologist can interpret these indigenous categories cross-culturally, in this case into English. Rather, the issue is the social and political conditions under which particular descriptive stereotypes of the family are sustained. I have already discussed the relevance of one descriptive typology, found in academic and popular commentary in English. It remains to elaborate Sesotho customary representations of the family.

The agnatic family and the kindred

As in English, terms in southern Bantu languages which may be translated 'family' are used in a variety of senses and in a variety of particular circumstances. In Sesotho the term *lelapa* may refer to any of the following: (1) the household which constitutes the basic unit of co-residence and consumption; (2) the physical space, the homestead or 'yard' which the household occupies; (3) the 'house' of the house–property complex, the basic property-holding unit in customary law, whose focal point is a married woman; and (4) the wider agnatic family or lineage which incorporates many such 'houses'. Basotho also use the term *leloko* which refers to 'all those people to whom you are related through your father and mother' and includes mother's brothers (*bo-malome*), father's sisters (*bo-rakhali*) and so on. In everyday usage they

113

employ the two terms somewhat indiscriminately and, as Adam Kuper (1975) has pointed out, writing of the Sotho-speaking peoples generally, people often contradict each other and experience difficulty defining these terms (or their equivalents) in the abstract. The reason, Kuper suggested, is that if all marriages reflected expressed preferences and took place between close kin, the *leloko* would be a bilateral descent group which overlapped with the agnatic descent group and would not, therefore, need to be distinguished from the *lelapa*; whereas, on the other hand, if no marriages took place between kin, the *leloko* would consist of an ego-centred bilateral kindred. Obviously in practice some marriages do take place between kin and many do not, and Kuper argued that the ambiguities in usage of the terms derive from failure to conform to an ideal of descent group endogamy.

The puzzle which arises out of this structural ambiguity for latter-day ethnographers of the Sotho is that of determining what kinship groupings are significant above the level of the individual household. In the terms used by anthropologists, the outstanding question is whether these groupings are agnatic lineages or bilateral kindreds. The answer, predictably perhaps, depends on the social context.[4] The identity of the agnatic lineage derives from its collective interest in externally defined political rights. If there are such rights, the effective boundaries and internal structure of the lineage will be readily discernible in the context of factional competition over succession to office (Appendix 3; Hamnett 1975: Appendix 1). This structure is not immutable but susceptible to redefinition depending on the outcome of the process of competition.[5] Arguments take place, and the idiom of conflict is often embarrassingly public, as at funerals where the order in which agnates of the deceased pour soil upon the coffin precisely reflects the seniority of houses within the *lelapa*. If there are no such externally defined political rights, the lineage will seldom emerge as a significant kinship grouping, in a sense that transcends local residential ties, since it lacks the necessary corporate interest.

Whether or not lineages are identifiable in this sense, individuals have kin on both father's side and mother's side who congregate on occasions such as marriages and funerals and feasts for the ancestors. The identity of the lineage in its political context is by no means incompatible with the observation that, in other contexts, paternal relatives and maternal relatives are not effectively distinguished. Instead, they merge to constitute what anthropologists call an ego-centred kindred. It is hardly surprising that modern studies of the Tswana emphasize the importance of the kindred as against the lineage, in view of processes of political decentralization and demographic dispersion that have been observed in

114

Botswana.[6] For example, Kooijman remarked of the population of Bokaa, an outlying community in the Kgatleng district of Botswana: 'As a general rule, paternal kin who do not belong to ego's ward are merged with his maternal kin as one single undifferentiated kindred and they do not fulfil any functions which set them apart from maternal kin' (1978: 99). In view of population pressure and the prevailing shortage of land, similar processes of political decentralization and demographic dispersion have not taken place in Lesotho.

The simplest pragmatic definition of significant kin was expressed by 'MaThabo (Household 120) in this way: '(the people) we are related to are those we wear the mourning cloth with' (*bao re amanang le bona ke bao re roalang thapo le bona*). The verb *ho amana* (reciprocal form) means 'to touch one another'. It is used with the appropriate qualifier to indicate agnatic ('through our fathers', *ka bo-ntate*), matrilateral ('through our mothers', *ka bo-'me*) or affinal ('through cattle', *ka likhomo*) ties. In its unqualified form it implicitly refers to agnates but not necessarily so. Close relatives of a deceased individual wear the mourning cloth (*thapo*) for the customary mourning period of a month following the death: men generally pin a small patch of black cloth to their jackets or blankets and women wear a black strip around their necks. The wearing of the *thapo* is not exclusive to agnates but it is obligatory for male agnates and their wives. Refusal to wear the *thapo* is the idiom by which distant branches of the *lelapa* segment and assume new boundaries in the natural course of their development. Vague memories may be retained of the relations between separate *malapa* within the clan but these are no longer of strategic relevance. The two largest families in Ha Molapo, Letlala and Manama, both belong to the Sia clan and acknowledge a common origin five or six generations ago, but they quarrelled over 'privileges' (*litokelo*) and neither family wears the *thapo* any longer for deaths in the other family. This is the empirical index of their independence.

Commoner families are seldom identified with reference to an apical ancestor more than three generations above the senior living generation. But the genealogical range and depth of the effective *lelapa* vary considerably within this limit. Appendix 3 contains a complete genealogy of the branches of the Letlala family whose members were domiciled in Ha Molapo and adjoining settlements in 1972–4, and also an extended account of the factional disputes which exercised more than fifty adult members of the family during these years. By contrast, the Polo *lelapa*, of the Koena clan, had only one surviving male agnate (Household 139). He was absent on migrant labour and could not attend the funeral of one of the family's 'wives' which took place in 1974. No-one was available to

115

throw earth into the grave and the structure of the *lelapa* was only discernible through a careful record of the female agnates who shaved their heads in mourning for the deceased.

The ethnographer's puzzle identified at the beginning of this section is epitomized in Sheddick's baffling remark that 'Descent follows the patrilineal system and is at the same time cognative' (1953: 28). It should be clear from the above discussion that the resolution of the puzzle does not lie in a more subtle translation of the Sesotho kinship 'code' and its several variants. Rather, there are alternative resolutions, which derive their validity from particular social contexts and also depend on the effects of variables such as the size of a community, its distance from the political centre, the range of family recruits evoked by shared political interests, and the degree of demographic dispersion that has taken place.

The house–property complex

The provisions of the customary law which govern the integrity and relative seniority of 'houses' within a polygynous menage, and which regulate the transmission of property and succession to office, are subsumed under the notion of the house–property complex, which is well established as the key to southern Bantu kinship systems (Sansom 1974; Preston-Whyte 1974). In 1903 the Basutoland National Council, an advisory body consisting mainly of chiefs, incorporated these provisions into the *Laws of Lerotholi*, a codification of Sesotho customary law which, with subsequent additions and emendations, remains today an extremely important repository of judicial guidelines and moral constraints. Thus what appear to have been ancient prescriptions are still directly relevant to the administration of justice in the modern state (Poulter 1972). Yet, as soon as the house–property complex is abstracted from history in this way, as a relatively static representation of custom, it cannot account for family structure as social process. Understanding of its operation in practice is inseparable from analysis of nineteenth- and twentieth-century social transformations. Crudely, these were, in the earlier period, structural differentiation between commoners on the one hand and senior members of the Koena aristocracy on the other, in respect of rates of polygyny, the distribution of heritable resources in livestock, and eligibility for succession to office;[7] and in the later period, the emergence of a monogamous and impoverished rural proletariat without substantial heritable resources and, by definition, ineligible from succession to office. We should not be misled by the evidence for the persistence of custom, which is real enough, into underestimating the fundamental nature of these transformations. The following three points illustrate problems of contemporary adjustment.

Firstly, the rule 'houses do not eat each other' (*malapa ha a jane*), which precludes the transfer of assets from one house to another without the specific approval of the heir and of his mother in each of the houses concerned, becomes effectively redundant, in the absence of polygyny, except in retrospective resolution of issues in the past. However, the concept of the jural independence of the house remains such an integral aspect of the customary law in its presumption and application that confusion may arise: either in cases of simple monogamy, where there is no necessary distinction between allocated and unallocated property, thus begging the question of the balance between the widow's and the heir's respective rights and obligations; or in cases of serial monogamy, where there may be difficulty in determining the number of houses with rights to inherit (Ramolefe 1969; Poulter 1976: 242–7).

Secondly, it is fallacious to draw the parallel which superficially presents itself between the 'relative autonomy' of married women in a polygynous regime and the 'relative autonomy' of monogamously married women who, in the absence of their husbands on migrant labour, assume a very great onus of domestic responsibility but have little control over the resources with which to carry out that responsibility. It is easy to discern ideological continuity in so far as women still invest the establishment of an independent house(hold) with significance and rationalize their behaviour with reference to customary law. But this does not relieve us of the need to trace in detail the changes in their economic position (see Chapter 7). For example, Schapera observed that migrant labour undermined household self-sufficiency but also allowed Tswana wives relatively greater freedom: 'the husband may find on his return that she will no longer submit so readily to his authority' (Schapera 1947: 185). In Keiskammahoek it was found that, while some women acquired greater economic independence than was the case traditionally, through limited employment opportunities, scarcity of land led to a deterioration in women's economic status (M. Wilson et al. 1952: 107–8).

Thirdly, the provisions of the customary law which govern house integrity cannot accommodate the circumstances of an increasingly large number of women who either remain unmarried or experience the failure of a conjugal union and return to reside in a 'matrifocal' household of the sort exemplified by 'MaBereng's household which I described above. The status of their children remains anomalous with respect to their incorporation into the agnatic family. Sesotho custom would require formal arrangements to incorporate 'women's children', and their ratification by the family council (*khotla la lelapa*). The evidence suggests that, where eligibility for succession to office is at stake, senior agnates whose interests would be threatened thereby seldom ratify such arrangements. Where succession is not at stake, the jural status of women's children is insufficiently important to justify their formal incorporation into the *lelapa*. Women's children, therefore, are just as important as any other units of human labour in strategies of household management. But they cannot expect to compete effectively with men's children where jural membership of the *lelapa* is of wider political relevance.

The appropriate inference from this discussion is that the persistence of custom is not a matter of counterposing the evidence for dissolution and the evidence for conservation of an allegedly traditional way of life. Rather, the apparent continuity of custom must be analysed as an integral and vital aspect of underlying structural transformation. The following Chapter is an attempt to indicate the lines along which this may be done, with specific reference to marital transactions.

6

Marital strategy: an essay in custom and conflict

In a general survey of African marriage law some thirty years ago it was pointed out that

The marriage transaction is normally a long-drawn out process and there is often some doubt, both as to the exact point in that process at which the parties become husband and wife, and also as to which (if any) of the accompanying ceremonies and observances are strictly essential to the conclusion of a valid marriage (Phillips and Morris 1971: 107).

The purpose of this chapter is to analyse the particular implications of this observation in Lesotho.

Firstly, marriage should be regarded as a process in time and not as a single point of transition between the unmarried and the married state. Indeed the Sesotho maxim *bohali ha bo fele* is perhaps best translated, 'affinity never ends'. Secondly, specific marital transactions remain outstanding for many years. The PEMS missionary, Duvoisin, commented on this nearly one hundred years ago: 'The Basuto are nearly all involved in a whole system of debts and of credit which is sometimes so intricate that anyone but a native would find it difficult to grasp' (CB: 536). In circumstances of dispute, the judicial process by which questions of marital status and thence of jural paternity are resolved offers opportunities for the exercise of speculative and manipulative skills by persons who may be identified as marital entrepreneurs. As I indicate in the last section of this Chapter, such judicial resolutions are particularly apposite for the purpose of distinguishing positivist and phenomenological approaches to the sociology of law. Thirdly, although bridewealth (*bohali*) is invariably reckoned in head of cattle, marital transactions do not constitute a 'sphere of exchange' discrete from that of cash earnings and 'subsistence' agriculture. On the contrary, marital transactions are often constituted in cash. Irrespective of the actual medium of payment, they are a vital element in household strategies of economic viability because of their consequences for jural filiation. In this sense, they are central to processes of social reproduction in the labour reserve.

In the following discussion I am concerned with Sesotho 'customary' marriage. About one third of marriages in Lesotho take place according to Christian rites, an estimate derived from Hastings (1973: 148). But most of these also involve the transfer of *bohali*, which is still generally regarded as a *sine qua non* of a legitimate conjugal union. In a survey of 87 conjugal unions identified as 'marriage' in a community in Mohale's Hoek district, Spiegel found that *bohali* transfers had taken place in 80 of the unions; that in 53 of these there had been no Christian or civil ceremony; and that where these had taken place they were often contingent on the transfer of *bohali* (Spiegel 1975: 40). Thus the overwhelming majority of conjugal unions in Lesotho fall within the terms of reference of Section 34 (1) of the *Laws of Lerotholi* (1973 edition), according to which a valid marriage requires firstly agreement between the parties and secondly the transfer of some *bohali* cattle. The attitude of the courts to marriage without cattle is equivocal but they appear to distinguish between civil and customary marriage in this respect.[1]

The most important elements of customary marriage today are *koae*, the sheep slaughtered respectively by the man's family and the woman's family to mark the formal arrival of a daughter-in-law and a son-in-law; *bohali*, the bridewealth cattle, which may be transferred over a period of many years; *tlhabiso*, the ox slaughtered by the woman's family to mark the fulfilment of the marriage contract; and *phahlelo*, the personal dowry provided for a married woman by her own family.[2]

The definition of marriage

Traditionally marriages were arranged by the parents of the boy and the girl. However, it is clear from an account by Azariel Sekese, who wrote prolifically on Sesotho oral tradition in the PEMS journal *Leselinyana*, that a young man could initiate the process. Rising early in the morning, he would release the calves to their dams and so prevent the cows being milked. Known as 'kicking the little dish' (*ho raha moritšoana*), this was a way of indicating to his father his anxiety to marry. His father would make enquiries and, when he had found a suitable girl, he would send to her father an intermediary with a beast, who would say, 'So-and-so sent me to you to beg for him a calabash of water (*mohope oa metsi*); the mouth that he speaks with is this beast' (Sekese 1970: 1). Nowadays a man may formally request (*ho qela*) a girl's hand in marriage and present her with small personal gifts, and an engagement is given public recognition. Otherwise there may be only an informal understanding

120

between the couple, followed by elopement (*chobeliso*), which occurs as a preliminary to more than half of all marriages today (Poulter 1976: 107; Spiegel 1975).

Whether a girl is 'properly' married or she elopes (*ho shobela*) one custom is still strictly adhered to. When the girl first arrives at her husband's home his people slaughter a sheep called *koae* (tobacco), and it is said, 'They give her *koae*'. Prior to this the girl cannot eat any food of her husband's household nor take part in any of its domestic activities. The meaning of the *koae* rite is always explained in terms of formally receiving the woman as a daughter-in-law (*ngoetsi*), and it marks her assumption of the privileges and responsibilities of a married woman. She dons the long skirt and headcloth typical of that status. The transition to full womanhood is a protracted process, however, and is achieved only by the formal presentation to her, often on the birth of a first child, of some sheep's intestine (*mala a nku*) which, like eggs, is taboo to an unmarried girl.

The *koae* rite initiates the domestic and sexual components of marriage.[3] In the past, according to some writers, the couple did not immediately engage in sexual relations, but waited a few days until the bride signified she was ready by placing a pot of water in her husband's hut (Ellenberger and Macgregor 1969: 277; Laydevant 1952: 67). However, Ashton observed in the 1930s that 'Nowadays, the couple usually sleep together immediately after the *koae* rite' (1952: 75). In my experience, people assume that whether or not the couple have been covertly sleeping together beforehand, they will start doing so 'officially' as soon as *koae* has been slaughtered.

The sheep of *koae* is slaughtered reciprocally by the woman's family for their son-in-law when the latter makes his first formal visit to their household. But this only takes place after the feast of *tlhabiso* which completes the marriage contract. Exegesis is similar but the inference is that a man is only acceptable as a son-in-law (*mokhoenyana*) in the full sense after he has transferred sufficient *bohali* cattle to allow the feast of *tlhabiso* to take place (see below). The sheep of *koae*, then, relates to the personal aspects of the relationship between husband and wife and their respective in-laws, but its significance cannot be divorced from that of *bohali* cattle, which relates to the transfer of rights in the woman's procreative capacity. Marrying is a differentiated and elastic process: a woman becomes a daughter-in-law through the killing of *koae*, and a man becomes a son-in-law through the killing of *koae*, but the latter rite often takes place years after the former. In formal terms, recognition by the woman's family of a son-in-law is by no means the immediate reciprocal of recognition by the man's family of a daughter-in-law.

121

The jural component of marriage, which presupposes an agreement between the respective parents or guardians (*bakhotsi*), is the transfer of *bohali* cattle. The principle which governs the allocation of rights of paternity – 'the child belongs to the cattle' (*ngoana ke oa likhomo*) – is essentially a neutral one. If sufficient cattle have not passed, the child's legitimate place is with the mother's family. If sufficient cattle have passed, the child is legitimately filiated to the father's family. What is the definition of sufficiency?

Although sexual intercourse with an unmarried girl is itself an action-able wrong (Palmer 1970: 152–6), damages commonly arise in practice when a girl is 'spoilt in the yard' (*o senyehetse lapeng*); and 'spoiling' (*ho senya*) is in effect synonymous with causing pregnancy (*kemariso*). The girl's parents will press for a standard compensation payment (*matšeliso*) of six cattle. This payment gives the man responsible no rights of paternity over the child, who will grow up in his mother's family and, normally, the child's mother's father or mother's brother (*malome*) is recognized as proxy father. A similar compensation payment is appro-priate in cases of elopement (*chobeliso*). Where a marriage agreement follows, the girl's parents usually accept the first six head retrospectively as marriage cattle (*likhomo tsa lenyalo*) although they are technically due as compensation cattle (*likhomo tsa matšeliso*).

Whereas payment of seven head of *bohali* cattle is said to be an act of derision on the part of the husband – 'he is insulting his mother-in-law'[4] – payment of eight head is said to 'lay the foundation' of the marriage (*ho thea bohali*). The transfer of ten head is said to 'complete a head' (*ho phetha hloho*) and to establish without question the husband's right to paternity of his children. After ten or more *bohali* cattle have been transferred the man's family will press the woman's family to 'smear them with fat' (*ho tlotsa likhomo mafura*). The woman's father must slaughter an ox and provide a feast known as *tlhabiso* for those who have married his daughter. In the past, according to Ellenberger and Macgregor, the pouring of the animal's gall upon the couple was the definitive ceremony at which they became husband and wife and 'were thereby solemnly recommended to the care of the Shades of their ancestors' (1969: 276). This rite is no longer observed. And nor does the feast of *tlhabiso* itself appear to be essential, before the courts, to the conclusion of a valid marriage (Poulter 1976: 120). Nevertheless it is the climax of a proper affinal relationship. Men familiar with the formalities of mine recruitment use the word *konteraka* (contract) to explain the significance of the *tlhabiso* feast which marks the fulfilment of the union. To celebrate this some special portions of meat (*litlhobohano*) are set aside and eaten together by the members of the two families; and the 'grandmothers' (*bo-nkhono*) on both sides are said to insist from beyond the grave on their particular entitlement of meat known as *matlala*.

Thus the transition to full married status is a protracted one. After the *koae* rite the woman is referred to in common parlance as somebody's daughter-in-law (*ngoetsi ea motho*) and as the wife of her husband. But 'he hasn't yet married her' and he will not be able to claim paternity of her children. This is accomplished in due course by the transfer of enough *bohali* cattle, which may take ten, fifteen or even twenty years. It is only after the feast of *tlhabiso*, itself contingent on the receipt of at least ten *bohali* cattle, that unanimity on the matter will prevail: 'Yes, he has married her properly now'. During the years between it is possible to say of the woman that, although she is certainly not 'unmarried', she is not yet properly 'married'.

The marriage contract satisfactorily fulfilled, the woman's parents should provide her with a personal dowry (*phahlelo*) of items of clothing and domestic equipment – blankets, skirts, cooking pots and dishes, grass mats and beer strainers, etc. These are delivered to the husband's village with elaborate ceremonial by women and girls of the wife's natal village. The feast of *tlhabiso* does not conclude the *bohali* obligations: some cattle are generally outstanding, as is evident from two typical agreements recorded in Ha Molapo:

25/11/73
This is an agreement at which M.R. [wife's mother] is receiving marriage cattle from M.H. [husband's mother's brother]. M.H. has paid twelve cattle, there remain outstanding six cattle and a horse and ten sheep or goats, since fulfilment (*khaolo*) of *bohali* is eighteen cattle, a horse and ten sheep or goats according to this agreement. And today we slaughtered an ox for him. We also gave him the sheep of receiving,[5] he found it today. The witnesses are ... [names]
[signed by chief's representative]

29/06/74
This is a marriage agreement. L.P. [husband's father] is handing over cattle to M.S. [wife's brother]. L.P. came with two cattle – one live beast and one made up of five sheep – having previously brought thirteen cattle. With fulfilment of *bohali* at twenty-two cattle there remain seven beasts outstanding. Those marrying each other are K.P. and S.S. The witnesses are ... [names]
[signed by chief's representative]

A schematic summary of the transactions in a proper marriage is given in Table 6.1. Multiple transfers of *bohali* cattle from the husband's kin to the wife's kin are followed by the feast of *tlhabiso* given by the wife's kin, the provision of her personal dowry and further outstanding transfers of *bohali* cattle. In most cases *bohali* transfers are staggered over many years and the wife's family may plan ahead in the meantime for the

123

Table 6.1. *Marital transactions: their cumulative significance.*

From husband's kin	From wife's kin	Significance
sheep of *koae*		to 'receive' the wife when she first arrives at husband's home
cattle: either		
6 *matšeliso*		compensation due for eloping with, abducting or 'spoiling' a girl
or		
6 *lenyalo*		where there is a previous agreement, this payment is evidence of serious intention to marry
7 *ho supa mohoehali*		to 'point at one's mother-in-law' (a gratuitous insult which achieves nothing and shows the husband is 'merely playing')
8 *ho thea bohali*		to 'lay the foundation' of the marriage
10 *ho phetha hloho*		to 'complete a head'; this establishes husband's paternity of children
	ho hlabisa bohali	feast provided by wife's family for husband's family, to mark receipt of 10 or more *bohali* cattle and to fulfil marriage contract
	sheep of *koae*	to mark first formal visit of husband to wife's natal home
	ho phahlela morali	to 'pack for' one's daughter: clothes and household goods for wife from her parents for use in marital home
ho khaola bohali		transfer of such additional cattle as necessary to complete number specified in original agreement

provision of her dowry, while the feast of *tlhabiso* represents a large capital outlay on a single occasion. In many unions *bohali* transfers do not reach ten head of cattle and the feast of *tlhabiso* never takes place. So the marriage contract is never formally fulfilled. But where *bohali* transfers have exceeded ten head of cattle it is very churlish of the wife's family to refuse to slaughter the ox of *tlhabiso*. The expense is prohibitive – at 1974 prices it cost R150 or more to buy a suitable beast, quite apart from the other associated expenses of a large feast – but failure may expose the family to mystical retribution. Two out of the five feasts of *tlhabiso* which I attended in Ha Molapo in 1972–4 were prompted by sickness which proved intractable to conventional medical treatment and which was eventually attributed to the anger of the ancestors at the wife's family's neglect of the obligations of affinity. The victims in both cases were the wives concerned: one had aching pains all over her body and in her stomach; the other was bent double and unable to walk. The intervals of twenty-four and thirty-eight years respectively between date of marriage and date of *tlhabiso* feast reveal a limit to the patience of the ancestors. The circumstances of one of these cases are described in Appendix 3.

Polygyny and marriage with cattle

Polygyny and marriage with cattle are deeply rooted in the Sesotho tradition. During the second quarter of the nineteenth century, in the unsettled circumstances of the post-*lifaqane* reconstruction period, Moshoeshoe and his principal subordinates were able to acquire large numbers of cattle through raiding. They exploited their accumulation of livestock in two ways: by the intensive practice of polygyny, which facilitated the demographic expansion of the dominant Koena lineage; and by the attachment of political clients called *bahlanka*, typically dispossessed refugees, through providing *bohali* cattle for their marriages and lending out cattle to them under the *mafisa* system (L. Thompson 1975: 52–69; Sanders 1975: 43–59). Differential control of livestock, indulgence in polygyny and high rates of *bohali* were the means by which Koena political patronage was expanded and consolidated during this period.

The connection between these features was aptly expressed by Duvoisin in 1885:

Marriage is so much a matter of speculation in this country, that a chief will often marry a woman with no other object than to present her to such and such of his subjects who may be too poor to buy one himself, but on condition that the latter's children will belong to him. Thus it is that numerous natives claim the title of sons and daughters of Moshoeshoe, without having any other bond of relationship with the late chief of the Basuto, than his payment of their mother's dowry [sic]. They are called by a rather significant name: *bana ba likhomo* (children of the cattle).

Thus it is that 'marriage by cattle' leads to polygamy. In a pastoral country where the herds constitute the principal wealth of the inhabitants and where, moreover, this wealth is the basis of power since, as the Basuto are at liberty to dispose of and to give themselves to the chief whom they prefer, he will have the most subjects who will know best how to attract or retain them with his presents; it follows that the more wives one has, the richer and the more powerful one will be. Provided that a man has the means, he will scarcely hesitate to treat himself to such profitable luxury; therefore, while the fairly well-to-do natives content themselves with two or three wives, while the rich and the subordinate chiefs permit themselves a larger number, the great chiefs have twenty, thirty, eighty, a hundred, whose huts often form a village around their lord's residence (CB: 537).

125

There was no doubt of the senior chiefs' extravagance in this respect. By 1864 Moshoeshoe was reported to have 150 wives, and he himself claimed about 200 (Sanders 1975: 272–3). In 1878 Moshoeshoe's senior son Letsie, who had succeeded to the paramountcy, was said to have some 50 wives (Burman 1976: 79); and his second son Molapo had 70 (Taylor 1972: 39).

The PEMS missionaries, who first arrived in Lesotho in 1833, regarded polygyny and marriage with cattle as the epitome of 'heathenism'. Moshoeshoe strove to maintain a judicious balance between the staunch defenders of Sesotho tradition, upon whose political support his chieftainship depended, and the missionaries as agents of moral reform, upon whose advice he had also come to rely in his conduct of diplomacy. Particularly in respect of the divorce of two of his wives who became Christian converts in 1841, he found himself in the uncomfortable position of having to appease both sides (Sanders 1975: 128–32). It is scarcely surprising that the old chief himself remained equivocal, until his death, in his attitude to Christianity.

In 1872 questions relating to the divorce of Christian wives and the custody of their children were the subject of a controversy between the PEMS and the Cape Governor's Agent in Maseru, Charles Griffith. In writing to express the Society's view Dr E. Casalis, son of Eugène Casalis, the first PEMS missionary in Lesotho, submitted as supplementary evidence a copy of an anonymous article which had been published in *Leselinyana*. The substance of this passionate diatribe was that marriages with cattle (1) constitute commercial transactions which are inimical to the spirit of a Christian union; (2) degrade, as mere chattels, women and their offspring; (3) render impossible all family life and the proper bringing up of children; (4) are not only unprofitable but also conducive to endless litigation, despite which their speculative potential 'dazzles the imagination of the natives, who are incapable of, and do not believe in, arithmetic'; (5) are therefore an 'insuperable barrier to progress, civilization and good government'; and (6) are so intimately connected with traditional social life that, were they abolished, heathenism would 'crumble away and cease to exist' (Report and Evidence 1873: 24–37).

At the end of the same year the Special Commission which had been appointed by the Cape Governor to investigate the laws and customs of the Basotho, under Griffith's chairmanship, conceded that there were three customs in particular which 'appear to be most injurious to the people, morally, socially and politically, and to retard them in the progress of civilization'. These were *lebollo* (circumcision), *sethepu* (polygyny) and *bohali* (marriage with cattle). However, the Commission also

126

acknowledged that polygyny and marriage with cattle 'are too deeply rooted to be easily abolished'; that it would be impossible to abolish them by legislation and therefore politically unwise to attempt this; and that such customs would, rather, atrophy with the passage of time and with the progress of the civilizing mission (Report and Evidence 1873: 5). As Basotho witnesses to the Commission made clear, the interpretation which the French Protestants placed on *bohali* constituted a parody of the institution, and their evangelical efforts alienated many people for this reason. Later, in recognition of this fact and in the face of inter-denominational competition for converts, the PEMS adopted a less intransigent attitude.

In respect of polygyny, the expectation of atrophy has been largely realized. According to census figures the rate of polygyny – the number of men with more than one wife expressed as a percentage of the number of men whose marriages are recorded – was 18.7 in 1911, 15.8 in 1921, 11.4 in 1936 and 8.9 in 1946 (calculated from Poulter 1976: 70). There are no comparable recent figures since later censuses did not investigate the extent of polygyny. My own survey of 105 men whose marriages were extant in 1974 revealed that only 3 (2.9 per cent) had more than one wife. It should be noted that, owing to the high rate of mobility of men and women and to the absence of a precise definition of marriage (see previous section), it is not always easy to distinguish genuine polygyny, serial monogamy and monogamy combined with an informal relationship of cohabitation known as *bonyatsi*.[6] But there is no doubt that the rate of polygyny has continued to decline since 1946. This has been attributed to the spread of Christian mission influence and of education and to the progressive emancipation of women. But there are also economic pressures which serve as a direct disincentive to polygyny. Even if a man could afford a second substantial outlay in *bohali* he would find it very difficult to make independent provision in land for another wife. He would merely be doubling his economic liabilities without proportionate return.

In respect of marriage with cattle, the expectation of atrophy has been very far from realized. Although rates of *bohali* have always varied with social status, there is evidence from published sources of high levels of *bohali* persisting through the latter part of the nineteenth century and the twentieth century. Arbousset, one of the first three PEMS missionaries, noted that poor men paid 'two or three cows with their calves, together with some sheep and goats'; whereas rich men paid 'ten, twenty, thirty or even forty head of cattle' (Arbousset 1968: 38). Most nineteenth-century sources refer to figures within the latter range. Casalis (1965: 182) recalled twenty-five to thirty head of cattle as typical of the period of his experience, from 1833 to 1856. In evidence submitted to the Special Commission of 1872, George Tlali Moshoeshoe explained that 'there is no fixed rule laid down for the number of cattle to be given for a wife: the usual number is from ten to fifteen head of cattle' (Report and Evidence 1873: 40). John Austen, a magistrate with thirty years of experience 'amongst all classes of natives on the frontier', stated that such high rates were not part of ancient custom but had been introduced by Moshoeshoe as a result of increased wealth in cattle (Report and Evidence 1873: 58). In 1885 Duvoisin wrote of 'ten, twenty, or thirty oxen or more, according to the social status or the personal charms of the young woman' (CB: 536). At the end of the century, Sekese (1970: 4) noted that the conventional expectation was twenty cattle or more, ten small stock (*setsiba*, loincloth) and a horse (*molisana*, herdboy); and that the rate amongst the aristocracy was thirty or forty head of cattle. He also remarked that the capacity for 'heavy' marriages was 'spoilt' in the aftermath of rinderpest. In his *History of the Basotho*, first published in English in 1912, Ellenberger wrote that *bohali* stood at fifteen to twenty head of cattle (Ellenberger and Macgregor 1969: 272). Ashton (1952: 71) recorded a relatively fixed standard of twenty cattle amongst the Tlokoa in the 1930s; while villagers in the Mafeteng district in 1963 stated that twenty-two cattle were the proper amount of *bohali*, plus ten sheep and a horse, but that this expectation was seldom realized in practice (Wallman 1969: 67, 70).

Thus marriage with cattle remains a vital aspect of contemporary Sesotho custom; and most Basotho remain committed to the normative proposition that 'the child belongs to the (bridewealth) cattle'. But bridewealth is not the 'same' institution in the latter part of the twentieth century as it was in the middle of the nineteenth century. High levels of *bohali* then reflected a process of structural differentiation between commoners on the one hand and senior members of the Koena aristocracy on the other hand. High levels of *bohali* today reflect the importance of access to able-bodied manpower in a monogamous and impoverished rural proletariat.

Interpreting the evidence

It is difficult to interpret the evidence on *bohali* transfers which is available from the published sources cited above. Firstly, the sources do not consistently distinguish between customary demand and actual payment, or between the levels appropriate for chiefs' and commoners' daughters respectively. Secondly, a relatively stable nominal rate of *bohali* expressed in numbers of 'cattle' transferred irrespective of media of payment does not of course imply no fluctuation in the real economic outlay that *bohali* transfers represent. Thirdly, it is meaningless to assert that *bohali* transfers are 'high' without some detailed reference to their socio-economic background. Fourthly, *bohali* transfers relating to one marriage are often staggered over a period of many years, and there are also significant flows of resources in the reverse direction, in respect of reciprocal obligations on the part of the wife's family. It is seldom easy, therefore, to isolate the transactions relating to a particular marriage from the general flows of income and expenditure that constitute a household's budget over a limited period of time.

In this section I discuss some of the variables relevant to an assessment of the actual *bohali* transfers which I recorded in Ha Molapo in 1972–4 and in 1978. The twenty-eight marriages to which they relate, over a period of more than fifty years, are a regrettably small sample. But this reflects the difficulty of obtaining reliable figures on real payments in an environment where a strong tradition of obfuscation prevails with regard to conversion between various media of payment; where a statement of *bohali* almost invariably carries political import and is seldom 'neutral' information; and where an instalment system renders the facts suscep-tible to re-interpretation over time. The details are recorded in Appendix 2.

There are at least four variables which it is necessary to consider, namely (1) the real earning capacity of Basotho migrant labourers; (2) the prevailing market price of livestock; (3) the nominal *bohali* rate of exchange between livestock and cash; and (4) the proportion of *bohali* transfers constituted in cash as against livestock. An approximate picture of the real economic outlay which *bohali* transfers represent may be derived firstly from a consideration of these four variables together and secondly from the detailed case studies which follow of the transactions undertaken by individuals.

The best single index of the earning capacity of Basotho was and is the average cash earnings of black labour on the South African gold mines. Francis Wilson (1972a: 46) has shown that real earnings in 1969 were approximately the same as they were in 1936. In the 1970s, by contrast, real earnings rose substantially (Table 1.7). The best available index of the cost to the migrant of buying large stock for the purpose of *bohali* transfers is the export price per head of cattle, since livestock prices prevailing within Lesotho generally follow those obtainable at the government markets. Table 6.2 shows a comparison for selected years between average cash earnings on the gold mines and the average export price per head of cattle from Lesotho. Such a crude comparison is obviously subject to considerable error, but it does suggest that in the

Table 6.2. *Average earnings and the average market price of cattle, selected years 1936–74.*

Year	Average monthly cash earnings, gold mines (current rands)	Index of real earnings	Average export price of cattle from Lesotho (current rands)
1936	5.67	100	10.39
1946	7.25	92	20.68
1956	11.00	89	29.18
1966	15.25	99	50.00
1969	16.58	99	60.00
1974	46.00		135.00

Sources: (1) Monthly cash earnings and index of real earnings 1936 to 1969 from F. Wilson (1972a: 46); monthly cash earnings for 1974 from SAIRR (1975: 186). (2) Average export price of cattle: 1936 to 1956 from Morse (1960: 372–3), converted at the pre-1967 rate of £1 = R2; 1966 and 1969 from Lesotho (1973); 1974 from ASB (1977: 84, 87).

period up to the 1970s the market price of large stock approximately doubled in real terms while earning capacity remained the same. During the 1970s inflation in the price of cattle may well have kept pace with wage increases; it certainly exceeded the general rate of inflation (Table 1.7). The inescapable inference is that it became increasingly difficult for the average wage earner to purchase livestock over the period in question. This is consistent both with folk memory and with the decline in the livestock ratio shown in Table 4.3. The changing livestock ratio itself is simply an indication of increasing scarcity of animals relative to potential demand for purchase. It is not a useful index of resources from which *bohali* transfers may be drawn, since it fails to take account of the distribution of livestock between rural households, which has been shown to be skew (Table 4.4), and since a significant proportion of *bohali* transfers is constituted in cash from migrant earnings (Appendix 2).

The experience of particular migrants amplifies the comparison shown in Table 6.2, for it suggests that in the 1920s and 1930s a beast could be bought for a month's wages or less. Levi (Household 118) recalled that he went to work in 1921 at the Vereeniging Power Station (Transvaal), where he earned £3 (R6) per month for seventeen years. He married in 1922 (Appendix 2, No. 2) with animals derived as follows: 4 cows bought at R4 per head; 2 bulls bought from the local chief at R4 per head; 1 horse (= 2 'cattle') bought from the local chief at R6; and 20 sheep (= 4 'cattle') which he had earned through previous service as a herdboy at

130

Mokhotlong. His total *bohali* fund was thus 12 'cattle', mostly bought with his own earnings. Malefetsane (Household 117) took his first mine contract in 1934 and worked for nineteen months at R5.50 per month. He married in 1937 (Appendix 2, No. 5) with 16 horned (i.e. live) beasts, all of which he claimed to have bought with his own earnings at rates of R4, R6, R4.50, R6, R4, etc. plus R6 in cash representing one beast. His total *bohali* fund was 17 'cattle'. In discussion of this he specifically recalled that a pair of trousers at that time cost R1.50, a shirt R0.25 and a blanket R1.80 or R2. In 1974, by comparison, it was quite impossible to buy a reasonable beast for a month's average earnings on the gold mines, despite the real wage increases of 1973 and 1974. Prevailing market prices may be judged from my records of one day's sales at Hlotse market in July 1974: 36 oxen were sold at an average price of R166 per head; 12 bulls at an average price of R142; and 5 cows at R65 each. As regards small stock, a sheep or a goat cost at least R10 in Ha Molapo in 1974, and some cost R14, R16 or even R20.

The availability of animals for purchase and the real earning capacity of migrants are relevant to a discussion of *bohali* transfers for two reasons. Firstly, it is often insisted that some of the items transferred should be animals 'walking on their own feet' (*tse tsamaeang ka maoto a tsona*). This demand is a prerogative of the woman's family and is not enforceable in court. But the expectation dies hard and the hapless husband may set about purchasing at a market-price per beast that is several times higher than the nominal cash equivalent. Secondly, despite inevitable lag the nominal *bohali* rate of exchange between livestock and cash is beginning to take account of soaring inflation in market values. Until the early 1970s, the usual nominal rate quoted was R20 per head, and the mean rate in the fifteen marriages from 1955 to 1973 for which details were recorded from Ha Molapo was R22.30 (Appendix 2). In 1974, however, in cases of default, the Local Court began to lay down a nominal rate of R30 per head, in recognition of the widening discrepancy with market prices established at government export outlets. Nominal rates demanded in the mid-1970s, ranging from about R35 to about R60 per head in Ha Molapo, with a mean of R45.50 (Appendix 2), still bore only tenuous relation to market prices; but they were no longer independent of prevailing rates of inflation. A substantial increase in the real earning capacity of migrants in the 1970s is reflected in a considerable increase in the proportional constitution of *bohali* transfers in cash, from one half (in the period 1955 to 1973) to three-quarters (in the period 1975 to 1977) of the 'cattle' transferred (Appendix 2). The decline in the real value of *bohali* transfers which this might have represented is offset by the recent doubling of the mean nominal rate of exchange between

131

livestock and cash. In this way *bohali* transfers have kept pace with the rate of inflation during the 1970s.

Detailed case studies

One household's marital budget

The following partial account of a particular household's marital budget illustrates the extent to which the performance of customary obligation is a matter of hard cash.

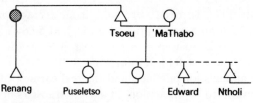

6.1 Household 120

Tsoeu and his wife 'MaThabo have a daughter Puseletso who was married in 1959 (Appendix 2, No. 9), when her husband's people paid eight 'cattle', made up of 4 cattle and 2 horses (= 4 'cattle'). Later they paid two more 'cattle' in cash equivalent plus R10 towards the eleventh head. In November 1973 they arranged to visit her parents, bringing a cash sum of R120. I attended the negotiations during which polite but tense haggling took place over the constitution of the eleventh head, part of which had already been paid. Eventually the money was laid on the table in four piles of R10 notes (3, 3, 4, 2), the first three piles representing one beast each and the fourth pile of R20 representing the part-beast left outstanding from the previous occasion. Renang, who grew up as a member of the household because his mother was never married, was instructed to 'drive the cattle to the kraal'. He took the money and formally handed it over to 'MaThabo, sitting in another hut, who slipped it into the recesses of her blanket and resumed chatting with the older women. Tsoeu meanwhile had passed out from hard drinking throughout the previous night. This money helped to pay for the large feast of *tlhabiso* which took place the following day, after the negotiations were completed. 'MaThabo told me later that she had also been able to buy food for the household, clothes for the grandchildren resident with her, and seed and fertilizer for the agricultural season. This payment of R120 meant that the marriage contract was fulfilled in respect of fourteen *bohali* cattle. For the feast of *tlhabiso* Tsoeu had arranged to exchange a still-fertile beast of his

132

Table 6.3. *Details of a single dowry, Ha Molapo, 1974.*

Items	Cost
6* blankets (2 for R17, 2 for R15, 1 for R11, 1 for R36).........	79.00
4 skirts, cloth bought for...	22.40
shoes/stockings/headscarf	6.35
plates/cups/dishes etc.	17.50
1 large cooking pot..	9.50
3 clay pots..	0.90
3 grass mats..	7.20
Total	**R 142.85**

* (One for Puseletso's mother-in-law; the most expensive one, of special type–*qibi*–for Puseletso's husband; the others for Puseletso herself)

own for the red ox of a neighbour. This animal was slaughtered together with the sheep of 'agreement' (*fomo*),[5] and the sheep of *koae* in due course when his son-in-law arrived. Both the latter animals were drawn from Tsoeu's household stock.

In September 1974 'MaThabo arranged to provide the dowry (*phah-lelo*) for Puseletso. The details of the items in it, all bought with cash, are shown in Table 6.3. From consideration only of the transactions in this marriage which I observed during 1973–4 (Table 6.4) it is quite obvious that, despite the receipt by Puseletso's family of a substantial sum in *bohali* 'cattle', their balance of marital payments was in the red. However, it is quite misleading to attempt to balance these items either against one another or against receipts and expenditure in respect of other marriages, because marital transfers in cash are part of the general household subsistence fund. In any case, the dowry items had been gradually accumulated over the years, representing a staggered outlay of cash.

The following transfers also took place. In March 1973, the household received a large sum (either R210, according to 'MaThabo herself, or R150, according to the son-in-law concerned, representing 7 and 6 'cattle' respectively) in respect of the marriage of Puseletso's younger sister. In August 1973 Renang came home with a large amount in cash from his mine contract at Welkom (Orange Free State). He eloped with a girl, spent R40 on clothes and household goods for her and sent R160 to her parents as a first instalment of 6 'cattle' (Appendix 2, No. 19), being short of R8 at an average rate of R28. After Christmas 1973 he returned to Welkom for another mine contract and his wife told me in July 1974 that he sent her R16 a month in regular remittances. Whereupon 'MaThabo, who 'wore the trousers' in the household owing to the 'weakness' of her

133

Table 6.4. *Recorded transactions in Puseletso's marriage, Ha Molapo.*

Date	Item	Credit	Debit
1959	8 *bohali* 'cattle'	4 cattle	
		2 horses	
?	2 *bohali* 'cattle'	cash	
	1 part-beast	R10	
Nov 1973	1 part-beast	R20	
	3 *bohali* 'cattle'	R100	
	feast of *tlhabiso*:		1 ox
	(a) slaughter of animals		2 sheep
	(b) estimate of expenses		R60
Sept 1974	provision of dowry		R143

husband Tsoeu, remarked it would be better if Renang sent R5 every month 'for a little soap and paraffin', and saved the rest towards further *bohali* payments so that his wife's family would not be able to make any claims on their children. By 1978 Renang had established his own household nearby, his wife had one child and was expecting her second, and he was no longer contributing to the household of 'MaThabo.

Tsoeu died in 1975. Edward and Ntholi, neither begotten by Tsoeu but both accepted as legitimate sons of the family, married in the same year. The former transferred all the family's small stock and a donkey, as well as contributing R160 from his own earnings towards a total fund of 11 'cattle' (Appendix 2, No. 21). The latter transferred R360 in a series of instalments representing 6 'cattle' altogether. In Ntholi's absence on his second mine contract at Welkom in October 1978, 'MaThabo explained: 'Whenever there's money enough to make up a beast, it goes along there to his wife's place' so that his two children will in due course be established as his own without doubt.

A question of paternity

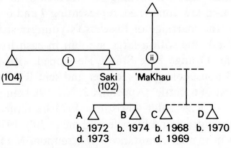

6.2 A question of paternity

134

Saki and his elder brother, members of the Thapelo family (Appendix 1), are heads of Households 102 and 104 respectively. Saki is a polygynist, his first wife being barren. In 1971, at the age of 53, he undertook negotiations to marry his second wife, 'MaKhau, who had already been 'spoilt in the yard' twice at her father's home. One of her children (C) had died. Saki paid five 'cattle', consisting of two donkeys, a sewing machine (= 2 'cattle') and the cash equivalent of one beast. Saki and 'MaKhau produced a son of their own (A) who died in November 1973 when only one year old. The circumstances of this death gave rise to the following dispute.

Shortly before the death of the child Saki and 'MaKhau had quarrelled and according to customary arrangement she had returned to her own home with their child who was still sucking, pending resolution of the quarrel. The child became ill; she sent news of this to Saki, who however did not visit but insisted that she should return to him with the child. The child died, and Saki and his elder brother went to 'MaKhau's home to recover the body for burial in Ha Molapo. An acrimonious exchange took place with her father who refused to let them have the child's body on the grounds firstly that Saki had not properly married 'MaKhau – he had not completed *hloho* (ten beasts) – and could not therefore claim the child as his own, and secondly that Saki had not shown proper concern for the child's welfare because he had failed to visit as soon as he had heard of its illness. The unofficial headman was called and the issue which dominated the argument was whether the 'cattle' which Saki had transferred constituted marriage cattle or merely compensation cattle. Because there was no immediate way of resolving the dispute Saki was forced to allow the child to be buried by his father-in-law.

The matter went to court, however, in the following weeks, and the decision went in favour of Saki who was able to produce evidence of a written agreement that, in view of 'MaKhau's double 'spoiling', Saki should only pay five cattle in respect of marrying 'MaKhau, and an additional five cattle if he wished to acquire paternity of her surviving child (D). The chief's court interpreted this agreement quite literally: Saki had fulfilled his obligation in respect of marrying 'MaKhau, but cattle remained outstanding to substantiate his paternity of the child (D). It followed that 'MaKhau's father had been wrong to bury the child (A) himself, and the court insisted that he allow 'MaKhau to return to Saki. In due course, late in 1974, she gave birth to another son (B). Saki was at pains to explain to me that, although a payment of five cattle was usually construed as compensation (*matšeliso*), nevertheless what was important was the specific agreement actually reached between the parties. In this case, five cattle were adequate to validate the marriage in jural

135

terms and thence Saki's jural paternity of the child whem he had begotten.

Marrying a mother-with-child

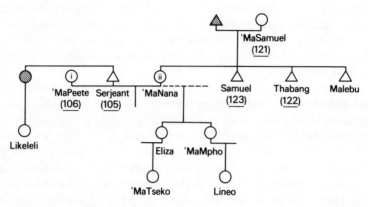

6.3 Marrying a mother-with-child

'MaSamuel was married by a member of the Taung clan in 1931 (Appendix 2, No. 3). Her husband died in 1963 and she continues to reside virilocally as a widow. She is the defendant throughout the dispute which follows. Serjeant, of the Kholokoe clan, was born in 1914 and has spent much of his life as a mine contract labourer, ending up as a 'boss-boy' on a gold mine. In 1955 he approached 'MaSamuel with a view to marrying her daughter 'MaNana as his second wife, his first wife 'MaPeete being barren. Agreement was reached that he should pay in *bohali* eighteen cattle, ten sheep and a horse to marry 'MaNana with her daughter Eliza (see below) for, in Sesotho, 'to love the mother is to love the child as well' (*serata 'me ke serata le ngoana*). 'MaNana went to the Republic to stay with her husband, and they both returned permanently to Lesotho in about 1964 because Serjeant had been bewitched for reasons connected with jealousy over jobs at the mine. This left him with a recurring condition of 'weakness in the head' and he was no longer able to work. Nor was he able to represent himself in the series of cases described below, in which he is the plaintiff.

In her youth 'MaNana had eloped with a man from another village and borne a child, Eliza. Unable or unwilling to marry her, the man had paid six head of cattle to her mother 'MaSamuel in compensation (*matšeliso*), and 'MaNana returned to her natal home. Later she eloped again with the same man, became pregnant again, and a further two

136

head of cattle were paid. At this point negotiations were undertaken for her marriage to Serjeant, and her second child, 'MaMpho, was born after she had taken up residence with her husband, who is thus recognized as pater to 'MaMpho. Subsequently 'MaNana bore five children to Serjeant – they are excluded from the diagram because they are not relevant to the dispute.

During the absence of Serjeant and 'MaNana in South Africa, Eliza and 'MaMpho and their younger half-siblings all resided with their grandmother 'MaSamuel in Ha Molapo. When their parents returned to Lesotho in about 1964 all the children came to live in their household except Eliza who remained at 'MaSamuel's place in response to her grandmother's insistence that she needed help with the domestic chores. Eliza eloped in August 1971 with a man from the next village who paid six 'cattle' (goats, a donkey and some cash) as compensation (*matšeliso*) to 'MaSamuel, who accepted this payment as an initial instalment of *bohali*. In due course Eliza became pregnant and according to custom – a woman's first child should be born in her natal home – she moved back to her grandmother's place where she gave birth to 'MaTseko in September 1973. She was still living there with her baby at the end of my fieldwork period in November 1974.

Serjeant's younger sister 'MaSmuts had been 'spoilt in the yard' by a village neighbour who paid six cattle to Serjeant in compensation. She remained attached to her natal home, but subsequently went to work in the Republic where she died (date unknown). Her daughter Likeleli thus belonged to Serjeant's household, for he is recognised as her pater in default of her mother's marriage. Likeleli was married in the mountains in the 1960s, and a payment of ten *bohali* cattle accrued to Serjeant. In the early 1970s 'MaMpho made an extended visit to Likeleli's marital home in the mountains. While there she eloped with a man who paid eight *bohali* cattle to Serjeant after marriage negotiations took place. Likewise according to custom, she returned to Serjeant's household when pregnant, where she gave birth to Lineo in April 1974. The two sisters, Eliza and 'MaMpho, who resemble each other closely (same genitor) and were both in a condition of recent maternity, were not allowed by their respective seniors to visit each other during 1974, owing to the hostility between the households (separated by a mere hundred yards) of 'MaSamuel and Serjeant.

Samuel and Thabang, both absent on migrant labour, have married and established independent households. They transferred nine and ten *bohali* cattle respectively (Appendix 2, Nos. 12, 13), allowing their fierce old mother to manage the negotiations in their absence. Malebu married a Tswana girl whose home is Mafeking and transferred three 'cattle' in cash to her uncles there. He resides with his wife in the Republic and in 1972–4 they seldom visited Ha Molapo, although two of their three children were living with his mother 'MaSamuel. By 1978 he had not yet built his own homestead.

Serjeant had no adult sons in 1973–4. His receipts of *bohali* in respect of the marriages of Likeleli and 'MaMpho were important since his only other apparent source of livelihood since his 'retirement' to Lesotho in 1964 was the cultivation of one field, by no means adequate for a large family, and the income from a few small stock and from hiring out two young sons as herdboys (about R24 per annum). His wife 'MaNana had come home from a spell of domestic service in South Africa at Christmas 1972, and she returned there in August 1974 for a further indefinite period. The following series of events which I witnessed during 1973–4 provide valuable insights into the nature of *bohali* obligations and of the judicial process. Serjeant was trying to use receipts from the marriages of two 'daughters' to whom he was pater by Sesotho custom but to neither of whom he was genitor (Likeleli and 'MaMpho), in order to acquire paternity of the elder sister of one of them to whom also he was not genitor (Eliza). Specifically, the issue was whether he could *sufficiently* marry 'MaNana-with-Eliza to claim receipt of the latter's *bohali*.

20 January 1973 Serjeant accused 'MaSamuel before the unofficial headman Morero Letlala of 'taking his child', by which he meant wrongly appropriating the *bohali* cattle she had received in respect of the marriage of Eliza. 'MaSamuel's defence was that Serjeant had not yet completed marrying 'MaNana-with-Eliza and, until he had done so, she was entitled to be regarded as pater to Eliza and therefore to receive any *bohali* payable for her. Witnesses were called who agreed that the original contract had specified eighteen cattle, ten small stock and a horse for marrying 'MaNana with her child Eliza. It was common cause that Serjeant had hitherto paid only ten cattle towards the settlement of this debt. The headman dismissed the claim and decided that Serjeant would be entitled to a refund of the six cattle paid to 'MaSamuel for Eliza and to any future *bohali* when he had completed the eighteen cattle specified in the original agreement.

16 February 1973 Dissatisfied with this decision, Serjeant took the matter to the Local Court (the lowest level in the official judicial hierarchy), but the Court President referred the matter back to a meeting between the respective families to try and resolve the matter themselves.

23 February 1973 A meeting between the two families took place at Serjeant's instigation. His representative (a distant patrilateral cousin) asked 'MaSamuel to give him the 'calves' (number unspecified since he did not know the details) she had received from Eliza's husband's people so that he would be able to complete the payments still outstanding for 'MaNana-with-Eliza. 'MaSamuel retorted that they had come to discuss one marriage only, that of 'MaNana, and 'when you have finished the one you have come about, then we can proceed to that other one'. In other words, she insisted that Serjeant complete his original obligations of eighteen cattle in full before she would discuss a refund of the six cattle she had received from Eliza's marriage. It was naturally in her interest to stall as long as possible, for she had already 'eaten' these latter – they had been partially disposed in an additional instalment on the marriage of Samuel.

Serjeant's side offered eight small stock as two 'cattle' towards the amount still due. In response 'MaSamuel scoffed and said that cattle were not what they used to be (i.e. they were very expensive nowadays) and as far as she was concerned eight small stock were worth one beast. After some heated altercation on this point agreement was reached at seven small stock per head of cattle and both parties witnessed a written record of this payment, which left one sheep over towards the twelfth head of cattle. Serjeant requested her to provide the ox of *tlhabiso* 'to smear me with fat because I have now married', but 'MaSamuel refused point blank saying that, in view of the wrangles that preceded this agreement, she saw that there was bad feeling between them and she was not prepared to slaughter for 'someone who just fiddles around' by dealing with one beast at a time. If he had brought the ten sheep and a horse as well she might have considered it. The written agreement implied, though it did not state explicitly, that the sum to conclude marrying 'MaNana was twelve cattle, ten small stock and a horse, leaving six cattle in respect of Eliza.

28 April 1973 Serjeant paid R24 which, with the single sheep left over from the previous agreement, made up the twelfth head of cattle: Subsequently there was some disagreement over the precise significance of these twelve head having been completed. 'MaSamuel argued that Serjeant had now finished marrying 'MaNana except for the horse and ten sheep outstanding. A letter to this effect was prepared by the headman who had first heard the case in January 1973 and who now wished to resolve the dispute once and for all, but Serjeant's side refused to sign it on the grounds that acceding to that arrangement would effectively renounce further claims over the *bohali* of Eliza. In other words, so long as the cattle for marrying 'MaNana-with-Eliza were undifferentiated, Serjeant could claim a continuing interest in the girl's paternity; but as soon as it was specified that, out of the eighteen cattle due, twelve were for marrying 'MaNana and six for marrying Eliza (as it were), his failure to render the final six cattle due would specifically undermine his claim to paternity over Eliza.

By this time Serjeant's distant kinsman who had been acting on his behalf was increasingly exasperated with the failure of successive attempts to get anywhere with the recalcitrant old woman who was still insisting on total fulfilment of the original demand, and withdrew from further participation in the case. 'MaNana remarked to me caustically that her mother had already received eight cattle in respect of her 'spoiling' and twelve cattle in respect of her marriage and still she was not satisfied. Family bitterness was exacerbated by a party-political split: 'MaSamuel was a prominent supporter of the BNP and her daughter 'MaNana was secretary of the local BCP committee.

12 July 1974 Serjeant took the matter to the chief's court, having failed to resolve it at family level and before the headman of their village section. His claim was, as before, that 'MaSamuel had 'taken' his child. Her defence was a direct denial of this and a counter-assertion that Eliza belonged to her household because of default by Serjeant on *bohali* obligations. Questions from the court concentrated on three issues:

(a) *the physical paternity of Eliza.* Who was her genitor and what was the status of 'MaNana's union with him? Was 'MaNana already the wife of another man when Serjeant undertook marriage negotiations with her mother? The court was satisfied with evidence that Serjeant had married 'MaNana from her mother's home, that he did not know Eliza's genitor, and that in any case the marriage agreement between Serjeant and 'MaSamuel had specified he could marry 'MaNana-with-Eliza, which agreement would have been impossible had there been paternity claims over Eliza from another source.

(b) *the upbringing of Eliza.* Who had been responsible for looking after her, feeding, clothing her, etc.? Had Serjeant contributed towards 'MaSamuel's expenses in this regard, since it was common cause that Eliza had been living in the latter's household until the time of her marriage? The plaintiff and defendant disagreed on this point, but Serjeant had already admitted his customary liability to pay 'MaSamuel one *seotla* beast – compensation due from a pater to those who have incurred the expense of bringing up his child – independently of the *bohali* dispute. Residence is thus nominally irrelevant to the determination of paternity, but in practice 'MaSamuel had the very considerable advantage of having received the initial instalment of six *bohali* cattle from Eliza's husband's people who, not unnaturally, had assumed that the 'owner' of the girl was the head of the household where she resided.

140

Had Eliza been married from Serjeant's household, and had Serjeant accordingly received her *bohali* himself, 'MaSamuel could have sued Serjeant on the same grounds as applied in the present case – that he had not yet established his paternity of Eliza – but Serjeant could have paid the outstanding debt of six cattle and would thus have been in a secure position for claiming future *bohali* payments made for Eliza. So Eliza's residence with her grandmother gave the latter a decisive *de facto* advantage in the case.

(c) *the significance of the two 'cattle' Serjeant had paid in 1973*. 'MaSamuel argued, as before, that they were in respect of marrying 'MaNana and this was confirmed by witnesses on both sides. Serjeant argued, not unreasonably since there are many precedents, that ten cattle were sufficient for marrying a woman who had already been 'spoilt' and that the two beasts transferred over and above the ten were in respect of Eliza. But he could not support this argument since the written agreement of 23 February 1973 was read to the court and it made no mention of the girl whose paternity was in question before the court. This proved to be a fatal oversight from Serjeant's point of view.

Nevertheless Serjeant also suffered from 'MaSamuel's unscrupulous conduct of her case. She had suborned two of her witnesses to confuse the issue by suggesting that the girl whose paternity was in question was in fact, 'MaMpho not Eliza. This was possible because Eliza's married name was 'MaMpho and Serjeant's new representative (another distant kinsman from a village some miles away) was not sufficiently familiar with the intricacies of the case effectively to dispel the confusion arising.

The decision of the court, administratively delayed for two months, went against Serjeant. His claim to the girl was rejected.

12 November 1974 In conversation with me, Serjeant explained his resignation, remaining bitterly resentful against his mother-in-law. Although the substance of the dispute was the *bohali* which would accrue to him had his claims of paternity been upheld, he expressed his views in terms of concern for the well-being of Eliza in the following manner:

There will be problems when the old woman dies, and it's not known where the girl's home is. It's this that upsets me ... because there are sometimes matters which compel someone to return to her (natal) home, for example if she dreams the ancestors ... Now (should this happen to Eliza) my own children will say to her, 'We don't know you, go away over there where they've eaten those *bohali* cattle'; but Samuel and his brothers have their own children and they won't have much to do with their cross-cousin (in such matters) ... But her own mother is here and I'm here, it's this that upsets me so much.

In other words, it is only a person's mother and father who can be relied upon in such circumstances.

This case stands by itself as an empirical illustration of the intricate system of debts and of credit in which the Basotho are involved today, and to which the missionary Duvoisin paid unwitting tribute in 1885 (CB: 536). I would stress two points in particular which arise from it. Firstly, the Sesotho principle 'debts do not cancel each other out' (*melato ha e lefane*) fully supported the defendant 'MaSamuel in her insistence that Serjeant should complete his obligation to her in full, in respect of 'MaNana and Eliza, before she would be in a position to consider a refund to Serjeant in respect of Eliza's *bohali*. Time was on her side also: Serjeant died in 1979. Even if the respective debts could have been weighed against each other in customary law, it was against 'MaSamuel's interest to terminate Serjeant's obligation to her for she would then renounce any claim to future instalments of Eliza's *bohali*. The speculative skill in the game of *bohali* lies in the politics of inflation, exchange rates and credit control. Secondly, the fact that the fundamental jural element of the marriage contract, the payment of *bohali*, is quantifiable is precisely the focus of many disputes. Had Serjeant sufficiently married his wife-with-her-daughter to be able to claim the latter's *bohali*? The area of uncertainty on this point provided the area of disagreement between the principals in the case.

The interpretation of marital transactions

An hypothesis well established in the anthropological literature relates the size of bridewealth in a general sense to the quantum of rights transferred. With reference to the Zulu, for example, Max Gluckman (1950) proposed a correlation, or mutual consistency, between high bridewealth and rare divorce in systems of 'marked father-right', in which a woman is 'incorporated' into her husband's family on marriage.[7] The fundamental premise of such a system is expressed with epigrammatic simplicity: 'the child belongs to the cattle'. In Sesotho, *ngoana ke oa likhomo*. Anthropologists interpret this idiom and its variants as follows: the passage of bridewealth cattle brings about the absolute transfer of rights in a woman's procreative capacity from the woman's family to her husband's family.

Gluckman's hypothesis has been extremely influential, mainly because it stimulated a number of vigorous debates in the 1950s.[8] Within the paradigm that was dominant in British social anthropology at that time, it exemplified very well the way in which comparative studies may be used to discover functional consistencies between variables of kinship structure within a relatively homogeneous 'society'. The debates confirmed the general relevance of a number of important analytical distinctions: between pater (social father) and genitor (physical father); between rights *in genetricem*, relating to a woman's child-bearing capacity, and rights *in uxorem*, relating to her sexual and domestic services; and – although Gluckman himself was criticized for neglecting this (Schneider 1953) – between criteria of conjugal stability, such as living together, and criteria of jural stability, such as the permanent disposition of rights over children.

In the following discussion I develop three lines of criticism of the Gluckman hypothesis, each of which serves the need to transcend its limitations. They relate, respectively, to the temporal distribution of significant transactions; to the way in which the customary law works in practice; and to the question of the appropriate unit of study.

The first line of criticism remains within Gluckman's positivist terms of reference. In other words, it takes for granted that the transactions identified as significant in customary law constitute the relationship 'marriage' between a man and a woman; and that it is the fact of his marriage to a child's mother that defines a man as the child's pater. But, the argument goes, the existence of such 'marriage' depends in practice on a series of transactions which are often distributed over a long period of time, so that it is difficult to identify empirically the point at which 'marriage' may be deemed to exist. For example, among the Zulu, marriage for a woman is being 'made to go on a long journey' symbolically from her natal home to her husband's home. The journey is marked by a series of prestations and counter-prestations and the beast which signals transition is above all the 'ox of the skin'. Harriet Ngubane's survey in the Valley of a Thousand Hills showed that this sacrifice had been performed in the marriages of 63 per cent of women (1977: 67). Many cases of illness or misfortune were attributed to non-fulfilment of marital obligations, such as sacrifice of the *imbeleko* goat by which a wife is properly 'introduced' to her husband's ancestors.

This line of criticism has been developed most explicitly by Adam Kuper (1970) in his account of Kgalagadi marriage, on the western fringes of the Tswana ethnographic area. He described the three most important transactions as follows: *kgobo*, a blanket or other small personal gift from the young man to the girl, gives him rights of sexual access; *pholo*, two he-goats or a cow and perhaps some cash, from the man and his close relatives to the girl's parents, marks the girl's move from her own home to her husband's home, his right to her labour and domestic services, and public acknowledgement of the union; and *bogari*, a valuable gift of perhaps six head of cattle, marks the irrevocable transfer of legal rights over the children of the union from the wife's father or brother to the husband. This payment is often made ten to fifteen years after *pholo*. Kuper collected details of 85 unions contracted by 37 adult men in one Kgalagadi village. With three anomalous exceptions, he was able to classify them all with respect to the three principal transactions that constitute 'marriage'. The 17 unions in which none of the three transactions had taken place were described as 'concubinage' involving a *nyetsi*, a 'wife who is not known to your family'; in 6 unions *kgobo* only had been paid; in another 32 both *kgobo* and *pholo* had taken place; and in the remaining 27 all three payments had been made. This classification reflects the distribution of significant payments over time, and from it may be inferred whether particular women are 'more' or 'less' married.

In summary of this approach, marriage must be seen as a developing process not as a single event; the process is marked by a cumulative series of transactions which signify various kinds of rights; and conflict arises over the distribution of such rights because, as Kuper put it, 'in the course of the development of the marriage, the locus of control over the woman and her children may be uncertain' (1970: 478).

The second line of criticism questions the validity of the assumption that particular transactions determine the distribution of significant rights, on the grounds that this is not how the customary law works in practice. Instead, it argues that the existence of a particular 'marriage' only comes into question in circumstances of dispute that require judicial resolution, that is, retrospectively, generally following conjugal dissociation. In such cases, all the circumstances will be taken into account, not simply those relating to the transfer or otherwise of bridewealth.

This approach is best exemplified in the work of John Comaroff and Simon Roberts on Kgatla marriage (Roberts 1977; Comaroff and Roberts 1977). In strictly formal terms, Kgatla stress the importance of two elements in particular in the formation of a marriage: a series of negotiations between the parties which culminates in the transfer of *dilo tsa patlo*, gifts accepted by the woman's guardian which signify his agreement to the union; and the presentation of *bogadi* cattle. Despite the formal clarity of this process, these elements are not 'prescriptive necessities in the constitution of a marriage' and, indeed, 'there may be considerable ambiguity surrounding the *de facto* definition of a particular union in the everyday context' (Comaroff and Roberts 1977: 112). Particular court cases demonstrate that failure to comply with formal procedures does not necessarily render a marriage invalid. Rather, there is scope for considerable argument over the question, for example, of whether a union is accepted and recognized by the kinsmen of the man and the woman. Definitional ambiguity is built into the logic of the marriage process; and the need to define the status of a particular union is contingent on the need to distribute rights over children and property which arises out of conjugal dissociation. In these circumstances, the protagonists to a dispute select, manage and counterpose evidence relating to the 'facts' of a particular situation. The judicial process involves retrospective and competitive constructions of events. Accordingly, the 'correct' resolution of a dispute is not simply determined by the law acting, as it were, 'out there'. It is, rather, a winning construction of the facts.

This account of the way the customary law works in practice is more realistic than the 'jural approach' exemplified above. However, Comaroff and Roberts laid too much emphasis on the derivation of the jural approach from western jurisprudence and the misleading consequences of its application to preliterate societies. In insisting on the dangers of 'ethnocentric extrapolation', the force of their argument is somewhat deflected from the ground where it properly applies: a confrontation between positivist and phenomenological approaches to the sociology of law.

The third line of criticism relates to the question of the unit of study. Even in the 1930s, at the time Gluckman studied them, the Zulu were deeply involved in migratory labour. His comparative study of bride-wealth (1950) therefore begs questions about the way in which social systems on the periphery of southern Africa are articulated with the larger political and economic system of the region as a whole. As Gluckman himself stressed elsewhere (1940, 1975), in common with other South African anthropologists, piecemeal ethnography can only make sense in its full political, economic and social context. In particular, participation in the larger economy has had effects on marriage payments which appear contradictory in the light of Gluckman's own hypothesis. On the one hand, increasing wage-earning opportunities, and a concomitant rise in levels of cash income, have generated an inflationary impetus in marriage payments.[9] At the same time as Gluckman published his essay on bridewealth (1950), Barnes observed that 'Payments rise as Africans participate increasingly in the money economy of southern Africa' (1951: 123). On the other hand, mass labour migration has undermined both the conjugal stability of marriage and its jural stability, whose structural basis was the traditional pattern of residence and authority within the agnatic family.

Thus high marriage payments may co-exist with highly unstable patterns of conjugal association. This is true of Lesotho today, and there is an obvious rationale for procrastination over marriage payments when the stability of unions is exposed to high risk in both conjugal and jural terms. In the circumstances of the southern African periphery, I would stress the importance of an analytical distinction between conjugal *separation*, an inevitable demographic feature of oscillating migration, and conjugal *dissociation*, which refers to the functional collapse of the marital relationship. As we have seen, repetitive conjugal separation is a condition of the viability of the nuclear-family form of the *de jure* household; conjugal dissociation almost inevitably dissolves that form of household.

How then are social relations sustained (1) within the rural household which consists of a migrant and his immediate family, and (2) between rural households in the labour reserve? The answers to these questions offer the key to understanding the persistence of *bohali* in Lesotho at levels at least as high as those prevalent in the nineteenth century. Marital transactions are competitive exchanges. Their moral idiom is the transfer of cattle for rights of paternity. Their practical purpose is to maintain the integrity of the rural household as an effective structure of supports and dependences. Migrant earnings materially sustain significant relationships of kinship and affinity. They also, through their partial disposition in *bohali* transfers, confer legitimacy upon those relationships. The implications of this point are extremely important. On the one hand, the persistence of *bohali* must be related to changes that have taken place outside the boundaries of Sesotho 'society'. On the other hand, this wider framework of analysis requires no less attention to the particular experience of Basotho and to the ways in which they articulate that experience.[10] Accordingly, it is impossible to isolate the material or 'economic' aspect of *bohali* transfers from their ideological or 'cultural' aspect, and to ascribe priority to one or the other. *Bohali* is 'cultural' in that Basotho effect resolutions of personal identity with reference to the transactions summarized in Table 6.1 above, and they also rationalize such resolutions retrospectively. The calculations that they make are constrained by custom and sanctioned by recourse to the courts. *Bohali* is also 'economic' in that transfers in livestock and cash are substantial items of income and expenditure in household budgets.

Bohali transfers in Lesotho today, at least in the Lowlands, are derived largely from the earnings of migrants. They are no longer provided in livestock by a variety of agnatic and matrilateral kin on the side of the husband and distributed amongst a similar variety of kin on the side of the wife (cf. Ashton 1952: 62–87). They are drawn from and contribute to a general subsistence fund concentrated largely within the household. However, to the extent that *bohali* transfers constitute items of expenditure for migrants and items of income for the heads of women's natal

146

households, they effect a redistribution of income in favour of the senior generation, which thus has a clear interest in continuing to demand high rates of *bohali*. Indeed, in the light of speculative exploits such as those of 'MaSamuel (Household 121) which I have described in detail above, it is often more realistic in contemporary practice to represent marital transactions as the result of bargaining conducted by senior women over the earning capacity of men, than as the result of bargaining conducted by senior men over the productive and reproductive capacities of women.

Migrants also have an interest in substantially fulfilling their *bohali* obligations, for their own long-term security is best assured by establishing access to legitimate dependants within a rural household. Given a high rate of conjugal dissociation, which is a consequence of oscillating migration, the migrant has to balance two considerations. On the one hand, the rationality of investment in the next generation, of the sort that *bohali* transfers represent, is qualified by his initially tenuous attachment to his own dependants. On the other hand, so long as *bohali* remains the idiom in which inter-household competition for the earning capacity of the next generation is rationalized and resolved, such investment remains the only way in which he can legitimately assert his own interests as against those of his affines. It is sensible for the migrant to dispose his resources accordingly: that is, both in maintaining his dependants in a rural household, which is a condition of conjugal stability, and in 'buying off' his affines by meeting their *bohali* demands, in order to validate in jural terms the relations of mutual dependence within his rural household.

It is therefore quite beside the point to criticize large *bohali* transfers on grounds such as the following:

> That such sums of money should be changing hands on marriage in a country of such dire poverty seems incredible and the fact that the majority of the male population have to put up with the appalling conditions and wages in South Africa to earn any money at all appears to make the whole process outrageous (Poulter 1976: 332).

Of expenditure of cash earnings on *bohali*, Poulter suggested that 'arguably they could be put to better use, for instance in purchasing necessary household articles and furniture for a new home' (1976: 332). Given that opportunities for capital accumulation in Lesotho are very limited, it is arguable, on the contrary, that no better investment can be made than the investment in human capital that *bohali* represents. Whether or not this is so, however, the points that Poulter missed are that every giver of *bohali* implies a receiver; and that the money is in any case spent on food, clothes and consumer-durables and non-durables of all sorts. From a macroscopic point of view, therefore, a reduction in the amount of *bohali* payable in customary law would not 'free family assets for more useful purposes' (Poulter 1976: 333).

At least two important conclusions may be drawn. Firstly, the rationality of the system cannot be reduced to the perspective of the individual migrant who needs to find the wherewithal to pay off his in-laws. Such reductionism is based on a false division of the migrant's behaviour into its implicitly rational 'economic' aspects (investing in the home) and its implicitly irrational 'social' aspects (adhering to custom). Secondly, the persistence of custom in this respect must be understood by reference to the structural relationships between migrants and their rural kin on the one hand and between rural households on the other. *Bohali* is a mechanism by which migrants invest in the long-term security of the rural social system, and by which rural kin constitute claims over absent earners. The outrage of liberal scholars is properly directed against the dire poverty in Lesotho and the appalling conditions of work in South Africa, not against the institution of *bohali*.

7

Women at home and at work

In her book on *Medieval Women* Eileen Power (1975) showed that none of the contradictory ideas about women which were prevalent during the Middle Ages accurately represented the position of women in different strata of society. She drew the salutary inference that 'A social position is never solely created by theatrical notions; it owes more to the inescapable pressure of facts, the give and take of daily life' (1975: 34). In this Chapter I am concerned on the one hand to identify some of the 'theatrical notions' which are used to evaluate the position of women in Lesotho, both inside and outside Sesotho terms of reference; and on the other hand to illustrate the variety of women's experience, both inside and outside the labour reserve.

Constrained as they are by the structures of apartheid and the imperative of migration, Basotho also conduct their lives with reference to ideas and practices which are recognized as 'proper Sesotho' (*Sesotho sa 'mankhonthe*) – the repository of a long tradition: the everyday observance of taboo, the fulfilment of ritual obligations towards the dead, and the invocation of Sesotho customary law. What I have elsewhere called the 'work of custom' (Murray 1979: 348) refers to the way in which these ideas and practices serve to reproduce social relations, between the living and the dead, between men and women, and between the generations. But an account of the work of custom cannot adequately represent the 'position of women' in abstract from the particular conditions of their lives in the labour reserve and of their participation in the labour market.

There are two complementary aspects of the position of women in Sesotho customary representation. A married woman is the focal point of house identity. As daughter to one family and daughter-in-law to another, she is also 'marginal' in respect of her status within both. These complementary aspects are structural corollaries of the integrity of the agnatic *lelapa*. Ideas and practices which define the position of women are therefore integral to the 'work of custom' as a whole. But these ideas

149

and practices are not crudely determinant. The experience of particular women must be related to phases in the developmental cycle, to the diversity of their material circumstances, and to the range of kin, affines and neighbours who are effectively accessible to them. There are multiple contradictions in the evidence available. For example, men in Lesotho rationalize the jural subordination of women in this way: 'women are weak, they lack sense' (*basali ba a fokola, ba hloka kelello*). As daughters, women are regarded as irrelevant to the perpetuation of their own agnatic family, and they are often 'forgotten' in the genealogical record. Yet, as wives and mothers, women are the nodal reference points in the diverse temporal processes of family constitution: the paternal dyad (father–child link) does not exist *sui generis* but is derivative, as I have shown in Chapters 5 and 6, from the overlap of a conjugal dyad (husband–wife link) with a maternal dyad (mother–child link) (cf. Adams 1971: 28). The strength and resilience of women, as managers of most rural households, are remarkable. Many men, by contrast, are transient visitors, strangers even, in their own communities.

Keeping house: the 'work of custom'

A woman starts off married life as a subordinate daughter-in-law in her husband's family. In her maturity, however, provided there are children born to the house established by her marriage, she is not only house keeper in the mundane sense but keeper of the interests of her house as against those of other houses within the agnatic *lelapa*. Some senior wives or widows develop into formidable protagonists in the conduct of family affairs. But their 'strength' in this position depends upon the importance of the issues at stake, which almost invariably relate to the disposition of property or office.

Implicit in the substantive definition of a house is its differentiation from other houses in respect of the operational management of domestic resources and of rights of inheritance and succession. A man has as many houses to administer as he has married wives; and he must allocate property from his estate to each house in an equitable manner. This property is heritable in due course by the sons of each house; while that portion of a man's estate which has not been allocated to his various houses passes on his death to the principal heir (*mojalefa*), namely the eldest son of the senior house. The integrity of house property is governed by the principle 'houses do not eat each other' (*malapa ha a jane*). Since the property-holding unit is the house and not the agnatic family as a whole, a woman's independent role as defender of the property interests of her own house is contingent on the presence of polygynous arrangements. Otherwise her identity is submerged, as it were, in that of her husband. Given the statistical infrequency of polygyny today, the wider political relevance of the role of house keeper is effectively confined to circumstances of competition for office. But such competition by definition preoccupies the 'owners' of the family (*beng ba lelapa*), the senior men acting through the family council. The logic of the house–property complex is that a woman's domestic autonomy is greatest where the interests of the wider agnatic family are most strongly articulated.

On marriage a woman moves from her natal place (*moo a tsoetsoeng*, where she was born) to reside at her husband's place (*moo a nyetsoeng*, where she is married). The presumption of virilocal residence in marriage is evident in the pointed ribaldry with which 'MaMorena and her eldest daughter commented on the circumstances of a migrant miner of the Thapelo family (Appendix 1, L), whose wife had deserted him in 1973 and who had quarrelled bitterly with his mother on account of this. On his occasional visits to Ha Molapo thereafter he stayed elsewhere in the village with an unmarried woman whose mother and brother had recently died (Household 146). In 1978 people were saying that this woman 'had married him'. The absurdity of this idea was conveyed in the reversal of conventional syntax by which a man marries (*ho nyala*) and a woman is married (*ho nyaloa*).

When a woman takes up residence at her husband's place she is no longer known by the personal name of her childhood and adolescence. Instead she is given a new name which usually takes the teknonymous form 'Mother-of-So-and-So' in anticipation of her reproductive fulfilment. Ideas about the proper place of a daughter-in-law are reproduced through the observance of *hlonepho* (respect, avoidance) prohibitions which require a married woman to avoid calling the names of her father-in-law and of other senior male agnates of her husband. She must also avoid homonyms of these. She rapidly learns the necessary verbal dexterity and discretion. The *hlonepho* prohibitions, which are still scrupulously observed today by most Basotho married women, are strikingly similar to those described by Caroline Humphrey (1978) for Mongol women, and they may be said to serve similar functions – 'suppressing attention' and dramatizing hierarchy within the agnatic family. In addition, in Lesotho a male child is often named after his paternal grandfather, so that it is not uncommon for a woman to be unable to call her son by his own name. She will either call him *ntate* (father) or use a nickname. The effect of this under circumstances of oscillating migration is that the elementary structure of the *lelapa* may be daily rehearsed by its daughters-in-law, since many of the linking males in the senior or middle generations are either absent or dead.

Although a married woman is progressively 'incorporated' into her

151

husband's *lelapa*, she never loses her membership of her natal *lelapa* and may throughout her married life claim protection by her own kin from maltreatment by her husband or his kin. For example, she has the right to return to her own home (*ho ngala*) following a marital dispute or trouble with her affines. If her husband is found to be at fault, he should approach his in-laws with the conciliatory gift of a sheep to precede a request for his wife's return. If, however, the conjugal rift is a permanent one, the woman generally remains in her natal home. In any case, when a man dies, the ritual to remove the death pollution (*ho tlosa sesila*) attaching to his widow must be performed at her natal home. The 'filth' (*sesila*) represented by the mourning clothes is said to derive from the 'sweat' of sexual congress and of co-operative labour. A sheep must be slaughtered, and the widow must be washed with a solution of the animal's gall into which pieces of the species of aloe known as *lekhala* have been placed. Her head is shaved, her nails cut and her black mourning clothes burned. Her own agnates must provide her with new clothes before she returns to her marital home. At the end of her own life she is buried by her husband's agnates according to their clan rites.

These customs reflect the fact that, as daughter to one family and daughter-in-law to another, a married woman experiences conflicting moral claims upon her, and ambivalent secular loyalties. She is also susceptible to mystical attack where either family has neglected its obligations in respect of the marriage, since she is the only target available through whom the ancestors (*balimo*) can exert moral pressure on affines reluctant to fulfil their obligations. As I suggested in Chapter 6, a common source of resentment is failure on the part of the wife's family to slaughter the ox of *tlhabiso* which constitutes acknowledgement of enough *bohali* cattle to fulfil the marriage contract. A similar ambivalence prevails with respect to a woman's clan identity. The question *seboko sa hao u mong?* – 'what is your clan?' – when put to a man evokes a direct and unequivocal response, except where his own paternity is susceptible to doubt. When the same question is put to a woman she will often require clarification of the sort: 'Do you mean where I am married or where I was born?' 'MaMorena resolved the problem by answering: 'On this side (right) I am Crocodile, on this side (left) I am Lion, here (touching forehead) I am Cat'. She meant, in order, her father's clan (Koena), her mother's clan (Taung) and her husband's clan (Sia).

Harriet Ngubane's book *Body and Mind in Zulu Medicine* (1977) well illustrates the strength and the weakness of an analysis of women's 'marginal' status in a kinship system constructed in the agnatic idiom. She identified a structural homology between the interstitial or marginal

152

role of Zulu women in the secular sphere and their marginal, and therefore dangerous and powerful, role in the mystical sphere. In the secular sphere, from the point of view of the men of a local descent group, their wives are outsiders. Such women are in an ambivalent position partly because they are never wholly 'incorporated' into the descent group into which they have married but retain membership in significant respects in their natal descent groups, and partly because they are the foci of internal differentiation of the descent group into sets of half-siblings and sets of full siblings. In the mystical sphere, an intensity of pollution attaches to birth and death, both seen as processes of transition between this world and the other world, where ancestors belong. Women give birth and women are chief mourners. In this way women control both entry into and exit from the world of the living. Women are therefore structurally appropriate to serve as mediators of mystical influence between the world of the living and the world of the dead. This is why Zulu diviners are women, for diviners experience mystical communion with the ancestors in the other world and interpret their moral authority to the living in this world.

Ngubane's analysis reveals a fascinating consistency of ideas concerning health, disease, imbalance in the universe and the mystical intervention of the ancestors. She also effected a pleasing compromise between two influential varieties of anthropological structuralism. In these respects her work is representative of an illustrious anthropological tradition. But, except in so far as alien spirits of 'colonialism' invade Zulu cosmology and afflict Zulu women, she did not relate the 'position of women' to the larger structures in which Zulu women necessarily participate and which generate the 'inescapable pressure of facts' of life in the haphazard aggregate of bits and pieces that constitute KwaZulu.

House keeping: the 'facts of life'

The predicament of Basotho as inhabitants of an impoverished labour reserve is expressed in the universal and bitter complaint *mosebetsi ha o eo*, 'there's no work'. Work in this sense refers to paid employment, opportunities for which are minimal within Lesotho. Most Basotho can only find employment as migrants who oscillate between the 'white' industrial areas of South Africa and their rural homes in Lesotho. Almost all adults spend part of their lives in South Africa. By definition they have no security of residence or employment there, and they cannot rear legitimate families in South Africa.

Since nine out of ten migrants are men, they depend on their wives, mothers and other kin who remain at home and who assume primary responsibility for the reproduction and socialization of the next generation. Together with the sick, the elderly, the children and the unemployed, women who assume these responsibilities comprise the 'superfluous appendages' to which the apologists of apartheid have repeatedly referred. They provide the essential services that are subsumed by marxists under the phrase the reproduction of labour power and that take up more than six and a half hours of the average woman-day.[1] Otherwise, women participate in the labour market under the following structural constraints. Firstly, entry into South Africa for the purpose of seeking work is illegal. Secondly, the wages and conditions of such work as they do nevertheless undertake are appalling. The largest single category of clandestine employment which is available to women is domestic service, in which wages in October 1972 varied between R15 per month in Bloemfontein and R29 per month in Cape Town, according to employers' estimates (SAIRR 1974: 312). I was told that wages in Lenasia, an Indian suburb of Johannesburg to which many women from Lesotho go, were between R16 and R24 per month at the end of 1974. Wages were so low, it was alleged, that South African women would not take jobs there. Thirdly, therefore, the decision by women to find employment in South Africa, despite the degrading conditions, social isolation and risk of arrest under the pass laws, is one of desperation. Women go because they have no alternative.

The economic viability of the rural household depends, above all, on the distribution of paid and unpaid labour. In Chapter 2 I showed that two variables of demographic composition – household size and sex of household head – are significant in this respect. Further elaboration will help to bring the role of women as house keepers into sharp relief. Table 7.1 shows the distribution of paid employees per household in Ha Molapo in October 1974 and October 1978, by size of household and sex of household head. Small female-headed households are at a striking disadvantage in respect of their direct access to the earnings of migrant labourers, since they predominate in the category of households without paid employees.

Approximately two-thirds of rural households have members in paid employment (Chapter 2; Table 7.1), most of whom are absent at any one time. Some of these absentees are identifiable as household heads; many others are subordinate migrants in households whose heads may or may not be permanently resident in the rural community. Irrespective of the distribution of paid employees, however, all households require someone who assumes effective responsibility for managing the affairs of the household at home. Thus it is necessary to distinguish in principle the

Table 7.1. *Distribution of paid employees, Ha Molapo, by size of household and sex of household head, October 1974 and October 1978.*

De jure size	Sex of head	October 1974 No. of paid employees					October 1978 No. of paid employees				
		0	1	2	3	Total	0	1	2	3	Total
Small	Male	4	8	1	—	13	4	11	—	—	15
	Female	16	2	—	—	18	13	6	—	—	19
Large	Male	3	19	5	1	28	4	14	5	3	26
	Female	2	5	5	2	14	3	5	5	—	13
All households		25	34	11	3	73	24	36	10	3	73

Notes: All figures refer to number of households. 'Small' households contain 1 to 4 members; 'Large' households contain more than 4 members (see Tables 2.3, 2.4).

roles of household head and household manager. As the histograms in Fig. 7.1 show, male household heads in Ha Molapo are concentrated in the age range 30 to 49, and the majority of them were absent in October 1974 and October 1978. In their absence their responsibilities of household management are vested in their wives. This fact qualifies the substantive importance of the classification by sex of household head, for in practice nearly 70 per cent of rural households are effectively managed by women.[2] These comprise (1) households whose female heads are concentrated in the age ranges 50 to 69 (Fig. 7.1), some of which are large and contain subordinate migrants, others of which are small and have no paid employees (Table 7.1); and (2) households whose male heads are absent migrants and which are managed in their absence by their wives left behind. The remaining third of households are managed by their male heads who are present in the community. At any one time, of course, the two groups of households effectively managed by women are empirically discrete: they are represented by case studies of particular households below. But they cannot be regarded as analytically discrete: as I suggested in Chapter 5, individual women in the course of their lives are likely to experience a series of movements between natal home, marital home and work-place in South Africa. The orthodox pattern is virilocal residence as a wife in the absence of the husband, followed by widowhood and, probably, the rearing of grandchildren. But there are many variations, involving perhaps a number of different conjugal associations, a period of absence as a migrant, a return to the natal home, and the rearing of children within a matrifocal household.

Thus the variety of women's experience reflects the exigencies of their

Families divided

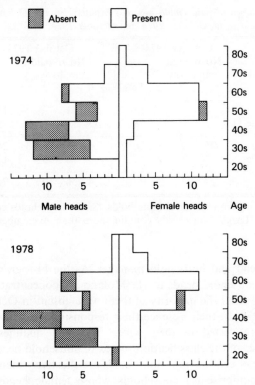

7.1 Histograms showing distribution of male and female household heads, Ha Molapo, by age cohorts and presence/absence, October 1974 and October 1978

marital and migrant careers. In their capacity as married women left behind by absent husbands, an extant conjugal relationship specifies a combination of heavy domestic responsibility with a variable degree of economic insecurity. Since effective household management depends above all on the reliability of cash remittances, it is not surprising that women's experience ranges from relative security to bitter frustration, acute personal stress and emotional desolation. In their capacity as single women, the failure of a conjugal relationship exposes them directly to the vicissitudes of a labour market heavily loaded against them; and exposes their children to the vicissitudes of rearing by more or less distant kin, to the high risk of malnutrition, and to a vicious circle of social deprivation. Some of the costs of desertion and illegitimacy may be assessed from the results of research in the Ciskei and KwaZulu: the incidence of malnutrition was found to be highest where mothers had no support from fathers and where children were in the care of relatives other than

156

their own parents (Thomas 1973; Schlemmer and Stopforth 1974). As widows, women face the deprivations of old age under circumstances where the capacity of the social relations of kinship to sustain their traditional functions has been undermined, to the disadvantage of the elderly, the sick and the unemployed. In some cases, however, they emerge as senior women in large households containing subordinate migrants; and, as we have seen, they may become effective local entrepreneurs in agriculture, village politics or family affairs.

In the light of the unequal distribution between households of paid and unpaid labour, respectively, it is important to investigate the effective distribution of migrant earnings within and between households. In a survey of 82 Basotho mining recruits in 1976, van der Wiel (1977: 82) found that 41 per cent of their cash earnings from their previous contract had been spent on themselves, 31 per cent on other household members, 19 per cent on communal items, and 9 per cent had been distributed in various ways outside the migrant's household, including 5 per cent on bridewealth transactions. These mean figures obscure wide variation in patterns of disposition. But they do reflect the concentration of earnings within the *de jure* household, and differential expenditure within it in favour of the migrant himself and to the relative disadvantage of his immediate dependants. However, the figure of 9 per cent of total cash earnings disposed outside the migrant's own household would assume greater significance relative to that proportion of these earnings, about 70 per cent (van der Wiel 1977: 79), which accrues to Lesotho. More importantly, however, this evidence is of limited value because any sample of migrants as opposed to rural households will obscure the differentiation that is taking place between rural households as a result of the intensification of general dependence on migrant labour (Chapters 1 and 4), the tendency for migrants' earnings to be disposed largely within their own households, and the increasing difficulty of finding employment at all. Only two-thirds of households, after all, have direct access to migrant earnings.

The question of indirect access to such earnings is therefore of crucial importance. Most forms of inter-household income transfer have already been referred to: occasional remittances in cash and kind; *bohali* transfers (Chapter 6); share-cropping arrangements and various other contractual and reciprocal arrangements connected with agriculture (Chapter 3). There is also a variety of other transfers such as beer-brewing, petty trading and 'concubinage' (*bonyatsi*). In circumstances of higher mine wages together with enforced marginalization of labour power, it is probable that activities in the 'informal sector' have been expanding in order to soak up migrants' surplus cash. Beer-brewing in particular is a widespread and popular way for women to generate a small but regular income at home. The white and green flags which signify the public sale of *joala* (Sesotho beer, made from fermented sorghum) and *hopose* (made from imported hops) are a common sight in the villages of Lesotho. Rather more nocuous recipes imported from the South African townships are also available. Depending on the nature of the brew, the profit varied from R1 to R2 in Ha Molapo in 1972–4. The keeping of pigs is often combined with regular brewing, for pigs live comfortably off the residue of the brewing process. Some women also engage in the itinerant retailing of fruit – peaches and apricots in season, or apples imported from South Africa – or of home-craft products such as knitted scarves and hats. Such petty trade relies on a high turnover and is not used to build up capital but to generate a small cash income for satisfying everyday household needs – paraffin, tea, sugar, soap. Some women form savings-clubs in order to have access, by turns, to the larger amount of cash necessary to hold a party or *setokofele* (from the English 'stock fair') at which people pay for the food, drink and entertainment provided.[3]

Wives left behind

Household 148   Mohao was aged 58 in 1974. He had spent twenty-five years employed by South African Railways and Harbours in Cape Town, and in 1971 he was transferred to Springs (Transvaal). He used to send his wife and family – two of his daughters had young illegitimate children resident in the household – a regular sum of R30 per month. He came home once a year, for about two weeks' leave over Christmas. In 1973 he spent a lot of money on brandy and on festive hospitality but his wife did not interfere in the drinking bouts because he had given her R34 to spend as she pleased. Mohao has no lands but his wife makes regular share-cropping arrangements, and they reaped ten bags of grain in 1974. She also supplements the income from wage earning with regular brewing of *joala* and *hopose*.

Household 137   In 1973–4 Motlalepula (Appendix 3, S18) was a truck operator in a coal mine at Vryheid (Natal), recruited through Vezamafa. His basic wage, he said, was only R0.80 per shift. Even with variable monthly bonuses these wages were appallingly low. His wife 'MaPuleng had three out of their four children resident with her in Ha Molapo, the fourth being resident in her natal home at Witsieshoek (Basotho Qwaqwa). Motlalepula came home for one month in June 1973, bringing some roofing materials to complete a new hut which they were building in response to the needs of a growing family. He took a new mine contract in July 1973 but the first remittance he sent following his departure was one of R45 in November, with instructions to 'MaPuleng to buy a table and chair set. The immediate priority at that time was to buy food for immediate consumption and to arrange for their single field to be ploughed. But she could not flout his direct instructions and she bought the cheapest table and chair set available in the wholesale store in Butha Buthe, for R29. Having paid R5 to hire oxen, plough and labour, bought seed for R1.50, repaid debts of R2 and bought half a bag of maize flour for R3, there was virtually nothing left of the R45 to buy paraffin, soap and other small but necessary household items. Less than two weeks after receiving the single large remittance of R45 'MaPuleng was deeply depressed about her budgeting problems. In December her husband sent her a parcel of clothes for herself and the children; and in January 1974 a sum of R15, one third of which went to repay local debts. Her husband arrived home at the beginning of May 1974 with very little money, for he had spent his earnings on buying three horses in the Republic and on expenses involved in smuggling them into Lesotho. The horses succumbed one after the other to an enzootic intestinal affliction (bots). The previous year Motlalepula had given R70 to an affine of his elder brother to invest in buying a beast on his behalf, but he was only able to recover a small calf worth a good deal less than that sum. His ventures into livestock were thus a notable failure and his wife was exasperated at the conflicts of priority in expenditure when, as so often, she and the children did not know where the next meal was coming from. 'A man hasn't got sense ... he doesn't know [our problems], yet if you don't do what he wants, he beats you ...' They only reaped two bags of maize from cultivation in 1973–4, a return that hardly covered even the minimal cash investment they had made. Motlalepula returned to work in September 1974 and sent 'MaPuleng a remittance of R30 in November, just in time to get their field ploughed.

The differences in standard of living and level of security between these two households were obvious ones. In the first case, that of a relatively well-off family, a regular monthly remittance relieved the wife of domestic insecurity and maintained a balance of authority firmly in favour of the absent husband, although there was no doubt of the wife's managerial competence during his absence. In the second case, that of a family constantly on the edge of hunger, a thoroughly irregular and inadequate cash income rendered the wife extremely vulnerable in her managerial capacity, since she had no alternative source of income; it also made her critical of what she regarded as her husband's poor

159

planning and his distorted priorities of expenditure. While she would not directly flout his wishes in the matter of furnishing the new hut, she frequently expressed the frustration she felt at having no control over the resources to meet her more realistic assessment of immediate needs – the purchase of food, the organization of ploughing, clothes and school fees for the children. It was impossible for Motlalepula, a sober and responsible man, to meet the most basic needs of his family on the wages he was paid in the South African coal-mining industry.

Female household heads

Household 116 'MaTau is an elderly widow aged about 80 in 1974, partially blind and infirm. She owns a few sheep herded out under a *mafisa* arrangement, and operates a small but modestly lucrative retail trade in 'European' liquor. Otherwise, cash income is derived from the earnings of Esther, her deceased son's wife, who is engaged in domestic service in the Johannesburg suburb of Lenasia, and whose two daughters were adolescent school girls in 1974. 'MaTau describes Esther as head of the household by virtue of the latter's residual exercise of her husband's authority. Felix, a young kinsman of the family who had been brought up in the household and normally resided there, took his first contract at an asbestos mine at Kuruman (northern Cape) in March 1974. Earning about R31 per month, he sent two small remittances home during a period of seven months' absence, and returned home at the end of October 1974. His classificatory grandmother 'MaTau appropriated the R30 cash he had brought with him and refused to let him have it, he told me, in order to stop him spending it on drink and girls.

This example brings out some of the variables of household composition which affect the distribution of authority within it. The old woman 'MaTau clearly deferred to her daughter-in-law Esther during the latter's stay at home for two months in mid-1974, a deference which is consistent both with Sesotho custom and with Esther's significant wage-earning role. In all other respects, 'MaTau retained the position of manager in a context in which the young Felix, lately returned from his first experience of migrant labour, was equally clearly regarded as irresponsible. She complained bitterly about the difficulty of hiring a tractor to plough her two fields – no contractor would take her seriously, she said, because of her infirmities. But she reaped a relatively good harvest of nine bags of grain in 1974.

Household 159 Anna is an unmarried childless woman, born in 1912. She lived with her aged and crippled mother who died in July 1974.

Thereafter she lived alone. Her mother held usufructuary title to a single field. The household has no migrant support: 'there is no-one who helps us'. This remark notwithstanding, Anna is well liked in the village and has a number of relatives who help out from time to time. She has a sister married some miles away who makes occasional contributions of grain to the household budget. Without such assistance Anna would be destitute. Lacking any source of cash income, Anna made a share-cropping contract in 1972–3 with the daughter of a cross-cousin, who supplied oxen, ploughing labour and maize seed. Planting was done by hand, and no fertilizer was used. The two women shared subsequent labour of weeding and harvesting, and the yield was divided between them. The same woman helps Anna from time to time with gifts of grain. In 1973–4 she was helped by another cousin, who ploughed for her and provided seed without charge.

My remarking on Anna's unmarried state provoked the specific comment from her neighbour 'MaMorena (Household 172): 'She brings bad luck ... when she's in love with men they just die ...', and she cited three or four times this had happened. 'Anyone without children is in great difficulty – boys go to the place of the whites (*makhooeng*) and get money, while girls get married and you get cattle'.

Household 142

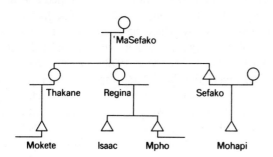

7.2 Household 142

'MaSefako was born in Ha Molapo in about 1890. She was married elsewhere; her husband died at the time of the Great Dust (the drought of the early 1930s); and she returned to settle in Ha Molapo with her three children Thakane (b. 1914), Regina (b. 1918) and Sefako. In due course Thakane was 'married' by a man of the Fokeng clan. She went to reside in his village where she gave birth to her only son Mokete. Her husband had paid seven cattle, an amount generally regarded as

161

insulting and as insufficient to establish jural paternity (Chapter 6, Table 6.1 and Note 4). While the child was still a baby he left to work in Natal and never returned. Thakane heard that he had got himself another wife there and so she returned to her own home where the child grew up in the care of her mother 'MaSefako while she herself went to work in Pimville (Transvaal) to support the family. Thakane has now retired to her mother's household – the two of them are sole permanent residents – where she rears pigs. Her son Mokete has married in his turn and established his own household nearby.

Thakane's younger sister Regina was 'married' by a member of the same family of Fokeng, a classificatory brother of Thakane's husband. He paid eight *bohali* cattle, barely adequate to 'lay the foundation' of the marriage (cf. Table 6.1). They both lived and worked for some years in Kroonstad (Orange Free State) while two boys Isaac and Mpho were born; he then deserted her and she returned with the two boys to her own home. Later she joined Thakane at work in Pimville and was said to be still there in 1974. She did not visit the household during the fieldwork period and made no contribution to its budget. Her sons Isaac and Mpho are active migrant members of 'MaSefako's household, the only home in Lesotho they have known, and they use their maternal grandfather's name as a surname; but they describe themselves as Fokeng by clan and recognize kinship links with surviving local kin of their father.

Isaac was aged 35 in 1974. A girl with whom he had eloped and had a child had lived in the household for about two years. Isaac had made a desultory payment of two cattle, by which he tried the patience of her father who eventually took her away altogether, with her baby daughter, saying 'You haven't married her ...' By May 1973 Isaac had completed at least four mine contracts, the latest at Impala platinum mine, Rustenburg. Mpho had also worked a number of mine contracts, but in the latter part of 1973 the two brothers were working together at a hotel in Braamfontein (Transvaal). Isaac came home in December 1973, explained to his grandmother 'MaSefako that he could not afford to give her any money at that time, and a few days later paid out six 'cattle' as a first instalment on Mpho's marriage to a neighbour's daughter (Appendix 2, No. 20). The 'cattle' were made up from R156 of their joint earnings, and a horse from the household in a thin and weak condition (= 1 beast). Mpho duly eloped with the girl when he came home a week later.

Throughout my fieldwork period Sefako was working as a police clerk in South Africa, and his wife lived with him. They were building a stone house next to his mother's homestead, in preparation for his retirement, and Sefako sent occasional remittances to support his mother and

162

resident sister. Sefako's only son Mohapi, an unmarried migrant miner, visited the household once only, in July 1974, when he gave 'MaSefako and Thakane a blanket each and some cash.

The matrifocal nature of this household developed as a result of the exigencies of two women's marital and migrant careers. The immediate factor determining the residential attachment of three sons, Mokete, Isaac and Mpho, was clearly conjugal default by their fathers but the fact that neither Thakane nor Regina had been 'properly' married in jural terms meant that 'MaSefako was able to insist on keeping the children of her daughters against any claims that might have been made by the family of Fokeng. The equivocal significance of fatherhood in this example is apparent from Isaac and Mpho's explicit acknowledgement of their father's clanship and of local kinship ties traced through him at the same time as they invoked a surname drawn from their mother's family in order to identify themselves. Foci of affection and patterns of material support are determined predominantly by the reciprocal obligations implicit in long-term membership of a household. But it is evident that the reciprocities of rearing do not necessarily coincide with the distribution of jural rights. Had the Fokeng family been able to exert stronger claims of paternity over Isaac and Mpho, for example, it is likely that conflict would have arisen between their father's kin and mother's kin.

A case of structural violence

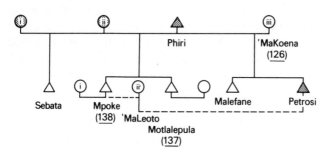

7.3 The three houses of Phiri

In 1966 Phiri's third wife 'MaKoena's younger son Petrosi handed over an initial 'beast' in cash to 'MaLeoto's family as an earnest of his engagement to her. He left her pregnant to take up another mine contract and was killed shortly afterwards in a mining accident. 'MaLeoto was officially acknowledged as his wife and she received a considerable sum in compensation. Sebata had by this time succeeded his father Phiri as head of this branch of the Letlala family (see Appendix 3 for full genealogy). He saw an opportunity in these circumstances to resolve a conflict between the three houses (his own, Mpoke's and Malefane's) which had previously arisen as a result of Phiri's unscrupulous abuse, in the disposition of bridewealth cattle, of the principle 'houses do not eat each other'. Sebata 'gave' 'MaLeoto to Mpoke as a substitute for the latter's wife who had either run away or been thrown out as a result of a complex series of adulterous indiscretions (involving an 'exchange' of wives between Mpoke and another member of the family in Johannesburg). This was a device to repay a debt outstanding from the third house to the second house but Sebata committed a new offence against the third house by acting in this way without consulting Malefane (absent at the time) or his mother 'MaKoena who could justifiably claim the girl as her daughter-in-law.

However, 'MaLeoto settled down with Mpoke and bore him two more children in due course. He transferred two 'cattle' in cash to her parents as a further instalment of bridewealth. He was an occasional migrant but continued philandering, and 'MaLeoto herself was not blameless in this respect. In 1972–3 two court cases were brought respectively by Mpoke and by a village neighbour who had had affairs with each other's wives during the other's absence. In 1974 their marital difficulties came to a head. Mpoke, morose and aggressive, was just wandering around the village, drinking and fighting, not working, no longer giving 'MaLeoto any money for herself or the children. He had previously fallen into bad company on the Rand (*Marasheaneng*, among 'Russians' or gangsters), and village gossip had it that he had been bewitched by a doctor there. He refused to consult a doctor in Lesotho to counteract this evil medicine. In a divorce case in July 1974 at the chief's court 'MaLeoto sued Mpoke for the return of her belongings. The division of property turned on the question of what clothes and household items she had bought with her own compensation money (from the death of Petrosi) and what items she had bought with the money Mpoke had sent her in remittances. She also claimed the corrugated-iron sheets from the roof of their hut. The resolution was that 'MaLeoto should return to her parents' home with the three young children. In view of Mpoke's derisory transfer of only two *bohali* cattle he had no paternity claim over them. Having no means of support, 'MaLeoto immediately left Lesotho to seek work in the informal sector in South Africa. She went to the shebeen run by associates of Lydia (Household 130) in Middelburg (Transvaal). Early in 1975 news reached the village that she had been killed in a drunken brawl.

164

Labour and value: some theoretical considerations

Unpaid labour is subject to contradictory evaluations. On the one hand, black people in 'white' areas who are not engaged in wage employment are not 'economically active' and may therefore be 'endorsed out' to the labour reserves without loss to the white economy. On the other hand, official South African declarations of their redundancy to the needs of the South African economy are belied by the long tradition of the 'subsistence wage' in central and southern Africa. Employers have always rationalized the 'subsistence wage' by reference to the partial livelihood that migrant workers' families are alleged to derive from cultivating the land in the African reserves; and by reference to the 'social services' available to migrants there, whose provision would otherwise, for a stabilized labour force, require expensive urban infrastructure (Schapera 1947: 204; Bettison 1960; F. Wilson 1972a, 1972b; cf. Meillassoux 1972, 1975).

Rationalizations of cheap labour by the apologists of apartheid are therefore self-contradictory. It is arguably more important to expose the inability of neo-classical economics, seen in its full ideological matrix as capitalism's self-image, to impute value to labour that has no price in the market place. For the neglect of unpaid labour is central to the practice of liberal economists who would dissociate themselves from the politics of Afrikaner nationalism and whose hard-headed 'realism', by contrast with the obstructive waffle of the rural sociologist, dominates the corridors of the international development agencies. For example, in a paper entitled 'Approaches to conceptualization and measurement of the social cost of labour migration from Lesotho' (Cobbe 1976), women are not mentioned at all. They are neither conceptualized nor measured. Economic costs, we are told, have mainly to do with the effects of migration on agricultural output and with the disutility to migrants of undertaking employment in a foreign country, far from home, etc. Cobbe himself has attempted to measure this disutility by comparing the 'shadow' wage rate with the real wage rate.

If one asks a worker with experience of migration the wage he last earned in the Republic, and the smallest wage for which he would have been willing to do the same work, but at home in Lesotho, the difference between the two should in fact measure, in rands and cents, the cost to that individual of being a migrant worker rather than working at home (Cobbe 1976: 85).

The precision implied in this exercise is quite spurious. It wholly fails to take into account that a migrant makes his decision to migrate not merely with reference to the differential that he observes between domestically generated income and his potential earnings as a migrant,

165

but also with reference to the distribution of labour within the rural household.

The domestic circumstances of Motlalepula (Household <u>137</u>) illustrate this point. His wife 'MaPuleng died in December 1977, of peritonitis following an operation for cervical cancer. Motlalepula could not undertake a further contract on the Natal coal mine where he was usually employed because there was no one he could trust to look after the four children (aged 8 to 15) properly in his absence from Lesotho. The point is this. The conventional economic analysis of Motlalepula's decision to migrate or not to migrate proceeds by reference to the marginal product of labour in agriculture. Could he earn more by taking up a mine contract than he could supplement the household's domestic income from agriculture by staying at home? These are not in fact alternatives, since agricultural output partly depends on cash investment from migrant earnings (Chapter 3). Even if they were alternatives, however, it can be seen that his dilemma has little to do with choosing between them. It could be argued, rather more plausibly, that the value of his wife's services was precisely the difference between Motlalepula's putative income as a migrant coal miner, that he could have earned in 1978 had his wife been alive and well, and his real income in the informal sector at home in 1978. I have absolute figures for neither income but the difference between them was clearly very great. The obvious solution to Motlalepula's dilemma, as the senior widow of the family observed, was for him to marry again. He duly did so in April 1979. This example demonstrates that a man's decision to migrate is conditional on the presence of someone at home who will carry out the essential tasks connected with the rearing of the family. This consideration has often been ignored by economists because a wife's domestic services have no price in the market place and therefore their value is not directly measureable.

All methods of accountancy involve arbitrary assumptions of one kind or another. But it is obviously more realistic to impute *some* value to women's domestic labour rather than none at all. Failure to take account of unpaid labour is still a critical source of bias in development project proposals. Its allocation is often unconceptualized, unmeasured and, literally, unrealized as a result of methodological preoccupation with the market price of factors of production. It is fair to point out in mitigation that in recent years the 'new home economics' has decisively expanded the boundaries of neo-classical discourse, from the market place into the home,[4] and that its influence is filtering through to southern Africa.

One example of its influence in Lesotho is Wykstra's (1978) argument that crop yields in Lesotho are low partly because of an absolute

166

shortage of female labour for the critical task of weeding. Another example of progressive accountancy is the recognition by a project-evaluation team (Feachem *et al.* 1978) that the introduction of piped water supplies has the sole significant benefit of reducing the time spent on drudgery, even though that time has negligible opportunity cost. It imputed a value to the time saved, 30 minutes per average woman-day, by relating the cost of a typical water supply, at R51 per adult woman, to the time saved over a period of ten years, discounted at a rate of ten per cent per annum, which amounted to 1,234 hours per adult woman. This worked out at a rate of 4 cents an hour. This figure has no reference to the 'real' cost of women's labour time, whatever that is. But it has the merit of recognizing the utility to women of a reduction in drudgery; and its relevance in cost-benefit analysis is that, if women's labour time is valued at 4 cents an hour, then the piped water supply is 'economically' justifiable; if it is given no value at all, the provision of piped water may not be 'economically' justifiable, in view of the team's conclusion that there are no other benefits which derive directly from it.

But the other limitations of neo-classical discourse still apply. In a paradigm that assumes harmony of interest between husband and wife and rational maximization of their pooled resources, a decision that the wife should remain at home to carry out household tasks, look after the family and so on is explained in terms of the fact that her labour in the market place would command a lower wage than that of her husband. Conversely, she commands a lower wage in the market place because she has spent a larger amount of time at home, and is therefore 'worth' less in terms of human capital investment – higher education, work training, experience, etc. Such tautology demonstrates the inability of neo-classical economics to explain structures of inequality, precisely because it takes them for granted in the first place. It is a significant step forward to recognize that decisions about the allocation of labour time have reference to the household or conjugal unit and not simply to the individual. But it does not follow from this that the household or conjugal unit must exhibit internal harmony of interest. In the southern African periphery women very often assume the onus of managing the rural household but have very little control over the resources with which to manage it effectively. Such disjunction between power and responsibility is the source of much bitterness, frustration and marital disharmony.

It is interesting to note that the partial advance represented by the 'new home economics' has taken place in parallel with an effusion of interest in the political economy of domestic labour. The marxists are also unable to measure the value of domestic labour but their vigorous debates of recent years represent an attempt to transcend this difficulty in

167

a theoretical context which Marx himself failed to elaborate. Their starting point is the distinction between use-value and exchange-value. The value of a thing is the expression of the average social labour embodied in its production. Its value is not made apparent if it is produced directly for use but it is made apparent if it is exchanged with other commodities. This means that, while value does not derive from exchange-value, it is only realized in the form of exchange-value (Marx 1976). Failing its realization in exchange-value, there is no way of measuring the value of domestic labour.

Within the British contribution to the domestic labour debate there are two main 'tendencies': the 'orthodox' and the 'unorthodox' (see Smith 1978). The difference between them relates to such issues as the nature of productive labour; whether or not domestic labour creates value; whether the value of labour power comprehends or excludes domestic labour; and the political implications of the analysis. In so far as they are relevant to the present discussion, the differences between the two 'tendencies' may be conveniently illustrated by reference to the debate between Seccombe and Gardiner in the *New Left Review*. Seccombe (1974) argued that the value created by female labour in the home is embodied in the exchange value of the commodities to whose production it contributes – labour power, in the case of domestic labour under capitalism. This leads him to assert that the value created by the wife's domestic labour is reflected in the value of the wage she receives from her husband's pay packet. Gardiner rejected this view on the grounds that 'the mystification of the wage form which Seccombe exposes and rejects in the case of wage labour is then applied unquestioningly to domestic labour' (1975: 50). Her criticism is based on Seccombe's alleged failure to acknowledge the economic dependence of women upon men in marriage, and the unequal exchange which derives from the relationship.

Behind this disagreement lies the question of whether the value of labour power is (1) the labour embodied in the reproduction and maintenance of labour power (i.e. including domestic labour); or (2) the value of commodities purchased by the wage and consumed by the worker's family. Proponents of the first view, who include Duncan Clarke (1976) and Harold Wolpe (1972), writing about 'primitive accumulation' in southern Africa, use the phrase the value of labour power in a sense that appears synonymous with the historically determined subsistence level for a worker and his family, although there is ambiguity in alternative phrases such as the value of the commodities that comprise necessary consumption. Gardiner argued that domestic labour does not create value, in the marxist sense, and therefore she adopted the second view, which implies that the value of labour power is not synonymous with the historically determined subsistence level. There is, however, agreement that domestic labour contributes to surplus value. According to the first view, it allows labour power to exchange at a wage below its value. According to the second view, it allows the value of labour power to fall below the subsistence level.

The terms of the debate relate to domestic labour under fully developed capitalism and are not therefore directly applicable to the rural proletariat of southern Africa which is not wholly 'freed' from the land. The pertinence of the controversy to the present discussion must be further qualified, firstly by the sensible recognition that 'subsistence' levels do not determine but are determined by wage levels (see Hubbard 1977); and secondly by the observation that the contemporary rationale of oscillating migration from the point of view of the South African state and of the various 'fractions' of capital is much less any direct economic subsidy of capital that it may provide and much more the sophisticated machinery of influx control and labour bureaux, which allows tight political control of the labour force, effective export from 'white' areas of the reserve army of labour, and political domination of the labour reserves by proxy, through the Bantustan administrations (see Chapter 1). It must be recognized, nevertheless, that such political control serves generally to depress wages and thereby to 'cheapen' labour.

The attempt by socialist feminists to theorize domestic labour, 'women's work' and capitalist accumulation is part of the ambitious project of relating the sexual division of labour to the labour process. Many of the issues which have arisen are presently unresolved (Edholm, Harris and Young 1977; Kuhn and Wolpe 1978). But it is possible to identify an approximate consensus on the following propositions which are directly relevant to the question of whether or not equal exchange takes place within the household or conjugal unit in peripheral economies subordinated to capital.

Firstly, the value of unpaid labour cannot be measured directly. But it is functional to the interests of capital in that it makes a vital contribution to the maintenance and reproduction of labour power over time. Therefore it contributes to the surplus value appropriated by capital. Secondly, the sexual division of labour is *not* explained by demonstrating this functional contribution and an approximate correspondence between 'women's work' and unpaid domestic labour. Gender hierarchies cannot be reduced to particular relations of production and reproduction. But they cannot be analysed independently of them. The implication of this is that an attempt to discover the elementary form, as it were, of the sexual division of labour must give way to an attempt to discover the transformations which have taken

169

Families divided

place through incorporation into social formations in which the capitalist mode is dominant. Thirdly, exchanges within the household or conjugal unit are non-commensurable. As Edholm, Harris and Young put it in the Women's Issue of *Critique of Anthropology*, 'the sexual division of labour acquires an ideological function of rendering non-comparable the different tasks performed by men and women, and correspondingly the portions of the product that are assigned to each sex' (1977: 124). In this way, the ideological construction of gender roles as complementary both obscures the dependence of women upon men in the conjugal relationship and legitimizes the unequal exchange between them.

8

Changing perspectives on migrant labour

Anthropologists and others have long been concerned with the effects of oscillating migration on the areas from which migrants are drawn. In his pioneering *Essay on the Economics of Detribalization in Northern Rhodesia*, Godfrey Wilson (1941–2) outlined systematic connections between the circulation of labour, the demographic 'disproportion' between town and country, and the impoverishment of the rural areas; and he related them all to contemporary conditions of uneven capitalist development. He wrote of the 'radical social contradictions' that had arisen in Northern Rhodesia, and of the 'objective necessity' of their resolution. Subsequent studies eschewed such a bold theoretical perspective but broadly endorsed Wilson's substantive findings. The most important of these were Schapera's (1947) report to the Bechuanaland Administration, and the report on the Keiskammahoek Rural Survey conducted in the Ciskei in 1949–50 (Houghton and Walton 1952; M. Wilson *et al.* 1952). They both drew attention to the destructive consequences of oscillating migration for family life. The prolonged absence of husbands and fathers was associated with high rates of conjugal breakdown and desertion; it induced a repetitive cycle of illegitimacy and instability in arrangements for rearing children; while the concentration of earning capacity among younger men subverted the authority of the senior generation. Monica Wilson's view, based on a lifetime's observation in central and southern Africa, is quite unequivocal: 'Migrant (oscillating) labour continuing over a long period of time and involving a substantial proportion of the population is, I believe, the single most destructive force in our society ... South Africa has lived on the capital of a very strong African family system and that capital has been squandered ...' (1975: 17–18). The present study of Lesotho confirms that a system in which large numbers of men spend long periods away at work, leaving their wives and children at home, generates economic insecurity, marital disharmony, material and emotional misery and problems relating to sexual morality and legitimacy of children irrespective of the cultural definition of these matters.

And yet there have been apparently conflicting views. Watson (1958) argued that tribal cohesion amongst the Mambwe of Zambia persisted not in spite of labour migration but because of the conditions under which Mambwe participated in the cash economy. There was a surplus of male labour arising out of the imposition of *pax Britannica* and the relative interchangeability of agricultural tasks between the sexes, so that co-operative labour relations were able to survive the absence of men. Migrants actively sustained their connections with their rural communities because their access to land there afforded them permanent security, by contrast with the endemic insecurity of life in the towns. Van Velsen (1959) reached a similar conclusion in his attempt to explain the 'apparent contradiction' between the exodus and return of large numbers of men who acquired new ideas, on the one hand, and the continued predominance of traditional values, on the other hand. Tonga migrants, he argued,

> do not fall back upon the security of a tribal social system which *happens* to have continued during their absence; the migrants themselves, during their absence, have been actively and consciously contributing to its continuance because they know that they have to rely on it when they are no longer usefully employed in their urban habitat (1959: 268, his emphasis).

How can these views be reconciled? Firstly, we should distinguish the domestic economies of northern Zambia and Malawi in the 1950s from those of what might be called the periphery in the narrow sense (Lesotho and the Bantustans) in the 1970s. The former had a much stronger agricultural base than the latter have today. Secondly, we should distinguish at least the following levels of analysis: (1) that of 'families' identified by reference to the individual household which contains a migrant and his immediate kin; (2) that of 'families' identified by reference to the wider kindred or the agnatic lineage; (3) that of the village or rural community as a whole; and (4) that of the larger political community defined by reference to the 'tribe' or to the territorial authority of a chief. Separation of these levels is a matter of analytical convenience only. The real consequences of a system based upon the premise, in Francis Wilson's words, 'that a human being can be broken into two parts: a "labour unit" working in town, separated from the other part – a man with parents and wife and children, with hopes and aspirations' (1972b: 188) reverberate through all levels of social aggregation. But it is possible that conclusions which apply at one level of analysis do not apply at another level. For example, Watson and van Velsen observed 'tribal cohesion', Monica Wilson and others have observed the destruction of families. A lively consciousness of ethnic

172

identity or a vigorous commitment to traditional values is surely not incompatible with the breakdown of family life, as is evident in the Bantustans. In any case, it is unrealistic to impute to a given population such uniformity of response as is implied in the notion of 'tribal cohesion', which weakly encapsulates a complex variety of social processes.

Thirdly, therefore, the apparent conflict of viewpoint clearly begs questions about the theoretical frameworks used to analyse conservation and change. The studies of both Watson and van Velsen have often been invoked to discredit the notion that a significant rate of out-migration either initiates or exacerbates a process which used to be described, misleadingly, as detribalization. But they have also, unwittingly, provided a rationale for complacency. For example, P. D. Banghart felt able to assure a conference on migrant labour at Umpumulo, Natal, in 1970, on the basis of a review of various studies in southern Africa:

I would like to reiterate that the effects migrant labour has on the homelands is [sic] not as great as most people like to think. I believe that this can be attributed to the generally conservative nature of the Bantu rural structure. In my research, both library and fieldwork, I found little or no evidence that labour migration is detrimental or disruptive, in any particular group's viewpoint. In most cases, I think, it can be shown that the opposite is the case, that labour migration has a stabilizing influence on the group and in particular on its social structure (1970: 102).

Banghart's views cannot be taken very seriously. But there is sufficient evidence of the persistence of custom in the periphery of southern Africa to pose the question whether custom persists in spite of or because of the transformations in social relations that have taken place. Those who make judgements about the relative integrity of a traditional social system misconceive the problem within a functionalist paradigm in which evidence of pathological breakdown is counterposed to evidence of continuity in or persistence of social relations, leading to conclusions which would appear to be mutually incompatible. On the other hand, those who recognize the fundamental transformations, yet also acknowledge the evidence for continuity, have to explain the systematic contradictions which generate the phenomena they observe.

Studies of migrant labour in the 1970s have been given further impetus by the new historiography in southern African studies, in which underdevelopment in the labour reserves of the rural periphery is analysed as a corollary of development in the South African industrial core (for references see Palmer and Parsons 1977; Ranger 1978). Migrant labour is no longer regarded as an extraneous or incidental phenomenon whose 'effects' can be analysed with respect to the integrity or otherwise of a traditional social system. Rather, it is regarded as a particular manifestation of a process of fundamental transformation which has been taking place in southern Africa for more than a hundred years, as a result of the penetration of capitalist relations of production under specific historical conditions. Detailed regional studies of migrant labour in historical perspective are now available for various parts of the periphery (in the wider sense): Mozambique (Maputo 1977); Zimbabwe (D. Clarke 1974, 1976; van Onselen 1976); Botswana (Kerven 1977; Cooper 1979a,b,c); and Namibia (Moorsom 1977). These studies convincingly demonstrate that capital accumulation has taken place in the core areas of southern Africa at the expense of the peripheral areas. Particular studies inside South Africa, of KwaZulu (Clarke and Ngobese 1975; Nattrass 1977) and the Transkei (Westcott 1977; Leeuwenberg 1977; Mayer 1980), amplify the picture of a fundamental structural imbalance in the regional economy.

This historical perspective transcends the increasingly refined attempts of economists such as Todaro (1971) to elaborate a theory of migration with reference to migrants' perception of income differentials between rural areas and urban areas (for further references see van Binsbergen and Meilink 1978). It is not necessary to pursue the point here, because criticism of neo-classical reductionism is a standard theme of radical critiques such as those of Magubane and O'Brien (1972) and Amin (1974). With respect to the question of the value of unpaid domestic labour, in Chapter 7, I have shown that 'explanation' of migration by reference to the motivations of people who migrate merely begs important questions about the structures of opportunity and constraint within which those individuals make their decisions. If only as a reminder of the transience of academic paradigms, however, it is perhaps salutary to recall that more than twenty years ago neo-classical economists such as Elkan (1959) and Barber (1959) played a notable part in rescuing *Homo oeconomicus africanus*, African economic man, from the obloquy of cultural stultification to which he had often been consigned in official reports and memoranda (cf. Houghton and Dagut 1972, 1973).

With regard to anthropology, the new historiography was broadly anticipated, perhaps, by Godfrey Wilson (1941–2) forty years ago. But it was not explicitly developed until recently (see for example van Binsbergen and Meilink 1978). In my view it implies a particular challenge for the anthropologist. On the one hand, it is no longer possible to apply paradigms of the sort that have been stimulating and influential in anthropological discourse, such as those of Gluckman (1950) and Ngubane (1977), without acknowledging simultaneous confinement within 'limits of naivete' that many students of southern Africa would find unacceptable today. On the other hand, the anthropological method of prolonged participant observation offers an invaluable opportunity of revising or elaborating, with appropriate empirical evidence, some of the rather abstract formulations proposed by the radical theorists of underdevelopment.

One such formulation is the 'dissolution/conservation contradiction', which I outlined in Chapter 5. This is an expression of the articulation of the capitalist mode of production with a pre-capitalist mode of production. Aspects of 'customary' behaviour in the labour reserve are identified as residual elements of the pre-capitalist mode which happen to be functional to the interests of capital. So long as they persist, it is difficult to discern, following this argument, at what point it would be possible to assert that a pre-capitalist mode no longer existed and that social relations were fully subsumed under capitalism. The suspicion remains, therefore, that advocates of this sort of theoretical dualism have implicitly endorsed an 'economism' that derives from 'the prior offence of capitalism in defining all relations in economic terms' and is accordingly deplored by some critics within the marxist tradition (E. Thompson 1978a).

There are at least three overlapping sets of theoretical issues involved here: (1) most narrowly, whether or not the notion of articulation of modes of production is useful in the southern African periphery (D. Webster 1978; Spiegel 1979; Foster-Carter 1978); (2) less narrowly, the question of how to interpret the concept of 'relative autonomy' in analyses of the South African state (Davies *et al.* 1976; Innes and Plaut 1978; S. Clarke 1978); and (3) most widely, the confrontation between 'grand theory' and 'socialist-humanism' which took place in some sectors of the British academic Left following the publication of Edward Thompson's polemic against Althusserian structuralism, *The Poverty of Theory* (1978b).[1]

My purpose has been to render an account of life in a southern African labour reserve in the 1970s rather than to elaborate these theoretical issues. But the facts of life do not 'speak for themselves'. This book represents a commitment to the importance of empirical detail but not to the pretence of empiricism with which, unfortunately, such a commitment is often confused. For I have tried to place the facts of life which confront members of rural communities in Lesotho in an analytical framework best defined as the political economy of migrant labour. It may be appropriate therefore to conclude with a brief statement of the wider implications of my analysis.

Firstly, in identifying the majority of Basotho as members of a rural proletariat, I assert that the conditions of their existence must be understood with primary reference to the development of industrial capitalism in South Africa. Secondly, these conditions are not derivative from the logic of capitalist accumulation 'in general'. Rather, they are derivative from the particular historical circumstances under which Basotho have been incorporated as wage labourers, together with their distinctive culture and their relative political autonomy, into the system of racial and class oppression in South Africa. Thirdly, 'traditional' social relations of hierarchy or of kinship should not be analysed as surviving elements, more or less functional to the interests of capital, of a non-capitalist or pre-capitalist mode of production. This would be to perpetuate the dualist illusion, albeit expressed in other terms, which I criticized in Chapter 1. Rather, the persistence or vitality of traditional social relations should be analysed as an integral aspect of more or less subtly conflicting processes of transformation.

Any analysis of the contemporary predicament of the Basotho must be duly sensitive to the changing face of apartheid and in particular to the question of whether southern Africa's vast rural proletariat can overcome the pressures of class fragmentation. These pressures are: (1) the imposition of multiple black nationalisms in South Africa itself; (2) the intensified division between permanent residents in 'white' South Africa and 'foreign' migrants and commuters; and (3) the conflicts of interest between the beneficiaries of ethnic nationalism on the one hand = the small peripheral elites = and its principal victims on the other hand = a steadily expanding relative surplus population (cf. Innes and O'Meara 1976; Legassick and Wolpe 1976). The notion of 'class suppression' is particularly helpful here. Several recent analyses have shown how conflicts in southern Africa which assume an overtly racial or ethnic form can be fruitfully interpreted in terms of mechanisms which suppress class consciousness and 'stunt' the emergence of a class through restricting its capacity to organize (E. Webster 1977; Phimister and van Onselen 1979). Shula Marks (1978) has shown likewise how a growing threat of proletarian consciousness amongst Zulu workers in the 1920s and 1930s induced a reversal of official attitudes towards the Zulu kingship and a deliberate promotion of the values associated with tribal tradition.

In describing Lesotho as an impoverished labour reserve I have deliberately drawn attention to the structural characteristics of southern Africa's rural periphery as a whole. In no way does this imply disrespect for the integrity of Lesotho as an independent nation state. Yet there are profound ambiguities in political autonomy combined with acute economic dependence. But for the Gun War one hundred years ago, in which the Basotho successfully resisted the Cape Government's attempt to disarm them, and which induced Britain to resume direct responsibility for Basutoland, it is likely that the constitutional history of Lesotho would have been very different. It may well have joined the Transkei, Bophuthatswana and Venda in the track of ethnic nationalism and the achievement of an abortive 'independence'. The parallels are obvious nevertheless: an overwhelming dependence on the export of labour; a debilitating preoccupation with domestic political rivalries and the suppression of internal dissidence; and a heavy reliance on foreign 'charity' = a massive international 'alms race' (Linden 1976) in the case of Lesotho, and hand-outs from 'white' South Africa in the case of the 'independent' Bantustans.

The Basotho have a justifiable pride in their long tradition of national resistance. But they are faced with larger and very difficult questions in the years to come. Can they develop a full historical consciousness of the structural processes which gave rise to the labour reserves? Can they transcend the social and political divisions which are explicit in the strategy of ethnic nationalism and implicit in the 'constellation of Southern African states' envisaged by South African prime minister P.W. Botha? In so doing, can they help to give political expression to the interests of southern Africa's rural proletariat as a whole? The answers to these questions will depend, in the first place, upon the evolving character of the post-colonial state. Subordinate as it is to the interests of foreign capital, and preoccupied as it is with repressing or co-opting internal opposition, the strategic possibilities for change, conceived within the confines of Lesotho's national autonomy, are very narrow. In the second place, therefore, the answers to the larger questions will depend upon the developing struggle within South Africa itself.

Appendix 1

Biographical notes on the
Thapelo family, Ha Molapo

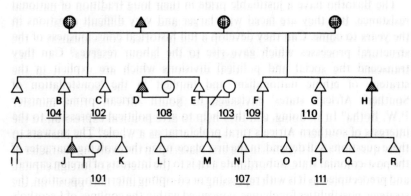

A.1 The Thapelo family

The genealogy above shows the male members (and wives where relevant) of the Thapelo family who were more than 15 years old in 1974 and identified as past or present members of households in Ha Molapo or one of the adjoining settlements. The founder of the family, of the Fokeng clan, came to settle in Ha Molapo from the Orange Free State in 1900, owing to the disruption caused by the Anglo-Boer war. The accompanying notes include date of birth (where known) and Ha Molapo household reference number, underlined where the individual concerned was household head in 1974, and in parentheses where the individual concerned was no longer a *de jure* household member.

House-hold	Date of birth	Brief biographical details
A		He has lived and worked at Standerton (Transvaal) since 1928. He visited Ha Molapo (104) briefly in October 1974.
B 104	1916	A retired migrant, he makes a living through cultivating his three fields and a brisk turnover in shoe-repairing. He also receives remittances from his unmarried son K and takes a prominent part in the affairs of the local Anglican congregation.
C 102	1918	After a career on the mines he appeared in 1974 to be 'retired' and working as a small-scale agricultural entrepreneur. His senior wife, who is childless, was in domestic service in Johannesburg. By 1978, however, she was at home and he was reported to have taken a further mine contract at Kuruman (asbestos), having been refused by the gold mines on account of his age.
D (108)		He died 'many years ago'. His childless widow (b. 1917) lives with her sister's grandson (b. 1967).
E (103)		He has not been seen in Ha Molapo for about twenty years, and his whereabouts are unknown. His deserted wife (b. 1928) is daughter of 'MaLebelo (116) and sister of Moeketsi (129). She continues to reside virilocally with her children, in the same village as her natal home. She receives remittances from M.
F 109	c. 1900	An elderly widower. Having contracted phthisis after long service in the mines, he retired many years ago with a lump sum of R400 as compensation. Remittances from his unmarried son O.
G 110	1914	The wealthiest stock owner in Ha Molapo, and an agricultural entrepreneur, he has achieved effective economic independence and stays at home permanently.
H		After a period of semi-retirement at home he resumed his migrant career in 1973. He took a job as a night watchman in Vereeniging (Transvaal) where he was murdered in August 1973.
I		A regular mine migrant.
J (101)		He died in June 1973 of a rapid wasting disease (undiagnosed). In 1978 his wife (b. 1944) had returned to the village with her children after a spell of work in South Africa. She claimed to be supported by her father-in-law B.
K 104		He left school in 1972 and took his first mine contract in April 1973, since when he has been a regular migrant. Still unmarried in 1978.

179

Appendix 1

House-hold	Date of birth	Brief biographical details
L (103)	1946	A migrant miner, he brought a girl home to be his wife in September 1973 but she left the household as soon as he departed on a new contract, finding his mother 'too fierce'. By 1978 he and his mother had bitterly quarrelled, he no longer had anything to do with her, and he had developed a liaison with an unmarried woman elsewhere in the village (146).
M 103	1957	In 1974 he was a youth in initiation school. In 1978 a migrant miner.
N 107	1937	He had been a migrant but was permanently and severely disabled in a mine accident. Having a large family, he ekes out a living in the village with the help of a substantial sum in compensation.
O 109	1940	An unmarried mine migrant, still resident in his father's household.
P 111	1944	A regular mine migrant. Married, he has built next door to his father's homestead.
Q		A regular mine migrant.
R		He took his first mine contract after his initiation in 1972.

Appendix 2

Bohali transfers recorded in twenty-eight marriages, Ha Molapo

Details of these *bohali* transfers are set out below. The first table (pp. 182–3) is a list of the items transferred, with dates of transactions (where known) and with their equivalence in cattle-units. The second table (p. 184) is a comparison of media of payment, over three periods: up to the 1930s (N = 5); 1955 to 1973 (N = 15); and the mid-1970s (N = 8). From this comparison may be inferred a steadily rising proportional constitution of *bohali* in cash (see Chapter 6). Names and household reference numbers are given, where appropriate, to allow cross-reference with information in the main text. The marriages themselves are also numbered, in chronological order. The letters m and f indicate sex of the individual concerned.

No.	Date of marriage	Date of transaction	Items transferred	Equivalent (in cattle-units)	Total	Cross-reference
1f	1914		10 cattle	10	10	'MaTau (116)
2m	1922	1922	4 cattle	4		
			2 cattle	2		
			1 horse	2		
			20 small stock	4	12	Levi (118)
3f	1931		11 cattle	11		
			1 foal	1	12	'MaSamuel (121)
4m	1937	1937	14 cattle	14		
		1937	2 cattle	2		Appendix 1,
			1 horse	2	18	G (110)
5m	1937		16 cattle	16		Malefetsane
			cash R6	1	17	(117)
6m	1955		small stock			
			cash	10		
		Feb. 1973	7 small stock	1		
			1 small stock			Serjeant (105)
		April 1973	cash R24	1	12	
7m	1958		2 cattle	2		
			2 horses	4		Elder brother
			cash R200	10	16	of Polao (135)
8m	1959		1 table			
			4 chairs	2		
			1 sewing machine	2		Sebata
			1 horse	1		(Appendix 3, S11)
			cash	3	8	
9f	1959	1959	4 cattle	4		
			2 horses	4		
			cash	2		Puseletso
			cash R10			(120)
		Nov. 1973	cash R120	4	14	
10m	1960	1960	2 horses	4		
			1 wedding outfit	1		
			cash R80	4		
		1963	cash R40	2		
		1965	cash R60	3		Polao (135)
		1970	cash R20	1	15	
11m	1960		7 cattle	7		Moeketsi (129)
			cash R160	8		(Appendix 3,
		Sept. 1973	cash R80	4	19	S48)
12m	1960		2 cattle	2		
		pre-1963	1 foal	1		
			1 saddle	1		
			4 small stock	1		
			cash R16	1		
		1972	1 donkey	1		Samuel (123)
			cash R20	1		
			cash R10			
			cash R30	1	9	

No.	Date of marriage	Date of transaction	Items transferred	Equivalent (in cattle-units)	Total	Cross-reference
13m	1962	1962	6 cattle	6		
			cash	2		Thabang (122)
			cash	2	10	
14m	1965	1965	5 cattle	5		
			4 sheep	1		
			1 horse	2		Levi's son
		1967	cash R36	1	9	(118)
15m	1966		cash R60	3	3	Mpoke (138)
						(Appendix 3, S16)
16f	1970		6 cattle	6		
			1 horse	2		
			3 donkeys	3		Sister of
			cash R40	2		Polao (135)
		June 1974	{ 1 cattle	1		
			{ 5 sheep	1	15	
17m	1970		2 cattle	2		Moeketsi (129)
			2 donkeys	2		marrying his
			cash R120	6	10	second wife
18m	1971	1972	{ 3 cattle	3		
			{ 2 horses	4		Teboho (130)
		1973	cash R300	15	22	
19m	1973	Aug 1973	cash R160	6	6	Renang (120)
20m	1973	Dec 1973	1 horse	1		
			cash R156	5	6	Mpho (142)
21m	1975		30 sheep	6		
			1 donkey	1		Edward (120)
			cash R160	4	11	
22m	1975	1975	cash R200 }			
		1977	cash R76 }	8	8	Thabo (172)
23f	1975		4 cattle	4		
			1 horse	1		received by
			cash R204	4		(110)
			cash R120	$1\frac{1}{2}$	$10\frac{1}{2}$	
24m	1976		cash R640	14	14	given by (139)
25f	1976		cash R300	8		received by
			10 goats	2	10	(103)
26f	1977		cash R200	4		daughter of
			1 donkey	1	5	Malefane
						(Appendix 3, S21)
27f	1977		cash R500	10	10	received by
						(139)
28f	1977		cash R400	8		daughter of
			1 horse	2		Polao (135)
			1 donkey	2		

Appendix 2

No.	Cattle	Horses/ donkeys	Small stock	Cash	Other Items	Total	Mean
1f	10	—	—	=	—	10	
2m	6	2	4	—	—	12	Period
3f	11	1	—	=	—	12	up to
4m	16	2	—	—	=	18	1930s
5m	16	—	=	1	—	17	
Total	59	5	4	1	—	69	13.8
%	(86)	(7)	(6)	(1)	—	(100)	
6m	—	—	6	6	—	12	
7m	2	4	—	10	—	16	
8m	—	1	—	3	4	8	
9f	4	4	—	6	—	14	
10m	—	4	—	10	1	15	
11m	7	—	—	12	—	19	
12m	2	2	1	3	1	9	
13m	6	—	—	4	—	10	Period
14m	5	2	1	1	—	9	
15m	—	—	—	3	—	3	1955 to
16f	7	5	1	2	—	15	
17m	2	2	—	6	—	10	1973
18m	3	4	—	15	—	22	
19m	—	—	—	6	—	6	
20m	—	1	—	5	—	6	
Total	38	29	9	92	6	174	11.6
%	(22)	(17)	(5)	(53)	(3)	(100)	
21m	—	1	6	4	—	11	
22m	—	—	—	8	—	8	
23f	4	1	—	$5\frac{1}{2}$	—	$10\frac{1}{2}$	Period
24m	—	—	—	14	—	14	
25f	—	—	2	8	—	10	1975 to
26f	—	1	—	4	—	5	
27f	—	—	—	10	—	10	1977
28f	—	4	—	8	—	12	
Total	4	7	8	$61\frac{1}{2}$	—	$80\frac{1}{2}$	10.1
%	(5)	(9)	(10)	(76)	—	(100)	

Note: All figures (except percentages) expressed in cattle-units. The 12 'cattle' in No. 6 made up of small stock and cash were arbitrarily assigned to small stock (6) and cash (6).

Appendix 3

The Letlala family, Ha Molapo

The various branches of this family that are domiciled today in Ha Molapo and adjoining settlements are all descended from Letlala and his younger brother Monyana, of the Sia clan. They were followers of Chief Molapo of Leribe, second son of Moshoeshoe I. The details of various disputes within the family are recorded here, with reference to the attached genealogy. The effective range and depth of the *lelapa* may be inferred from the summary which follows of the occasions in 1972–4 when I observed its members acting as 'children of Letlala'.

Of the sons of the first house of Letlala, Letsolo (Q1) died without male issue; Mota (Q2) was *ramotse* for a short time during the 1920s but subsequently emigrated to the Orange Free State, and the headmanship rights passed to Jack (Q4). Jack also left the village to settle in the remote Malibamatšo valley, in the steep ranges of the Maloti mountains to the east. Leohla (Q5) had previously emigrated to the Free State, where his only son died without issue. The headmanship therefore passed, laterally again in default of lineal heirs, to Rafutho (Q6). On the latter's death in the 1930s the family council (*khotla la lelapa*) acknowledged Kholu's (R3) right to succeed; and this arrangement was specifically ratified by Mpeli (R1), whose father Jack had by his 'removal' effectively abrogated his claim and that of his lineal heirs to exercise the *ramotse* rights in Ha Molapo. The rights were thenceforth heritable in the line of descent from Kholu exactly as if he had been the original holder.

Following the death of the area chief Molapo in 1928 there was a succession dispute between his son Mohlomi by his first (but commoner) wife and his surviving second wife who, as a sister of Motšoene, Jonathan's successor as Chief of Leribe, enjoyed the support of a powerful Koena faction. Motšoene, as head of the family council which met to resolve the succession, unsurprisingly decided in favour of his sister – a classic example of the decisive political weight of powerful affines following a father's-brother's-daughter-type marriage. However, on the failure of her house as a result of the death of her daughter-in-law without surviving issue in 1956, Mohlomi succeeded to the area chieftainship and ruled until his own death in 1964, when he was succeeded in his turn by his son Mosoang.

The details of this dispute in the ruling Koena clan are relevant to the events recorded below because the two protagonists were supported by different factions of the Letlala family. In particular, Phiri (R13), head of the second house of Letlala, had married Mohlomi's sister as his first wife and he later married his daughter as his third. Phiri exploited his close relations with Mohlomi in order to undermine Kholu's (R3) position as surviving local head of the senior house of Letlala and, therefore, as *ramotse*. Conflict between these two men, who were of an age, had flared up many years previously in the initiation lodge, over which of them should be scarified first with protective medicine – the order of precedence follows seniority in the family. On appeal to the Paramount Chief's (King's) court at Matsieng, the court upheld the 'official' version of the genealogy given here, namely that Letlala had married three wives (P1, P3 and P4) in that order and that their respective houses ranked accordingly first, second and third. The verdict therefore confirmed Kholu's legitimate tenure of the *ramotse* rights but the bitterness was transmitted to their successors and was manifest during fieldwork in 1972–4 in recurrent personal clashes between Kholu's youngest brother Morero (R6), who had become *ramotse*, and Phiri's eldest son and heir Sebata (S11). The terms of reference are their rival versions of descent from Letlala.

Sebata claims that his house is senior to that of Morero on the following grounds. Tsele, he asserts, was the senior brother of Letlala (P2) and Monyana (P5). Tsele died without male issue and his wife 'MaMolipe was taken over in the levirate (*kenelo*) by Letlala who had already married his own senior wife (P1). Molipe was born (genitor = Letlala, pater = Tsele). In due course Letlala married another wife (P4) with cattle belonging to the house of Molipe, thus infringing the principle that a man cannot marry with cattle belonging to a house other than his own. 'MaMolipe advised her adolescent son Molipe of this infringement and urged him to lay claim to Letlala's young wife on the grounds that she had been married with his (Molipe's) cattle. Molipe made sexual advances to her and was caught in the act by Letlala who shot him dead. 'MaMolipe insisted that Letlala marry a further wife, but to the name of Molipe (*lebitla*, a form of marriage 'for the grave' no longer sanctioned in customary law), so that his line should not die out. Letlala did so, and the offspring of this woman (P3) constitute the legitimate descendants of Tsele and are therefore senior to the descendants of Letlala's first house. Though plausible, this version is not even generally accepted within the second house of Letlala but is maintained only by Sebata who received it from his father Phiri. Both used the family name of Molipe, rather than Letlala, as an *ex post facto* device to justify their claim.

Morero, on the other hand, maintains that Tsele was in fact Letlala's father, and that Molipe was the offspring of a casual union of Letlala with a widow 'MaMolipe, quite independently of his three jurally established marriages to P1, P3 and P4. Accordingly Molipe, of whom elderly members of the family profess only the most scanty memory, has no place in the genealogy. However, as the Matsieng court pointed out, if they assumed for the sake of argument that Phiri was the legitimate descendant of Molipe in a collateral line senior to that of Letlala, then why did not Phiri go and take up his full political rights at Molipe's place? This rhetorical question clinched the argument in favour of Kholu's version, for everyone knows there is no place where Molipe's descendants have political rights. The *ramotse* rights at Ha Molapo are vested in the senior house of the Letlala family: the successor must be recruited from among the descendants of Letlala himself.

The decision of the court illuminates Phiri's dilemma. He could only claim

186

agnatic seniority to Kholu by denying his own descent from Letlala, the undisputed original holder of the rights, and therefore by opting out of the political competition for succession to those rights. Conversely, he could only retain a plausible claim to compete for the rights by accepting junior agnatic status in relation to Kholu. But the decision also demonstrates a fundamental aspect of political rights in Lesotho – that they are defined in relation to a particular territory and do not inhere in descent relations *per se*.

The corollary of this definition is that citizenship and descent are independent criteria of access to office. Citizenship derives from accepting the political authority of a chief, and is manifest in residence and payment of tax in that chief's area; it is not automatically ascribed by descent (cf. Fortes 1975). It follows that an individual can abrogate his citizenship in one area and offer allegiance to a chief in another area, although I suggested in Chapter 5 that land shortage throughout Lesotho now inhibits the freedom to 'remove' elsewhere. 'Removal' (*ho falla*) does not affect a man's membership of a *lelapa* with respect to inheritance rights, throwing earth at funerals and participation in family councils, although he is less likely for reasons of distance to maintain active ties in this manner. But a man cannot exercise political rights *in absentia*: his 'removal' from the area in which his family holds political rights effectively disqualifies him from eligibility to succeed to the office irrespective of the validity of his claim of descent. In such circumstances his claim does not die but remains dormant so long as he is not an active citizen of the area in question. Were he to 'remove' from elsewhere in Lesotho and take up citizenship in the original area he could revive his claim to succeed by descent. But the following case suggests that abrogation of Lesotho national citizenship may preclude a man and his descendants from reviving a claim by descent in this way.

Kholu died without surviving issue in 1959. The *ramotse* rights remained with his widow 'MaTseko (R2), who is said to have resented Morero because he was her husband's favourite. Aware of the antagonism between them, Morero's elder brother Likoto (R5), a resident of Vereeniging (Transvaal), arranged for his son Leboha (S2) to look after the widow 'MaTseko's interests. Leboha ran a taxi business in Maseru (see Figure 1.1) and seldom visited Ha Molapo. But he paid some medical bills on 'MaTseko's behalf and in 1968–9 he undertook the cash expenditure in a share-cropping contract she made with a third party, Malefetsane (117), in respect of the latter's field. 'MaTseko died before the harvest of 1969, but when Leboha came to Ha Molapo to recover her share of the crop he found that the yield had already been divided between Malefetsane and Morero. The latter presumed the right to appropriate 'MaTseko's share of the produce in his capacity as her heir, for he had already been confirmed as successor to the position of *ramotse* by resolution of the family council following 'MaTseko's death. It was this presumption on Morero's part that Leboha contested. Morero attempted to consolidate his position in 1973 through a formal application to the Chief of Leribe to be listed on the gazette of officially recognized headmen, a recognition which depends on the number of taxpayers in the area of jurisdiction. Leboha opposed the application on the grounds that he, Leboha, was the senior representative of the family, his father Likoto having died in 1972, and that the area chief of Ha Molapo had already recognized him as such when Likoto had formally introduced him in the 1960s. The issue concerns primarily criteria of citizenship and secondarily criteria of legitimacy of descent.

Likoto had been born in Harrismith (Orange Free State) in 1904 but, owing to the disruptions caused by the Anglo-Boer war, his family moved back in the same year to their original home at Ha Molapo in Lesotho, where Likoto grew up until he was 19 years old. Then he went to work in Vereeniging (Transvaal) and remained there permanently, lodging with a family there. He settled down with the woman of the house and had three children by her, without marrying her, for she never obtained a divorce from her husband. The only male child was Leboha, who grew up in Vereeniging but afterwards came to Lesotho to run a taxi business in Maseru.

In 1964, as a result of new immigration restrictions on aliens imposed by South Africa in 1963, Likoto requested a formal letter from the area chief of Ha Molapo to substantiate the facts that he had been born in South Africa, that he was a resident of Vereeniging and that he had married there; furthermore, he had never paid tax in Lesotho, and did not have a house in the village where his parents had settled. The letter constituted evidence to the South African authorities to the effect that Likoto was in every respect a citizen of the Republic, and its purpose was undoubtedly to secure his right to live and work in Vereeniging. Morero, literate, sophisticated and scrupulously aware of the importance of written evidence, had retained a copy of this letter, which in effect abrogated Likoto's citizenship rights in Lesotho and with them the right to assume the local headmanship in Ha Molapo.

Likoto died in Vereeniging in 1972. There was collusion between Leboha (S2) and Sebata (S11) who, as recorded above, had grievances of his own against Morero, over the funeral arrangements and over the disposal of Likoto's movable property. They acted without consulting Morero whose prerogative it was to make such arrangements, as senior agnate of the deceased. There was no explicit confrontation over these matters in 1972-4, but they were a lively source of antagonism between Morero and Sebata, the two senior resident members of the Letlala family. Leboha himself, as a self-employed business man in Maseru, was undoubtedly paying tax in Lesotho, but the status of his father is neverthe-less the critical factor. It seemed likely that, if the question of the *ramotse* rights went to court, the 1964 letter would prove definitive, being a denial by Likoto himself of the rights of citizenship in Lesotho, and positive evidence of his 'removal' from the area where he might otherwise have exercised political rights. Even if it did not prove definitive, however, Morero would argue that Leboha in any case had no right of succession because, although Likoto is known to be Leboha's genitor, he never married Leboha's mother, either by civil process or by the transfer of *bohali*.

This case illustrates the manner in which families may be dispersed throughout Lesotho and the Republic. Morero's own sons (S4, S5) both live and work with their families in Natalspruit (Transvaal) and take no active part in family affairs in Ha Molapo, so that Morero is the only representative of the first house of Letlala who is resident in the village. Until his death in 1978, his position as *ramotse* was one of isolated eminence, threatened by the numerical preponder-ance of men who belong to junior houses. The demographic dispersal which arises from the economic pressure to migrate has the effect of stressing the important principle that rights of succession to office, which appear to be defined by criteria of agnatic descent, do not exist *in vacuo* and must be validated by the primary criterion of citizenship.

Nor was the rest of the *lelapa* immune from similar conflicts. In the branch descended from Letlala's younger brother Monyana (P5), Tlokotsi's (Q16) widow 'MaMuso (Q15) had refused to be taken in the levirate by his younger brother RaNtja (Q18) on the grounds of indignity, since it was she who had brought him up. She had one son Kotsi (R19). Nevertheless, in lieu of a leviratic arrangement, she approved RaNtja's use of cattle from her house to marry another wife, whose children would be affiliated to Tlokotsi. RaNtja already had his own wife 'MaNanai (Q17) and children, but he married another woman 'MaThabo (Q19) supposedly to Tlokotsi's name. The seniority of 'MaThabo's house was apparently recognized for a generation, for it was her son Thabo (R27) who in due course undertook arrangements for the burial of Kotsi (R19) and slaughtered a beast for his funeral, a prerogative of the closest agnate of the deceased. In the following generation, however, it appears that 'MaNanai's sons (R21, 22, 24, 26), who were considerably older than Thabo and resented their junior genealogical status, were able to assert successfully that their father had in fact married 'MaThabo to his own name and not to that of his elder brother Tlokotsi; and, accordingly, that Thabo belonged to the second house of RaNtja. The *de facto* precedence of 'MaNanai's house is now apparent in the order of throwing earth at funerals and it is accepted as senior to Thabo's house by the majority of the family. In 1973–4 only one elderly woman (S30) claimed accurate knowledge of the circumstances which justify the reverse position in strict law. The issue, however, is not a live one for the 'privileges' involved are insubstantial. Neither house is in a position to compete for the office of *ramotse* which is vested in the senior collateral branch of the family; while both vicariously experience the prestige of belonging to the politically and numerically dominant family in Ha Molapo.

These circumstances illustrate the potential confusion which arises from transgression of the principle that 'houses do not eat each other'. The disposal by one house of animals belonging to another house, for *bohali* or other purposes, almost invariably causes trouble between those houses, sooner or later, for 'a debt does not decay' (*molato ha o bole*). Phiri's (R13) conduct of marital affairs was notoriously unscrupulous in this respect and he created a lasting legacy of ill feeling. 'He was very good at receiving *bohali*', his surviving third wife 'MaKoena remarked drily, 'and not so good at paying it out'.

Phiri's elder sister (R11) had been 'married' in the Orange Free State but, on the death of her husband, she returned to Lesotho and her two daughters were brought up in the household of Phiri, their mother's brother (*malome*). He was thus the arbiter of their marriages. He received twelve cattle from the marriage of his younger niece Selloane (S8) but refused to slaughter the ox of *tlhabiso* for her husband's kin because, he said, 'the cattle were too few'. Some years later, however, his own senior son Sebata (S11) married Selloane's husband's sister (S10). Instead of transferring *bohali* cattle, Phiri quickly pressed for both parties to slaughter the ox of *tlhabiso* to seal a bargain of mutual exchange = not an arrangement of which he could boast. Selloane's husband's people refused, not unreasonably insisting that Phiri should transfer twelve cattle first, but there the matter rested. Phiri died in 1962. In 1973 Selloane, who had been immobilized

Appendix 3

The structure of the Letlala *lelapa*, Ha Molapo, defined in terms of participation in family affairs (numbers refer to genealogy pp. 192–3).

Event	Date
1 Signatories to decision of family council which met to determine the succession to the *ramotse* rights following the death of R2	8/4/69
2 Meeting of family council to resolve dispute between R6 and R8 over the former's right to safeguard a lump sum in cash which the latter received in compensation for the death of her husband R9 in a road accident	20/12/72
3 Family summoned by R6 for ritual head-shaving, in mourning for an agnate in the (Q4) branch of the family which removed to the Malibamatšo valley	19/3/73
4 Feast of *tlhabiso* in respect of marriage of R48: (a) men's party set off to his affines' village with final instalment of *bohali*; (b) women's party: initial prayer at home	28/9/73
5 Two meetings of family council to resolve dispute between S24 and S25 following their mother's (R17) unilateral disposal of her field to S25	13/5/73 9/6/73
6 Witnesses to written agreement made at the feast of *tlhabiso* in respect of the marriage of Alice, daughter of S32	25/11/73
7 Funeral of S25. Order of throwing earth on the grave reflects genealogical seniority within each generation. R6 was the last to throw, as only surviving male in R generation and as head of the *lelapa*	4/74
8 Meeting to resolve disputes between S16 and S17 over disposition of household goods following their divorce	5/7/74

190

Gen	Agnates Males	Females	Wives	Remarks
R	16			
S	1 16 21 24 25			
R	6			There was alleged to be a secret letter denouncing the conduct of R6, signed by all of S generation indicated here
S	11 16 24 38 39 46 47			
R	6		17	
S	11 24 25 39		19 40 43 45 49	
R			7 28	Women's prayer led by S32 as senior 'wife' of the junior (P5) branch of the family. Married 'daughters' also took part
S	24 25 35 36 39 42 50	30 33	32 45	
R	6		17 23 28	
S	11 24 25 39		29 45 49	
R				Seniority and numbers not significant here but participation indicates range of interest
S	21 34 39 42			
R	6			S21 refused to throw earth after S16 on account of inter-house seniority dispute (for details see text)
S	11 16 38 39 41 42			
R	6		7 15	Seven unrelated neighbours also took part in the meeting
S	16 18 21 34 42 49 50		17 19	

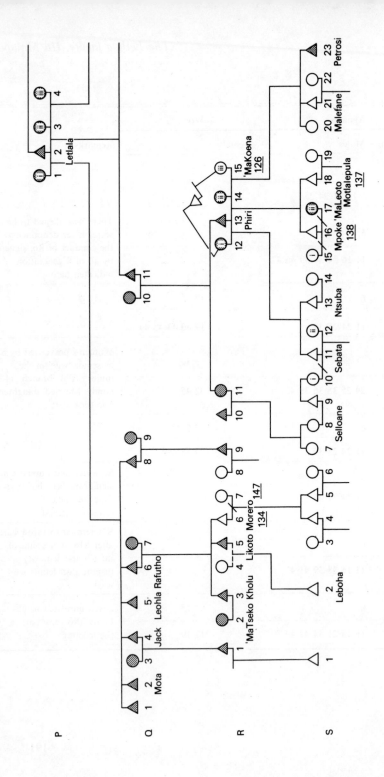

A.3 The Letlala *lelapa*, Ha Molapo

for two years with 'bodily pains', went to a diviner who diagnosed the reason for her affliction as Phiri's failure to finish the original marriage contract by slaughtering the ox of *tlhabiso*. Confronted with Selloane's husband's request that he finish the matter, Sebata could not refuse to comply, especially since he had paid no cattle for his own wife who had gone off to Johannesburg without trace many years previously. Nevertheless he replied that he had no animals, which was true. So anxious was Selloane's husband to bring relief to his wife that he gave Sebata an ox and the feast of *tlhabiso* for Selloane's marriage took place at Sebata's home in September 1973, thirty-eight years after the date of their marriage.

Phiri also created inter-house debts. The respective heirs of his three houses were actively involved in family politics: Sebata (S11) of the first house was a permanent resident of the village, while both Mpoke (S16) of the second house and Malefane (S21) of the third spent extended periods in the village during 1972–4, between spells of migrant labour. But relations between them were so confounded by the effects of their father's manipulations that they were seldom able to present a united front vis-à-vis Morero in respect of the larger issues, related above, which concerned the *lelapa* as a whole.

Phiri had disposed of cattle accruing to his second house from the marriage of Mpoke's sister by making a contribution towards the marriage of Malefane in the third house. In order to help Mpoke (second house) to marry he used some cattle from the first house. The latter action mollified Mpoke's grievance over the original transgression but also created a new inter-house debt. Sebata, the heir in the first house, wanted this repaid but Mpoke insisted on settlement of the debt outstanding from the third house before he could himself repay the first house. It was this debt that prompted Sebata to 'give' 'MaLeoto to Mpoke under circumstances fully described in Chapter 7. Malefane resented Sebata's interference but he had a separate reason for quarrelling with Mpoke. He claimed that Phiri had married his mother 'MaKoena as a substitute (*seantlo*, 'sister' marriage) for his first wife (R12) on the latter's death. These women were, respectively, sister and father's sister to Mosoang, the area chief of Ha Molapo. As chiefs' daughters, they ranked higher than Mpoke's mother who was a commoner. Accordingly, in Malefane's view 'MaKoena's house should be granted the precedence attaching to the first house. This argument is no longer legally viable in view of the present reluctance of the judicial authorities to accept that a *seantlo* union can interfere with the ranking established by the chronological order of marriages (Poulter 1976: 160).

Notes

Chapter 1 From granary to labour reserve

1. Heights are given in metres in the text to conform with modern practice. Almost all existing maps of Lesotho show contour heights in feet (hence Fig. 1.1). However, a new edition of the 1:250,000 map was published in 1978, with metric contours.
2. 1976 census, preliminary figures, Bureau of Statistics, Maseru.
3. There are two recent biographies of Moshoeshoe which cover this early period in the nation's history. See Sanders (1975) and L. Thompson (1975).
4. See especially Basutoland (1958), Spence (1968), Khaketla (1971), Weisfelder (1971), Breytenbach (1975) and Ström (1978).
5. The Lesotho Order No. 13 of 1973, dated 13 April, provided that the Assembly should consist of
   (a) the twenty-two Principal and Ward chiefs;
   (b) 'sixty persons nominated by the King acting on the advice of the Prime Minister provided that before tendering advice to the King in that behalf, the Prime Minister shall have consulted such persons as are in his opinion representative of the various shades of political opinion in Lesotho'; and
   (c) eleven persons, nominated in the same manner, who 'have rendered distinguished service to Lesotho and who have knowledge of matters affecting the various interests of the inhabitants of Lesotho'.
6. See CB (569–71) and Sanders (1975: 238, 242) for maps illustrating the complex history of successive boundary-making between Lesotho and the Free State.
7. The principal sources are CB; the Cape Parliamentary Papers (Burman 1976); the Colonial Annual Reports on Basutoland (CARs) in British Parliamentary Papers (1882–1919) and in Colonial Office Publications (1920–65); the Pim Report (Pim 1935); the Morse Report (Morse 1960); and recent statistical material available from the Bureau of Statistics, Maseru. I am also indebted to the following secondary reviews of the primary sources: Leys (1979), Spray (n.d.) and Kimble (1976).
8. The Keiskammahoek Rural Survey report found that production in a drought year (1948–9) was only one twentieth of the consumption requirement, estimated at 20 bags of maize per annum per family of 5.8 persons,

195

while in the relatively good season of 1949–50 production was less than half the consumption requirement. The report concluded that 'without the income from migrant labour, the vast majority of the families would starve. Cash surpluses from migrant-labour earnings in the cities constitute from one-third to one-half the family's total annual cash income of about £45' (Houghton and Walton 1952: 159, 183).

9. Calculated from figures available in the Annual Statistical Bulletins. The five-year rolling average has the effect of suppressing extraordinary inter-seasonal fluctuations.

10. For references on and discussion of these points see Turner (1978) and Chapter 3 below.

11. It is not easy to estimate the total number of migrants. For informed guesses from which this figure is derived, see van der Wiel (1977) and Wykstra (1978).

12. This legislation is extremely complex. The best recent summaries may be found in Horrell (1978) and Davis (1978). Some case histories which illustrate the appalling consequences for individuals of the rigid enforcement of the provisions of Section 10 (1) are published in Black Sash (1974).

13. In February 1980 the government announced that the 72-hour 'curfew' in Section 10 (1) would be suspended on a trial basis in Pretoria and Bloemfontein, following the recommendations of the Riekert Commission (*Guardian*, 6 February 80).

14. The validity of these findings must be qualified by the fact that average annual cash earnings relate to man-years of labour, not to the earnings of particular migrants. Their accuracy for Basotho miners depends on their average length of service and also on whether or not they are representative of all miners in terms of their distribution between occupational grades. The average length of service for Basotho miners was 12.1 months in 1975 and only 10.6 months in 1976 (van der Wiel 1977: 43).

15. The question of the level of structural unemployment in South Africa is discussed in the *South African Labour Bulletin* (SALB) 4, No. 4, July 1978.

16. For sources see SALB 3, No. 9, November 1977, and SALB 5, No. 4, November 1979.

17. A summary and critique of Wiehahn may be found in SALB 5, No. 2, August 1979, and of Riekert in SALB 5, No. 4, November 1979.

18. National Press Club, Washington D.C., Lunch meeting on 15 June 1979.

19. One official expression of this was a speech in 1976 by R. F. ('Pik') Botha, then South African Ambassador to the United Nations and now South Africa's Minister of Foreign Affairs:

> The problem in Southern Africa is basically not one of race, but of nationalism, which is a world-wide problem. There is a White nationalism, and there are several Black nationalisms ... My Government's principal aim is to make it possible for each nation, Black and White, to achieve its fullest potential, including sovereign independence, so that each individual can enjoy all the rights and privileges which his or her community is capable of securing for him or her (*The Star*, Johannesburg, 2 July 76).

196

Dugard (1979) has clearly analysed the fraud involved in terms of the concepts of international law.

20. The gold price reached 500 dollars an ounce in December 1979 and, briefly, 800 dollars in January 1980. The recent gold bonanza is expected to stimulate economic growth in South Africa. There is no evidence that it will be used by the South African state to alleviate the appalling conditions of over-crowding, poverty and unemployment in the black rural areas. Indeed, these conditions are being deliberately reproduced.

21. The text was completed before I had the opportunity of reading the recent substantial ILO report (JASPA 1979) on Lesotho, *Options for a Dependent Economy*. One of its major emphases was the establishment of a regional association of labour-supplying states which would negotiate with the mining companies and if necessary with the South African government on 'uniform attestation fees, more flexible arrangements for deferred pay, regular paid return visits (home), comprehensive sickness benefits, old-age pension payments, pay-as-you-earn taxation of migrants' earnings, general improvements of working and living conditions, and, finally, higher wages' (JASPA 1979: 75–6). No formal suggestion has yet been made that such an association should include the 'independent' South African Bantustans.

Chapter 2 Migrant labour: a way of life

1. In view of the volatile nature of politics in a small country of which it is not mere hyperbole to assert that everyone knows everyone else, and in view of the obligation of the anthropologist to protect his sources, I have judged it best to preserve their anonymity. Well-known chiefs and place names are not disguised, as will be apparent to anyone who knows Lesotho.

2. Some earlier information on these points is available in McDowall (1973).

3. To facilitate cross-reference throughout the text I have identified individuals as members of numbered households. The first digit in the number refers to the village to which the household belongs. Thus, for example, households in Ha Molapo (village no. 1) are numbered from 101 to 173. The listing relates to the surveys carried out in 1974 (see Table 2.1). Where the individual concerned is head of the household, the reference number is underlined.

4. The terms 'rate' and 'incidence' are here used in what I construe as their common senses, which correspond neither with Mitchell's well-known (1959) distinction between 'rate' and 'incidence' in the study of labour migration nor with the usage conventional in epidemiology or statistical demography. It may be helpful to illustrate the differences. In 'common sense' usage incidence refers to a synchronic frequency distribution, such that the incidence of smoking may be compared between the sexes or between social classes, or the incidence of absenteeism of male labour migrants may be compared between age strata or between administrative districts, at any one time. Thus, Mitchell (1975) writes of *rates* of male absenteeism in Rhodesia but he is properly referring to its *incidence* between districts, since the figure for each

197

district is

$$\frac{(E-P)}{E} \times 100$$

where E is the expected number of males in the age stratum $16\frac{1}{2}$–46 years, derived from a standard population, and P is the actual number of males in that age stratum, derived from the 1962 census. By contrast, the rate of labour migration would properly have a time-period reference, such that X per cent of a particular population went away on migrant labour during a specified period, say one year.

Epidemiologists and statistical demographers distinguish between *incidence*, with a temporal reference, and *prevalence*, with a spatial reference, while both are loosely referred to as rates. Thus, the incidence of measles in a given population would refer to the weekly, monthly, seasonal or annual variation in numbers of people contracting the disease. The prevalence of measles would refer to the number of people who had contracted the disease in a given period in various areas or administrative sub-divisions of a population. Applied to labour migration, incidence in this sense would refer, for example, to variation in the number of migrants recruited at different seasons of the year; prevalence would correspond to Mitchell's (1975) use of rate and my 'common sense' use of incidence.

5. For example, Mr Dennis Etheredge of the Anglo American Corporation claimed in September 1978 that '56 per cent of Basotho mine workers visit their homes every 6 weeks' (*Lesotho Weekly*, 21 September 78) as a result of the introduction of a fortnightly shift system and the proliferation of direct taxi services between Lesotho and the Corporation's mines at Welkom in the Orange Free State.

6. Spiegel's distribution (1979: 53) for 83 households in Qacha's Nek district is slightly different but, I would argue, justifies the same distinction between 'small' and 'large' households.

7. This explains why, in an earlier published attempt to work out dependency ratios (Murray 1978: 136), children less than 15 years old were not identified as a separate category of dependants. Their inclusion as 'dependants' in Table 2.3 is not, of course, intended to suggest that their labour does not make an important contribution to household activities. The question of the value of unpaid domestic labour is considered in Chapter 7.

8. Further detailed evidence is available in Spiegel (1979) and Judy Gay's forthcoming (1980) Ph.D. thesis, University of Cambridge.

9. A form of pollution known as *seqoma* is thought to attach to a child born following a still-birth or death in infancy. Such a child always carries a prominent tuft of hair left unshaven at the back of the head. This tuft must be shaved prior to initiation and the ritual to remove the pollution (*ho tlosa seqoma*) should be performed by the child's mother's brother, the true *malome*. This involves ritual washing with gall and an animal must be slaughtered for the purpose.

Chapter 3 Managing the land

1. For detailed examples of particular placings and their consequences see Ashton (1952: 186–221), Jones (1966) and Hamnett (1975: Appendix 1).
2. *Paballo* was an administrative arrangement whereby lands within one chief's territorial boundaries were ceded for the temporary or permanent use of subjects of another chief. An edict from the Paramountcy repudiating any legal recognition of *paballo* was incorporated into the revised (1959) edition of the *Laws of Lerotholi* (Duncan 1960: 70–3; 150–1).
3. Sections 7 (2) and 7 (3) of the 1973 edition. In view of the prevailing shortage of land, inspections based on the second provision must have reference to principles of equity rather than to criteria of adequacy for 'subsistence'. For a discussion of the status of the *Laws of Lerotholi* in the legal system of Lesotho, see Poulter (1972).
4. For example, use of these under experimental conditions has been shown to increase maize yields dramatically, from an average of about 3 (200 lb) bags per acre on an unimproved holding to perhaps 12 bags per acre (Williams 1972: 16). But such yields depend on the coincidence of favourable conditions and have not been consistently maintained.
5. In his analysis of the Senqu project, John Gay drew attention to 'the serious and obvious flaw that no arrangements have yet been made for competent local farmers to manage the land and livestock of those who have left the village to earn money' (1977: 27).
6. In seeking to explain the importance of contract among the Birwa of Botswana, Mahoney argued that

> contracts among close kin are made only in regard to specific kinds of transactions and that the purpose of the transacting parties is one of insulating that aspect of their relationship which is characterized by freely given assistance and in which no one counts the cost, from transactions which all hold to be potentially disruptive and which are a regular cause of complaint and dispute. The circumstances of production in neighbourhood sets are such that generous exchanges and potentially disruptive transactions have to be made between the same people. It is here that contracts can be effective (1977: 62).

This argument is much more convincing than Wallman's attempt to explain 'the unexpected non-use of kinship as a consistent organizing principle in Lesotho' (1975: 331). Wallman rightly observed the pragmatism of Basotho in making share-cropping arrangements; but she implausibly invoked a typology of discrete behavioural motivations to explain this: three principles identified as kinship, a-kinship and anti-kinship. Such a typology begs more questions than it answers. Firstly, the dividing line between kin and non-kin is an arbitrary one. Secondly, the moral weight of kinship varies between particular relationships. Thirdly, she wrongly supposed that these principles are mutually exclusive. It is impossible to determine with any confidence whether particular partners interact because they are kin (the kinship principle), because it is mutually convenient (the a-kinship principle), or because they are not kin (the anti-kinship principle).

7. This summary relates to arrangements observed in Ha Molapo in the 1972–3 and 1973–4 agricultural seasons. They are not necessarily typical of Lesotho as a whole. For other detailed accounts see Sheddick (1954), Turner (1978) and Spiegel (1979). For comparable studies elsewhere in southern Africa, see Curtis (1972) for south-eastern Botswana, and Holy (1977) for a Tonga-speaking part of Zambia.

8. The inadequacy of agricultural production in the periphery is commonly assessed against estimates of grain requirements per household per annum. But both production and consumption estimates, on which elaborate policies of agricultural improvement are based, can be extravagantly inaccurate, as Merle Lipton (1977) has shown. The following examples illustrate the range of discrepancy in estimates of consumption requirements in Lesotho:

   (a) a Basutoland Government official estimate that a family of 5 persons requires 20 bags of grain per annum to meet subsistence requirements (Wallman 1969: 75);

   (b) a recent estimate by a project evaluation team that the average *de facto* household of 4.4 persons in rural Lesotho requires 14 bags of grain per annum to meet its energy requirements (Feachem et al. 1978: 19);

   (c) my own estimate that the average *de facto* household of 4.4 persons in rural Lesotho requires 7 bags of grain per annum to meet *that proportion* of its calorie requirements that can properly be met by the consumption of maize meal, according to a localized FAO construction of the dietary requirements of the 'reference' man (Marres and van der Wiel 1975: 28). Other food resources are of course necessary to constitute an adequately balanced diet.

   The comparison shows that estimates of 'subsistence' needs made on such a basis can convey significantly different impressions of the inadequacy of agricultural output. In any case the actual variation in age and sex composition of the household and the frequency distribution of rural household sizes (see Figure 2.3) render the concept of the 'average' household somewhat absurd in this context.

9. These figures are based on self-assessment by the household head or household manager. No attempt was made to check their accuracy, and as records of crop yields they are susceptible to all the uncertainties discussed by Lipton (1977).

10. One Sesotho acre is approximately, but not consistently, 12×100 paces. The difficulties of converting indigenous measurement in Sesotho acres into English acres are discussed by Wallman (1965) and Helman (1973: Appendix C). Helman has stated that the conversion will depend on 'the method of measurement used, the average length and width of fields and their shape'. He found that the average size of 84 fields measured in the Leribe district was 7.2 Sesotho acres and 3.2 English acres, though the correlation varied with size of field.

200

Chapter 4 Differentiation, poverty and class formation

1. It is not fully specified how the calculations were made but information in van der Wiel's (1977) Appendix B may be summarized as follows:
   (a) Income from crops was calculated by imputing a market value to all crops produced (using producers' prices obtained from the Produce Marketing Corporation), and subtracting the cost of inputs in the form of hire charges (real or imputed) and of seed and fertilizer (prices obtained from Co-op Lesotho; estimates used for use of own seed).
   (b) Income from livestock was calculated by using the Livestock Marketing Corporation's standardized estimates of the annual net return per adult animal.
   (c) Migrant income was calculated by using average occupational wage norms in cash (i.e. *excluding* income received in kind in the Republic of South Africa but *including* cash income spent by the migrant himself in South Africa).
   It should be borne in mind that, while the inclusion of a migrant as a *de jure* member of a rural household is essential to its material integrity, inclusion of *all* his cash earnings as household income greatly exaggerates the income disposable by and on behalf of the *de facto* rural household. See discussion on this point in Chapter 7.
2. The 1974 figure is taken from an unpublished survey of farm household income in the Thaba Bosiu Rural Development Project area. The 1970 figure is the World Bank's estimate for Lesotho as a whole (IBRD 1975: 40).
3. For the method of construction of the PDL in Lesotho, see Marres and van der Wiel (1975), and for a theoretical evaluation of methods of measuring poverty, see Townsend (1979).
4. For discussion on this point I am indebted to David Cooper who has developed a similar argument in a series of stimulating working papers (1979a,b,c) on labour migrants, wage differentials and patterns of investment in livestock and agriculture in Botswana.

Chapter 5 Changing family structure

1. See, for example, Thomas (1973), Clarke and Ngobese (1975) and Leeuwenberg (1977) in addition to other sources cited in this Chapter.
2. Sheddick (1954: 21) explained this as follows: 'A man's parents will remind him that he must treat his wife reasonably well because he is after all only her guardian; that she really belongs to them by virtue of the fact that they provided the *bohali* payment; and furthermore that her children are in fact their children.' This statement fairly represents Sesotho 'custom', but precisely because parents seldom provide *bohali* cattle nowadays (see Chapter 6) it does not explain why so many children live with their grandparents.
3. M. Wilson (1969: 76–7); Curtis (n.d: 76); Comaroff (1973: 136); Murray (1976: 161–80); Cooper (1979a: 12–13).
4. The summary which follows is based on an analysis fully set out elsewhere. See my chapter on 'Kinship: continuity and change' in Lye and Murray (1980).

5. In his study of succession disputes among the Tshidi Rolong of Bophuthatswana, John Comaroff (1978) has shown that the winner 'fixes' the official genealogy so as to legitimize his accession.

6. In Botswana there are population movements taking place of such variety and complexity as to vitiate facile generalization. These are (a) regular oscillating migration to work in South Africa; (b) traditional seasonal movement between villages and lands; (c) a drift 'outwards' to more permanent settlement at the lands; (d) a drift 'inwards' to the large tribal capitals and particularly to the 'new' urban centres of employment; and (e) partial disintegration of the ward as a political and social entity. The results of the National Migration Study of 1977–80 are expected to clarify the dynamics and the relative scale of these movements.

7. See Monica Wilson's important generalization .of process: 'Only the combination of patrilineal descent, polygyny and marriage with cattle allows wealthy lineages to increase fast at the expense of the poor' (1969: 79).

Chapter 6 Marital strategy: an essay in custom and conflict

1. See Poulter (1976) and the decision in Maqutu v. Hlapane (Lesotho Civil Appeal No. 1 of 1971) reported in the *Journal of African Law* 17 (1973), 307–9.

2. For idealized accounts of the traditional sequence of marriage ceremonies, see Ellenberger and Macgregor (1969: 272–7) and Ashton (1952: 66–9).

3. See Murray (1975) for a full exegesis.

4. This is derived from the Sesotho method of counting by which the index finger of the right hand, the 'pointing' finger, is used to denote seven. Hence *likhomo tse supileng*, seven cattle, from the verb *ho supa*, to point. To point at someone in this way is very insulting.

5. More commonly described as the sheep of 'agreement' (*fomo*), it often accompanies the ox of *tlhabiso*, but many Basotho describe it as a piece of Setebele (Nguni) custom.

6. The term *nyatsi* is commonly translated as 'concubine'. This is unsatisfactory since it is used irrespective of sex to refer to either partner in a sexual or conjugal relationship that on the one hand is not merely casual or transient but on the other hand is not sanctioned by customary law. Its distinctive connotation is of an extra-marital affair and the word is used whether the relationship is irregular and clandestine or regular and overt.

7. This is one form of 'strong' patriliny. Subsequent debate (cf. Lewis 1965) was concerned *inter alia* with distinguishing another form of 'strong' patriliny, in which sibling solidarity prevails over the conjugal bond.

8. For references see Goody (1971).

9. There appears to be more evidence to support this proposition than to controvert it. See, for example, Watson (1958: 40–2), Kuper (1970: 472, 477) and M. Wilson (1976). The main Tswana tribes appear to be exceptional to the general trend in this respect.

10. In the course of their subtle and convincing analysis of the transformations that have occurred in the perception and treatment of extra-marital sexuality

among the Kgatla, Comaroff and Roberts insisted, rightly, that

> History does not occur in a cultural vacuum; to ascribe the particularities of the Kgatla situation to the generalities of sub-continental material processes is to end the analysis where it should properly begin... In order to explain the Kgatla variant, therefore, it is necessary to examine certain critical aspects of the cultural logic which underpins their marriage system (1977: 112).

Yes. But they propose a false antithesis between Kgatla cultural particularities, on the one hand, and the generalities of sub-continental material processes, on the other hand. For the generalities to which they refer are best exemplified through study of their impact on particular communities. Accordingly I would reverse their dictum and insist that culture cannot be studied in a historical vacuum. I have elaborated this view in my introduction to Lye and Murray (1980).

Chapter 7 Women at home and at work

1. Little systematic study has been carried out of the disposition of women's labour time, in Lesotho or in any other part of the periphery. The figure cited here is derived from time budgets for 57 women at various seasons of the agricultural year, compiled by a team responsible for evaluating the effects of a rural water supply programme (Feachem *et al.* 1978). Observation of 79 woman-days revealed the following distribution of time in the average woman-day:

water collection	13 mins;
household work (cleaning, washing, cooking, etc.)	391 mins;
agricultural work	142 mins;
social and leisure activity (eating, resting, visiting)	312 mins.

2. This percentage figure is surprisingly consistent, cf. van der Wiel (1977: 37) and Wykstra (1978: 14).
3. Further details of 'informal sector' activities, particularly *bonyatsi* and *litokofele*, are contained in Spiegel (1979).
4. For a representative sample of the 'new home economics', see the *Journal of Political Economy* 81, 2 (II), March/April 1973, and 82, 2 (II), March/April 1974; and for a review of its development and recent trends, see Cawhill (1976).

Chapter 8 Changing perspectives on migrant labour

1. See especially the contributions by R. Johnson, McLelland, Williams, McLennan and S. Clarke, respectively in *History Workshop Journal* No. 6, 1978, and Nos. 7 and 8, 1979.

Bibliography

Adams, R. N. 1971. 'The nature of the family.' In *Kinship*, ed. J. Goody. Harmondsworth: Penguin Books.

Amin, S. 1974. Introduction to *Modern Migrations in West Africa*, ed. S. Amin. London: OUP for the International African Institute.

Arbousset, T. 1968. *Narrative of an Exploratory Tour to the North-East of the Colony of the Cape of Good Hope*. Cape Town: Struik. Facsimile reprint of 1846 edition.

Arrighi, G. 1973. 'Labour supplies in historical perspective: A study of the proletarianization of the African peasantry in Rhodesia'. In *Essays in the Political Economy of Africa*, G. Arrighi and J. Saul. Monthly Review Press.

ASB. *Annual Statistical Bulletins*, 1966–78. Maseru: Bureau of Statistics.

Ashton, E. H. 1939. A sociological sketch of Sotho diet. *Transactions of the Royal Society of South Africa* 27, Part II, 147–214.

1946. 'The social structure of the Southern Sotho ward'. University of Cape Town: Communications from the School of African Studies (New Series No. 15).

1952. *The Basuto*. London: OUP for the International African Institute.

Banghart, P.D. 1970. 'The effects of migrant labour on the social structure of the Bantu homelands'. In *Migrant Labour and Church Involvement*. Umpumulo: Missiological Institute.

Barber, W. J. 1959. 'Economic rationality and behaviour patterns in an under-developed area: a case study of African economic behaviour in the Rhodesias'. *Economic Development and Cultural Change* 8, 2, 237–51.

Barker, A. 1973. 'Community of the careless'. In *Outlook on a Century*, ed. F. Wilson and D. Perrot, 490–3 (reprinted from *South African Outlook*, April 1970). South Africa: Lovedale Press and Spro-cas.

Barnes, J. A. 1951. *Marriage in a Changing Society*. Rhodes–Livingstone Papers No. 20. London: OUP.

Basutoland 1958. *Report on Constitutional Reform and Chieftainship Affairs*. Maseru: Basutoland Council.

Basutoland Records II, 1853–1861, collected and arranged by G. M. Theal. Cape Town: Struik, 1964. Originally published 1883.

Bawden, M. G. and Carroll, D. M. 1968. *The Land Resources of Lesotho*. Ministry of Overseas Development: Land Resources Division, Directorate of Overseas Surveys, Tolworth, Surrey.

204

Beinart, W. 1973. 'Peasant Production, Underdevelopment and the Traditionalist Response in Pondoland, c. 1880–1930'. M.A. thesis, University of London.

Berg, E. J. 1961. 'Backward-sloping labor supply functions in dual economies – the Africa case'. *Quarterly Journal of Economics* 75, 468–92.

Bettison, D. G. 1960. 'Factors in the determination of wage rates in Central Africa'. *Human Problems in British Central Africa* 28.

Black Sash 1974. 'Memorandum on the Pass Laws and Influx Control'. *Sash* 16, No. 8. Johannesburg.

Böhning, W. R. 1977. 'Black Migration to South Africa: What are the Issues?'. World Employment Programme, Working Paper 10. Geneva: International Labour Office.

Breytenbach, W. J. 1975. *Crocodiles and commoners in Lesotho*. Pretoria: Communications of the Africa Institute No. 24.

Bundy, C. 1979. *The Rise and Fall of the South African Peasantry*. London: Heinemann.

Burman, S. B. 1976. *The Justice of the Queen's Government: The Cape's Administration of Basutoland 1871–1884*. African Social Research Documents, vol. 9. Leiden: Afrika-studiecentrum.

Casalis, E. 1965. *The Basutos; or Twenty-Three Years in South Africa*. Cape Town: Struik. Facsimile reprint of 1861 edition.

Cawhill, I. 1976. 'Economic perspectives on the family'. *Daedalus* 106, 2, 115–25.

Clarke, D. G. 1974. *Contract Workers and Underdevelopment in Rhodesia*. Gwelo: Mambo Press.

1976. 'Subsistence wages and primitive accumulation on plantations in Rhodesia'. Paper presented at SALDRU Farm Labour conference, University of Cape Town, September 1976.

1977a. 'Social security and aged subsistence: roots of the predicament in Zimbabwe'. *South African Labour Bulletin* 3, No. 6, 38–53.

1977b. 'Foreign Migrant Labour in Southern Africa: Studies on accumulation in the labour reserves, demand determinants and supply relationships'. World Employment Programme, Working Paper 16. Geneva: International Labour Office.

Clarke, L. and Ngobese, J. 1975. *Women Without Men*. Durban: Institute for Black Research.

Clarke, S. 1978. 'Capital, fractions of capital and the state: "neo-Marxist" analyses of the South African state'. *Capital and Class* 5, 32–77.

Cliffe, L. 1978. 'Labour migration and peasant differentiation: Zambian experiences'. *Journal of Peasant Studies* 5, No. 3.

Cobbe, J. H. 1976. 'Approaches to conceptualization and measurement of the social cost of labour migration from Lesotho'. In *South Africa Today: A Good Host Country for Migrant Workers?* Transvaal: Agency for Industrial Mission.

Comaroff, J. 1973. 'Competition for office and political processes among the Barolong boo Ratshidi of the South Africa–Botswana Borderland'. Unpublished Ph.D. thesis, University of London.

1978. 'Rules and rulers: political process in a Tswana chiefdom'. *Man* 13, 1, 1–20.

Comaroff, J. and Roberts, S. 1977. 'Marriage and extra-marital sexuality: The dialectics of legal change among the Kgatla'. *Journal of African Law* 21, No. 1, 97–123.

Cooper, D. 1979a. 'Rural urban migration and female-headed households in Botswana towns'. National Migration Study, Working Paper No. 1, March 1979. Gaborone: Central Statistics Office.

——— 1979b. 'Economy and society in Botswana: some basic national socio-economic co-ordinates'. National Migration Study, Working Paper No. 2, June 1979. Gaborone: Central Statistics Office.

——— 1979c. 'Migration to Botswana Towns'. National Migration Study, Working Paper No. 3, October 1979. Gaborone: Central Statistics Office.

Cowen, D. V. 1967. 'Land tenure and economic development in Lesotho'. *South African Journal of Economics*, 57–74.

Curtis, D. 1972. 'The social organization of ploughing'. *Botswana Notes and Records* 4, 67–80.

——— n.d. 'An Analysis of Development Agencies in Agricultural Communities in Botswana'. An unpublished report for the Ministry of Overseas Development, London.

Davies, R., Kaplan, D., Morris, M. and O'Meara, D. 1976. 'Class struggle and the periodization of the state in South Africa'. *Review of African Political Economy* No. 7, 4–30.

Davis, D. 1978. *African Workers and Apartheid.* Fact Paper on Southern Africa No. 5. London: International Defence and Aid Fund.

Doke, C. M. 1967. *The Southern Bantu Languages.* London: International African Institute.

Douglas, A. J. A. and Tennant, R. K. 1952. *Basutoland: Agricultural Survey 1949–50.* Maseru: Basutoland Government.

Dugard, J. R. 1979. *Independent Homelands – Failure of a Fiction.* 1979 Presidential Address. Johannesburg: South African Institute of Race Relations.

Duncan, P. 1960. *Sotho Laws and Customs.* Cape Town: OUP.

Eckert, J. and Wykstra, R. 1979. 'The Future of Basotho Migration to the Republic of South Africa'. LASA Research Report No. 4. Maseru: Ministry of Agriculture.

Edholm, F., Harris, O. and Young, K. 1977. 'Conceptualizing women'. *Critique of Anthropology* 3 (9 and 10), 101–30.

Elkan, W. 1959. 'Migrant labour in Africa: an economist's approach'. *American Economic Review* 49, 1, 188–97.

Ellenberger, D. F. and Macgregor, J. C. 1969. *History of the Basuto, Ancient and Modern.* New York: Negro Universities Press. First English edition published in 1912.

Feachem, R. G. A., Burns, E., Cairncross, A., Cronin, S., Cross, P., Curtis, D., Khan, M., Lamb, D. and Southall, H. 1978. *Water, Health and Development: An Interdisciplinary Evaluation.* London: Tri-med Books.

FFYDP. *Lesotho First Five Year Development Plan, 1970/71–1974/75.* Maseru: Central Planning and Development Office, 1970.

Fortes, M. 1975. 'Strangers'. In *Studies in African Social Anthropology*, ed. M. Fortes and S. Patterson, 229–53. London: Academic Press.

Foster-Carter, A. 1978. 'Can we articulate articulation?'. In *The New Economic Anthropology*, ed. J. Clammer. London: Macmillan.

Gardiner, J. 1975. 'Women's domestic labour'. *New Left Review* 89, 47–58.

Gay, J. 1977. 'Rural Sociology Technical Report on Senqu River Agricultural Extension Project'. Food and Agriculture Organization of the UN. Mohale's Hoek.

Germond, R. C. 1967. *Chronicles of Basutoland*. Morija Sesuto Book Depot.

Gluckman, M. 1940. 'Analysis of a social situation in modern Zululand'. *Bantu Studies* 14, No. 1, 1–30, and No. 2, 147–74.

    1950. 'Kinship and marriage among the Lozi of Northern Rhodesia and the Zulu of Natal'. In *African Systems of Kinship and Marriage*, ed. A. R. Radcliffe-Brown and D. Forde. London: OUP for the International African Institute.

    1975. 'Anthropology and apartheid: The work of South African anthropologists'. In *Studies in African Social Anthropology*, ed. M. Fortes and S. Patterson, 21–39. London: Academic Press.

Goody, J. ed. 1971. *Kinship*. Harmondsworth: Penguin Books.

Gordon, E. 1978. 'The Women Left Behind: A study of the wives of the migrant workers of Lesotho'. World Employment Programme, Working Paper 35. Geneva: International Labour Office.

Hailey, Lord. 1953. *Native Administration in the British African Territories*. London: HMSO.

Hamnett, I. 1973. 'Some problems in the assessment of land shortage: a case study in Lesotho'. *African Affairs* 72, 37–45.

    1975. *Chieftainship and Legitimacy: An Anthropological Study of Executive Law in Lesotho*. London: Routledge and Kegan Paul.

Harrison, M. 1975. 'Chayanov and the economics of the Russian peasantry'. *Journal of Peasant Studies* 2, No. 4, 389–417.

Hastings, A. 1973. *Christian Marriage in Africa*. London: Society for Promoting Christian Knowledge.

Helman, C. 1973. 'Economic Surveys of a Random Sample of Farmers (1970/71–1972/3)'. Leribe Pilot Agricultural Scheme.

Hirschmann, D. 1979. 'Changes in Lesotho's policy towards South Africa'. *African Affairs* 78, No. 311, 177–96.

Holy, L. 1977. 'Toka ploughing teams: towards a decision model of social recruitment'. In *Goals and Behaviour*, ed. M. Stuchlik. Belfast: Queen's University Papers in Social Anthropology, vol. 2.

Horrell, M. 1973. *The African Homelands of South Africa*. Johannesburg: South African Institute of Race Relations.

    1978. *Laws Affecting Race Relations in South Africa, 1948–1976*. Johannesburg: South African Institute of Race Relations.

Houghton, D. H. 1973. *The South African Economy*. 3rd edition. Cape Town: OUP.

    1974. 'The process of economic incorporation'. In *The Bantu-Speaking Peoples of Southern Africa*, ed. D. Hammond-Tooke, 397–414. London: Routledge and Kegan Paul.

Bibliography

Houghton, D. H. and Dagut, J. eds. 1972, 1973. *Source Material on the South African Economy: 1860–1970.* Vol. 1 (*1860–1899*), 1972; Vol. 3 (*1920–1970*), 1973. Cape Town: OUP.

Houghton, D. H. and Walton, E. M. 1952. *The Economy of a Native Reserve.* Keiskammahoek Rural Survey, vol. II. Pietermaritzburg: Shuter and Shuter.

Hubbard, M. 1977. 'Notes on the concept of subsistence in wage theory and policy'. Mimeo, Department of Economics, University College of Botswana.

Humphrey, C. 1978. 'Women, taboo and the suppression of attention'. In *Defining Females*, ed. S. Ardener. London: Croom Helm.

IBRD 1975. *Lesotho: A Development Challenge.* Washington: International Bank for Reconstruction and Development.

IBRD 1978. 'Migration from Botswana, Lesotho and Swaziland'. Report No. 1688-EA. Washington.

Innes, D. and O'Meara, D. 1976. 'Class formation and ideology: the Transkei region'. *Review of African Political Economy* No. 7, 69–86.

Innes, D. and Plaut, M. 1978. 'Class struggle and the state'. *Review of African Political Economy* No. 11, 51–61.

JASPA 1979. *Options for a Dependent Economy: Development, Employment and Equity Problems in Lesotho.* International Labour Office: Jobs and Skills Programme for Africa. Addis Ababa.

Jeeves, A. 1975. 'The control of migratory labour on the South African gold mines in the era of Kruger and Milner'. *Journal of Southern African Studies* 2, No. 1, 3–29.

Jingoes, S. J. 1975. *A Chief is a Chief by the People.* London: OUP.

Johnson, R. W. 1977. *How Long Will South Africa Survive?* London: Macmillan.

Jones, G. I. 1951. *Basutoland Medicine Murder: A report on the recent outbreak of 'Diretlo' murders in Basutoland.* Cmd. 8209. London: HMSO.

1966. 'Chiefly succession in Basutoland'. In *Succession to High Office*, ed. J. Goody. Cambridge Papers in Social Anthropology, No. 4. Cambridge: CUP.

Kerblay, B. 1971. 'Chayanov and the theory of peasantry as a specific type of economy'. In *Peasants and Peasant Societies*, ed. T. Shanin, 150–60. Harmondsworth: Penguin Books.

Kerven, C. 1977. 'Underdevelopment, migration and class formation in the North East District of Botswana'. Unpublished Ph.D. thesis, University of Toronto.

Khaketla, B. M. 1971. *Lesotho 1970: An African Coup under the Microscope.* London: C. Hurst and Co.

Kimble, J. 1976. 'Aspects of the economic history of Lesotho, 1830–85'. Paper presented to the History workshop, National University of Lesotho, July 1976.

Kooijman, K. F. M. 1978. *Social and economic change in a Tswana village.* Leiden: Afrika-studiecentrum.

Kowet, D. K. 1978. *Land, Labour Migration and Politics in Southern Africa: Botswana, Lesotho and Swaziland.* Uppsala: Scandinavian Institute of African Affairs.

Kuhn, A. and Wolpe, A-M. (eds.) 1978. *Feminism and Materialism.* London: Routledge and Kegan Paul.

208

Kuper, A. 1970. 'The Kgalagari and the jural consequences of marriage'. *Man* 5, 466–82.

1975. 'The social structure of the Sotho-speaking peoples of Southern Africa'. Parts I and II, *Africa* 45, 1, 67–81 and 2, 139–49.

Laws of Lerotholi. 1973 edition. Morija Sesuto Book Depot.

Laydevant, F. 1952. *The Basuto*. Roma: St Michael's Mission.

Leeuwenberg, J. 1977. *The Transkei. A study in economic regression*. London: Africa Bureau.

Legassick, M. and Wolpe, H. 1976. 'The Bantustans and capital accumulation in South Africa'. *Review of African Political Economy* No. 7, 87–107.

Leistner, G. M. E. 1966. *Lesotho: economic structure and growth*. Pretoria: Communications of the Africa Institute No. 5.

1967. 'Foreign Bantu workers in South Africa: their present position in the economy'. *South African Journal of Economics*, 30–56.

Lesotho 1972. *1970 Census of Agriculture Report*. Maseru: Bureau of Statistics.

1973. 'Agricultural statistics 1950, 1960 and 1965–70'. Maseru: Bureau of Statistics.

1975. *Report of the Lesotho pilot survey on population and food consumption May 1973*. Maseru: Bureau of Statistics.

Lewis, I. M. 1965. 'Problems in the comparative study of unilineal descent'. In *The Relevance of Models for Social Anthropology*, ed. M. Banton. ASA Monographs 1. London: Tavistock.

Leys, R. 1975. 'South African gold mining in 1974: "the gold of migrant labour"'. *African Affairs* 74, 196–208.

1979. 'Lesotho: non-development or under-development. Towards an analysis of the political economy of the labour reserve'. In *The Politics of Africa: Dependence and Development*, ed. T. M. Shaw and K. Heard. Longman and Dalhousie University Press.

Linden, E. 1976. *The Alms Race*. New York: Random House.

Lipton, M. 1977. 'South Africa: two agricultures?'. In *Farm Labour in South Africa*, ed. F. Wilson, A. Kooy and D. Hendrie, 72–85. Cape Town: David Philip.

Lusaka 1978. 'Country Case Study of Lesotho'. Presented at the Conference on Migratory Labour in Southern Africa, Lusaka, Zambia, 4–8 April 1978, under the auspices of the Economic Commission for Africa.

Lye, W. F. and Murray, C. 1980. *Transformations on the Highveld. The Tswana and Southern Sotho*. Cape Town: David Philip.

Magubane, B. and O'Brien, J. 1972. 'Migrant labour in Africa: a critique of conventional wisdom'. *Critical Anthropology* 2, 2, 88–103.

Mahoney, N. 1977. 'Contract and neighbourly exchange among the Birwa of Botswana'. *Journal of African Law* 21, No. 1, 40–65.

Maputo 1977. *The Mozambican Miner: A study in the export of labour*. Maputo: Universidade Eduardo Mondlane, Centro do Estudos Africanos.

Marks, S. 1978. 'Natal, the Zulu royal family and the ideology of segregation'. *Journal of Southern African Studies* 4, No. 2, 172–94.

Marres, P. J. Th. and van der Wiel, A. C. A. 1975. *Poverty Eats My Blanket. A Poverty Study: the Case of Lesotho*. Maseru.

Bibliography

Marx, K. 1976. *Capital*, vol. 1. Harmondsworth: Penguin Books, in association with *New Left Review*.

Mayer, P. ed. 1980. *Black Villagers in an Industrial Society: Anthropological Perspectives on Labour Migration in Southern Africa*. Cape Town: OUP.

McDowall, M. 1973. 'Basotho Labour in South African Mines – An Empirical Study'. Maseru: Bureau of Statistics.

Meillassoux, C. 1972. 'From reproduction to production'. *Economy and Society* 1, 1, 93–105.

  1975. *Femmes, Greniers et Capitaux*. Paris: Maspero.

Mitchell, J. C. 1959. 'The causes of labour migration'. *Bulletin of the Inter-African Labour Institute* 6, 1, 12–46. Reprinted in *Black Africa*, ed. J. Middleton. London: Macmillan, 1970.

  1975. 'Factors in rural male absenteeism in Rhodesia'. In *Town and Country in Central and Eastern Africa*, ed. D. Parkin, 93–112. London: International African Institute.

Monyake, A. M. 1973. 'Report on the Demographic Component of the Rural Household Consumption and Expenditure Survey 1967–69. Part 2: Presentation and Analysis of the Data'. Maseru: Bureau of Statistics.

Monyake, L. B. 1974. 'Lesotho – Land, Population and Food. The Problem of Growth in Limited Space'. Paper presented at the National Population Symposium, Maseru, 11–13 June 1974.

Moorsom, R. 1977. 'Underdevelopment, contract labour and worker consciousness in Namibia, 1915–72'. *Journal of Southern African Studies* 4, No. 1, 52–87.

Morojele, C. M. H. *1960 Agricultural Census: Basutoland*, eight parts, 1962 etc. Maseru: Government Printer.

Morris, M. 1976. 'The development of capitalism in South African agriculture'. *Economy and Society* 6, No. 3.

Morse, C. 1960. *Basutoland, Bechuanaland Protectorate and Swaziland*. Report of an Economic Survey Mission (chairman Chandler Morse). London: HMSO.

Murray, C. 1975. 'Sex, smoking and the shades'. In *Religion and Social Change in Southern Africa*, ed. M. G. Whisson and M. West, 58–77. Cape Town: David Philip, and London: Rex Collings.

  1976. 'Keeping House in Lesotho'. Unpublished Ph.D. thesis, University of Cambridge.

  1977. 'High bridewealth, migrant labour and the position of women in Lesotho'. *Journal of African Law* 21, No. 1, 79–96.

  1978. 'Migration, differentiation and the developmental cycle in Lesotho'. In *Migration and the Transformation of Modern African Society*, eds. W. M. J. van Binsbergen and H. Meilink, 127–43. Leiden: Afrika-studiecentrum.

  1979. 'The work of men, women and the ancestors: social reproduction in the periphery of southern Africa'. In *The Social Anthropology of Work*, ed. S. Wallman, 337–63. London: Academic Press.

Nattrass, J. 1977. *Migrant Labour and Underdevelopment: the case of KwaZulu*. Department of Economics, University of Natal, Durban.

Ngubane, H. 1977. *Body and Mind in Zulu Medicine*. London: Academic Press.

Nobe, K. C. and Seckler, D. W. 1979. 'An Economic and Policy Analysis of Soil-

Water Problems and Conservation Programs in the Kingdom of Lesotho'. LASA Research Report No. 3. Maseru: Ministry of Agriculture.

Palmer, R. and Parsons, N. (eds.) 1977. *The Roots of Rural Poverty in Central and Southern Africa*. London: Heinemann.

Palmer, V. 1970. *The Roman-Dutch and Sesotho Law of Delict*. Leiden: Sijthoff.

Perry, J. A. G. 1973. 'The broker in a rural Lesotho community'. *African Studies* 32, 137–52.

1977. 'Law codes and brokerage in a Lesotho village'. In *Social Anthropology and Law*, ed. I. Hamnett, 189–228. London: Academic Press.

Phillips, A. and Morris, H. F. 1971. *Marriage Laws in Africa*. London: OUP for the International African Institute. Originally published 1953.

Phimister, I. and van Onselen, C. 1979. 'The political economy of tribal animosity: a case study of the 1929 Bulawayo Location "Faction Fight"'. *Journal of Southern African Studies* 6, No. 1, 1–43.

Pim, A. 1935. *Financial and Economic Position of Basutoland*. Cmd. 4907. London: HMSO.

Plaatje, S. 1916. *Native Life in South Africa*. London: P. S. King and Son.

Poulter, S. 1972. 'The place of the Laws of Lerotholi in the legal system of Lesotho'. *African Affairs* 71.

1973. 'Family Law and Litigation in Basotho Society'. Unpublished D.Phil. thesis, Oxford University.

1976. *Family Law and Litigation in Basotho Society*. Oxford: Clarendon.

Power, E. 1975. *Medieval Women*, ed. M. M. Postan. Cambridge: CUP.

Preston-Whyte, E. 1974. 'Kinship and Marriage'. In *The Bantu-Speaking Peoples of Southern Africa*, ed. D. Hammond-Tooke, 177–210. London: Routledge and Kegan Paul.

Ramolefe, A. 1969. 'Sesotho marriage, guardianship and the customary law heir'. In *Ideas and Procedures in African Customary Law*, ed. M. Gluckman. London: OUP.

Ranger, T. O. 1978. 'Growing from the roots: reflections on peasant research in central and southern Africa'. *Journal of Southern African Studies* 5, No. 1, 99–133.

Report and Evidence of *Commission on Native Laws and Customs of the Basutos*. 1873. Cape Town: Solomon. Reprinted Morija Sesuto Book Depot.

Roberts, S. 1977. 'The Kgatla marriage: concepts of validity'. In *Law and the Family in Africa*, ed. S. Roberts, 241–60. The Hague: Mouton.

Rogers, B. 1976. *Divide and Rule. South Africa's Bantustans*. London: International Defence and Aid Fund.

Rugege, S. 1979. 'Legal Aspects of Labour Migration from Lesotho to the South African Mines'. World Employment Programme, Working Paper 40. Geneva: International Labour Office.

Sadie, J. L. 1960. 'The social anthropology of economic underdevelopment'. *The Economic Journal* 70.

SAIRR. Annual *Survey of Race Relations in South Africa*. Johannesburg: South African Institute of Race Relations. References are to year surveyed, not date of publication, e.g. SAIRR (1974) is vol. 28, published 1975.

Sahlins, M. 1974. *Stone Age Economics*. London: Tavistock.

211

Bibliography

Sanders, P. 1975. *Moshoeshoe, Chief of the Sotho.* London: Heinemann.

Sansom, B. 1974. 'Traditional Economic Systems'. In *The Bantu-Speaking Peoples of Southern Africa*, ed. D. Hammond-Tooke, 135–76. London: Routledge and Kegan Paul.

Schapera, I. 1935. 'The social structure of the Tswana ward'. *Bantu Studies* 9, 203–24.

1947. *Migrant Labour and Tribal Life.* London: OUP.

Schapera, I. and Roberts, S. 1975. 'Rampedi revisited: another look at a Tswana ward'. *Africa* 45, No. 3, 258–79.

Schlemmer, L. and Stopforth, P. 1974. 'A study of malnutrition in the Nqutu district of KwaZulu'. Fact Paper No. 2. Durban: Institute for Social Research.

Schneider, D. M. 1953. 'A note on bridewealth and the stability of marriage'. *Man* 53, 55–7.

Sebatane, E. M. 1979. 'An Empirical Study of the attitudes and perceptions of migrant workers'. World Employment Programme, Working Paper 42. Geneva: International Labour Office.

Seccombe, W. 1974. 'The housewife and her labour under capitalism'. *New Left Review* 83, 3–24.

Sekese, A. 1970. *Mekhoa ea Basotho.* Morija Sesuto Book Depot. Originally published 1893.

Selwyn, P. 1975. *Industries in the Southern African Periphery.* London: Croom Helm.

SFYDP. *Kingdom of Lesotho Second Five Year Development Plan, 1975/76–1979/80.* Maseru.

Sheddick, V. G. J. 1948. 'The morphology of residential associations as found among the Khwakhwa of Basutoland'. University of Cape Town: Communications from the School of African Studies (New Series No. 19).

1953. *The Southern Sotho.* London: International African Institute.

1954. *Land Tenure in Basutoland.* Colonial Research Studies No. 13. London: HMSO.

Smith, P. 1978. 'Domestic labour and Marx's theory of value'. In *Feminism and Materialism*, ed. A. Kuhn and A.-M. Wolpe. London: Routledge and Kegan Paul.

Smits, L. G. A. 1968. 'The distribution of the population in Lesotho and some implications for economic development'. *Lesotho (Basutoland) Notes and Records* 7.

Spence, J. E. 1968. *Lesotho. The Politics of Dependence.* London: OUP for the Institute of Race Relations.

1971. 'South Africa and the Modern World'. In *The Oxford History of South Africa*, vol. II, ed. M. Wilson and L. Thompson, 477–527. Oxford: Clarendon.

Spiegel, A. D. 1975. 'Christian Marriage and Migrant Labour in a Lesotho Village'. B.A. (Hons) thesis, University of Cape Town.

1979. 'Migrant Labour Remittances, the Developmental Cycle and Rural Differentiation in a Lesotho Community'. M.A. thesis, University of Cape Town.

212

Spray, P. n.d. 'A tentative economic history of Lesotho from 1830'. Mimeo, University of Sussex.

Stahl, C. W. 1979. 'Southern African Migrant Labour Supplies in the past, the present and the future, with special reference to the gold-mining industry'. World Employment Programme, Working Paper 41. Geneva: International Labour Office.

Stahl, C. W. and Böhning, W. R. 1979. 'Reducing Migration Dependence in Southern Africa'. World Employment Programme, Working Paper 37. Geneva: International Labour Office.

Ström, G. W. 1978. *Development and Dependence in Lesotho, the Enclave of South Africa.* Uppsala: Scandinavian Institute of African Studies.

Taylor, H. 1972. *Doctor to Basuto, Boer and Briton 1877–1906: Memoirs of Dr Henry Taylor,* ed. P. Hadley. Cape Town: David Philip.

Thomas, T. 1973. *Their Doctor Speaks.* Cape Town.

Thompson, E. P. 1978a. 'Folklore, anthropology and social history'. *Indian Historical Review* 3, No. 2, 247–66. Reprinted as a Studies in Labour History pamphlet, 1979.

1978b. *The Poverty of Theory and other essays.* London: Merlin Press.

Thompson, L. 1975. *Survival in two worlds: Moshoeshoe of Lesotho 1786–1870.* Oxford: Clarendon.

Todaro, M. P. 1971. 'Income expectations, rural–urban migration and employment in Africa'. *International Labour Review* 104, 5, 387–413.

Townsend, P. 1979. *Poverty in the United Kingdom.* Harmondsworth: Penguin Books.

Turner, S. D. 1978. 'Sesotho Farming: The Condition and Prospects of Agriculture in the Lowlands and Foothills of Lesotho'. Unpublished Ph.D. Thesis, University of London.

Van Binsbergen, W. M. J. and Meilink, H. (eds.) 1978. *Migration and the Transformation of Modern African Society.* Leiden: Afrika-studiecentrum.

Van der Wiel, A. C. A. 1977. *Migratory Wage Labour: Its Role in the Economy of Lesotho.* Mazenod: Mazenod Book Centre.

Van Onselen, C. 1975. 'Black workers in Central African industry: a critical essay on the historiography and sociology of Rhodesia'. *Journal of Southern African Studies* 1, No. 2, 228–46.

1976. *Chibaro: African Mine Labour in Southern Rhodesia 1900–1933.* London: Pluto Press.

Van Velsen, J. 1959. 'Labour migration as a positive factor in the continuity of Tonga tribal society'. *Economic Development and Cultural Change* 8, No. 2.

Wallman, S. 1965. 'The communication of measurement in Basutoland'. *Human Organization* 24, 3.

1969. *Take Out Hunger. Two Case Studies of Rural Development in Basutoland.* London School of Economics Monographs on Social Anthropology No. 39. London: Athlone.

1972. 'Conditions of non-development: the case of Lesotho'. *Journal of Development Studies* 8, 2, 251–61.

1975. 'Kinship, A-kinship, Anti-kinship: Variation in the logic of kinship situations'. *Journal of Human Evolution* 4, 331–41.

1976. 'The modernization of dependence: a further note on Lesotho'. *Journal of Southern African Studies* 3, No. 1, 102–7.

Watson, W. 1958. *Tribal Cohesion in a Money Economy*. Manchester: Manchester University Press.

Webster, D. 1978. 'Migrant labour, social formations and the proletarianization of the Chopi of southern Mozambique'. In *Migration and the Transformation of Modern African Society*, ed. W. M. J. van Binsbergen and H. Meilink, 157–74. Leiden: Afrika-studiecentrum.

Webster, E. 1977. 'The 1949 Durban "Riots" – a case study in race and class'. In *Working Papers in Southern African Studies*, ed. P. Bonner. African Studies Institute, University of the Witwatersrand.

Weisfelder, R. F. 1971. *The Basotho monarchy: A spent force or a dynamic political factor?* Denver: African Studies Association.

Westcott, G. 1977. 'Obstacles to agricultural development in the Transkei'. In *Farm Labour in South Africa*, ed. F. Wilson, A. Kooy and D. Hendrie, 139–53. Cape Town: David Philip.

Williams, J. C. 1970. 'Problems and Prospects of the economic development of agriculture in Lesotho'. Unpublished Ph.D. thesis, University of Natal.

1972. *Lesotho: Land Tenure and Economic Development*. Pretoria: Communications of the Africa Institute No. 19.

Wilson, F. 1971. Farming, 1866–1966. In *The Oxford History of South Africa*, vol. II, ed. M. Wilson and L. Thompson, 104–171. Oxford: Clarendon.

1972a. *Labour in the South African Gold Mines 1911–1969*. African Studies Series No. 6. Cambridge: CUP.

1972b. *Migrant Labour in South Africa*. Johannesburg: South African Council of Churches and Spro-cas.

1975. 'The political implications for Blacks of economic changes now taking place in South Africa'. In *Change in Contemporary South Africa*, ed. L. Thompson and J. Butler, 168–200. Perspectives on Southern Africa, 17. Berkeley: University of California Press.

1976. 'International migration in Southern Africa'. *International Migration Review* 10, No. 4, 451–88.

1979. 'Directions for the future'. *Race Relations News* 41, No. 8, Johannesburg.

Wilson, G. 1941–2. *An Essay on the Economics of Detribalization in Northern Rhodesia*, Parts 1 and 2, Rhodes–Livingstone Papers No. 5, 1941 and No. 6, 1942.

Wilson, M. 1969. 'Changes in social structure in southern Africa: the relevance of kinship studies to the historian.' In *African Societies in Southern Africa*, ed. L. Thompson, 71–85. London: Heinemann.

1971. 'The Growth of Peasant Communities'. In *The Oxford History of South Africa*, vol. II, ed. M. Wilson and L. Thompson, 49–102. Oxford: Clarendon.

1973. 'Let no man put asunder'. In *Outlook on a Century*, ed. F. Wilson and D. Perrot, 468–71 (reprinted from *South African Outlook*, January 1964). Cape Province: Lovedale Press and Spro-cas.

1975. 'So truth be in the field.' The Alfred and Winifred Hoernle Memorial Lecture, 1975. Johannesburg: South African Institute of Race Relations.

1976. 'Zig-zag change'. *Africa* 46, 4, 399–409.

Wilson, M., Kaplan, S., Maki, T. and Walton, E. M. 1952. *Social Structure.*
Keiskammahoek Rural Survey vol. III. Pietermaritzburg: Shuter and Shuter.
Wolpe, H. 1972. 'Capitalism and cheap labour power in South Africa: from
segregation to apartheid'. *Economy and Society* 1, No. 4, 425–56.
Wykstra, R. A. 1978. 'Farm Labor in Lesotho: Scarcity or Surplus?' LASA
Discussion Paper No. 5. Maseru: Ministry of Agriculture.

Index